INITIATED BY THE SPIRITS

Healing the Ills of Modernity through Shamanism, Psychedelics and the Power of the Sacred

Frédérique Apffel-Marglin and Randy Chung Gonzales

Illustrations by Randy Chung Gonzales

Green
Fire
Press

Housatonic
Massachusetts

Cover painting and interior art by Randy Randy Chung Gonzales
Cover design by Javier Veliz Benzaquen

Library of Congress Control Number: 2022919359
Paperback ISBN: 979-8-9858064-2-7
Ebook ISBN: 979-8-9858064-3-4

Green
Fire
Press

Green Fire Press
PO Box 377 Housatonic MA 01236

Publisher's Cataloging-in-Publication data

Names: Apffel-Marglin, Frédérique, author. | Gonzales, Randy Chung, author.
Title: Initiated by the spirits : healing the ills of modernity through shamanism , psychedelics and the power of the sacred / Frédérique Apffel-Marglin and Randy Chung
Gonzales; illustrations by Randy Chung Gonzales.
Description: Includes bibliographical references. | Housatonic, MA: Green Fire Press, 2022.
Identifiers: LCCN: 2022919359 | ISBN: 979-8-9858064-2-7 (paperback) |
979-8-9858064-3-4 (ebook)
Subjects: LCSH Shamanism. | Hallucinogenic drugs and religious experience. | Mind and
body. | Mind and body therapies. | BISAC SOCIAL SCIENCE / Anthropology / Cultural
& Social | RELIGION / Indigenous, Folk & Tribal | BODY, MIND & SPIRIT / Shamanism |
BODY, MIND & SPIRIT / Healing / Prayer & Spiritual
Classification: LCC BL2370.S5 .A64 2022 | DDC 201/.44—dc23

Praise for *Initiated by the Spirits:*

The loss of enchantment—that natural disposition of children, mystics, and Indigenous People to wonder and remain at peace with cosmic mysteries—may be recovered through psychedelics and shamanism, suggest Randy Chung Gonzales and Frédérique Apffel-Marglin. Not everything has a rational answer and silence itself may be needed to ground our wisdom once again in awe. This extraordinary book, written by a heretical anthropologist and an unorthodox shaman in a profound mystical and intellectual dialogue, is proof that we modern individuals are still in time to recover and practice the ancient, original, and indigenous wisdom that may heal the cosmos.

—Stefano Varese, Professor of Indigenous Studies, University of California, Davis

Initiated by the Spirits offers an utterly fascinating story of transformation: the unsought transformation of Randy Chung Gonzales—the secular Peruvian assistant to US anthropologist Frédérique Apffel-Marglin—into a shamanic visionary and healer, and how this experience, in turn, transformed Apffel-Marglin personally and professionally. The book pairs a dramatic autobiographical account of shamanic initiation with a wide-ranging exploration of how western modernity has sought to eradicate shamanic practices and a sacred worldview, much to our detriment and peril. This brilliant book points toward a re-enchantment of the world and a recovery of soul in its many aspects. It represents an important contribution to the growing body of research that defies the disastrous taboo against integrating spiritual wisdom into modern scholarship.

—Richard Sclove, author of *Escaping Maya's Palace: Decoding an Ancient Myth to Heal the Hidden Madness of Modern Civilization*

This book explores the return of a therapeutic understanding of visionary altered states, of substances that alter psychic perceptions, and of medicines that speak to us of their potentials. Just as the Book of Job says, "Look to the Earth and she shall teach you," we read here the story of teachings and wisdom that come from plants.

—John Grim, Co-Director, Yale University Forum on Religion and Ecology

In this book, Frédérique Apffel-Marglin documents the spontaneous and deliberate development of Randy Chung Gonzales as an ayahuasquero and spiritual healer, while also sharing her own transformation into an advocate for the global acceptance of the healing power of this indigenous spiritual path. Together they help us understand how the indigenous spiritualties that have survived the onslaught of the West can help heal the world, eco-logically and socially.

—**Dr. Michael James Winkelman, author of** *Shamanism: A Biopsychosocial Paradigm of Consciousness and Healing*

The Peruvian forest and its healing powers come alive in this remarkable book, written in the dual voices of a western scholar and a Peruvian shaman. Presenting a scathing critique of modernist devastation, *Initiated by the Spirits* affirms our primal connection with the Great Mother, who reveals herself in magical ways, especially in visions that Shaman Randy Chung Gonzales draws with beauty and precision. His stories echo many indig-enous accounts, heard across eons and cultures, when human hubris did not interfere with our ability to recognize the pulse of the mountain, the flight of the eagle, and the call of the medicinal plants. *Initiated by the Spirits* argues convincingly that it is possible to emerge from the nightmare of the Anthropocene and reinvigorate the Anima Mundi.

—**Neela Bhattacharya Saxena, author of** *Absent Mother God of the West: A Kali Lover's Journey into Christianity and Judaism*

INITIATED BY THE SPIRITS

Healing the Ills of Modernity through Shamanism, Psychedelics and the Power of the Sacred

Frédérique Apffel-Marglin and Randy Chung Gonzales

Illustrations by Randy Chung Gonzales

CONTENTS

PART I: INTRODUCTION By Frédérique Apffel-Marglin 1

1. Introduction: Science and Shamanism in the Peruvian Rainforest . . . 3

2. Shamanism in the Upper Amazon 15

3. Relations Between Kichwa-Lamas and Mestizos 21

4. Situating Ourselves in Our Social Contexts 35

PART II: INITIATED BY THE SPIRITS: RANDY'S VOICE AND
   ILLUSTRATIONS 51

Introductory remarks by Frédérique Apffel-Marglin 53

1. The Initial Session at Don Aquilino Chujandama's Center, June
   2016 55

2. Randy Receives Shamanic Knowledge/Power from a Discarnate
   Master, June 2016 61

3. Randy's First Visit and Ceremony at Takiwasi Drug-addiction
   Treatment Center, July 2016 65

4. A Shattering Event: Report by Frédérique Apffel-Marglin, August
   2016 69

5. Randy Receives Mentoring from Dr. Jacques and a Vision, July
   and August 2016 71

6. Randy's First Encounter with Sorcery/Brujeria, September 2016 . . 73

7. Second Session with Don Aquilino in Chazuta; Randy Acquires
   More Tools and Powers, September 2016 75

8. Randy Receives Mentoring from Dr. Jacques Mabit, September to
   December 2016 79

9. Randy's First Dieta in Takiwasi in February 2017, Followed by
   Four Months of Depression 85

10. Randy Learns How to Prepare Ayahuasca, July 2017 89

11. Randy Leads His First Ayahuasca Session and His First
    Workshop, August 14–16, 2017 93

12. Randy Decides to Abandon the Path of Curandismo; Session
    with Grimaldo on December 8, 2017 95

13. Randy's Turning Point on December 12, 2017: The Virgin of
    Guadalupe Empowers Him 99

14. Randy Fulfills the Virgin's Wish
    Reported by Frédérique Apffel-Marglin, December 2017–April
    2018. 105

15. Prophetic Session with Karen and the Virgin, December 15,
    2017. 107

16. Prelude to Receiving Powers from the Sacred Mountain,
    February 16, 2018 109

17. The Sacred Mountain Comes to Randy and Gives Him Powers,
    February 23, 2018 111

18. Randy Learns to Exorcise a Possession, April–May 2018. 115

19. Randy is Healed by Plant Spirits and Receives a Protection from
    the Virgin, June 5, 2018 119

20. Pilgrimage to Tepeyac in Mexico and the Virgin of Guadalupe
    Reported by Frédérique Apffel-Marglin, September 2018. . . . 121

21. Randy is Blinded by a Jealous Curandero, March 2019; and
    Second Dieta in Takiwasi, April 2019 125

22. Randy Has a Beautiful Vision, Late Spring 2019. 129

Concluding Remarks on Part II by Frederique Apffel-Marglin . . . 131

Coda: A Few of Randy's Fugitive Visions. 133

PART III: REFLECTIONS ON THE ERADICATION OF SHAMANISM
    IN THE WEST By Frédérique Apffel-Marglin 137

1. The Oldest Destructions of Cosmocentric Worldviews in the West . . 139

2. The Burning Times as a Foundation for the Scientific Revolution . . . 149

3. The Enclosure of Land in Europe Then and in South America Now . . . 161

4. The Enclosure of the Self and Cosmocentric Reciprocity 173

5. Implications for Society and the Non-Human World 189

6. Spirits and Other Discarnate Beings 201

7. Collective Memory in the Cosmos 215

8. Academia and its Discontents 225

9. Psychedelics and the Healing of Modernity's Ills 245

Conclusions 257

Bibliography 265

Endnotes 279

Acknowledgments 305

DEDICATION

For my grandchildren:
Noah, Mira, Louise, Micah, Jordan, Jasmine,
Suzanne and Emmanuelle

— Frédérique Apffel-Marglin

For my parents:
Jaime Chung Rengifo and Ida Gonzales Flores

and for la Doctora

— Randy Chung Gonzales

One conclusion was forced upon my mind at that time, and my impression of its truth has ever since remained unshaken. It is that our normal waking consciousness, rational consciousness as we call it, is but one special type of consciousness, whilst all about it, parted from it by the filmiest of screens, there lie potential forms of consciousness very different...No account of the universe in its totality can be final which leaves other forms of consciousness quite disregarded.

—William James [1]

Puhpowee...translates as "the force which causes mushrooms to push up from the earth overnight." As a biologist, I was stunned that such a word existed. In all its technical vocabulary, Western science has no such term, no words to hold this mystery. You'd think that biologists, of all people, would have words for life. But in scientific language our terminology is used to define the boundaries of our knowing. What lies beyond our grasp remains unnamed.... The makers of this word understood a world of being, full of unseen energies that animate everything.

—Robin Wall Kimmerer [2]

La civilization occidentale, qui produit les crises de la globalization, est elle-même en crise. Les effets égoistes de l'individualisme détruisent les anciennes solidarités. Un mal-être psychique et moral s'installe au coeur du bien être matériel.... La crise de la modernité occidentale rend dérisoires les solutions modernisatrices aux crises.
Western civilization, which produces the globalization crises, is itself in crisis. The egotistical effect of individualism destroys the ancient solidarities. A psychic and moral unease settles at the heart of material well-being.... The crisis of Western modernity makes modernizing solutions to those crises laughable.

—Edgar Morin [3]

When and how did a small group of humans come to believe that other beings, including the majority of their own species, were incapable of articulation and agency? How were they able to establish the idea that nonhumans are mute, and without minds, as the dominant wisdom of our time...It is essentially another elite idea that gained ground with the onward march of the mechanistic metaphysics.

—Amitav Ghosh [4]

PART I

INTRODUCTION

By Frédérique Apffel-Marglin

1. INTRODUCTION: SCIENCE AND SHAMANISM IN THE PERUVIAN RAINFOREST

This book tells the interlinked stories of the transformation of each of the two authors. Randy Chung Gonzales was transformed in a sudden and radical way, one not welcomed initially but impossible to refuse and eventually accepted, which completely changed his life. My own final breakthrough, the result of my directly witnessing Randy Chung's journey, was the last step in a long and slow transformation. Randy was initiated by discarnate beings in an ayahuasca shamanic ceremony to which I insisted he accompany me. This kind of initiation is extremely rare in the region, where typically a neophyte shaman seeks the teachings of an older living shaman.[1] Randy tried, unsuccessfully, to reject that path. At the beginning it left him totally disoriented and confused. His three-year initiation by disembodied beings eventually transformed him from a materialist secular person into an effective healer, an empowered shaman, and a deeply spiritual person. As far as my own final breakthrough is concerned, it led me to ask new questions concerning the sustained efforts to eradicate shamanism in the Western tradition. It allowed me to perceive how the eradication of shamanism is embodied in our contemporary modern institutions, and to recognize that shamanism can be a powerful tool for addressing some of modernity's most intractable ills: the ecological crisis and the growing epidemics of mental illness, including drug addiction.

The recent renewal, around the year 2000, of the scientific study of shamanic psychedelic substances—referred to as "the

3

psychedelic renaissance"—along with other neuroscientific breakthroughs, have contributed greatly to my recognition of the potential for shamanism to play a role in addressing the ills of modernity. These shamanic substances are still classified as Schedule I illegal drugs in most countries, although not in Peru. This renaissance of the scientific study of psychedelics, taking place in many universities and hospitals in North America and Europe, as well as a few in Latin America, has been given new urgency by the dire epidemics of mental illness world-wide, combined with the limited efficacy of legal treatments. I am part of an interdisciplinary research project funded by the National Autonomous University of Mexico focusing on "magic mushrooms" containing psylocibin.[2] The Nahuatl name for those mushrooms is *teonanácatl*. This project is unique in that it works collaboratively with indigenous Mexican shamans and their communities, something that is not happening in the psychedelic renaissance in the global north.

Randy's narration and black and white line drawings, which form Part Two of this book, are based on his telling me his most important visions and other experiences during his three-year initiatory journey. Randy is not loquacious; his medium is not the word but visual expressions: drawing, architecture, and landscaping. He has designed and overseen all the build-ings and landscaping in our non-profit center in the Peruvian Upper Amazon, in the town of Lamas in the department of San Martin.[3] Now, because of his initiation, he is also healing a growing number of patients seeking his help in ayahuasca ceremonies.[4] It is important to note that the shaman leading such ceremonies will also ingest the ayahuasca potion. This radically differentiates the shaman from the doctor or psycho-therapist who must remain clearly separate from the patient and does not partake of their medicines or treatments.

My voice in the third part of the book is a more intellec-tual one, reflecting on the meaning, implications, and results of the longterm eradication of shamanism in the West. I espe-cially reflect on the demonization of shamanism during the "scientific revolution" in the 16th and 17th centuries in Western Europe, known as "the burning times," which destroyed a worldview rather like the Amazonian indigenous worldviews. The successful erasing of the Medieval and Renaissance worldview known as Anima Mundi (the Soul of the World), as well as the wars of religion, were instrumental in the invention of a mechanical, insentient, and purely material understanding of Nature and the cosmos. This enabled the creation of a system of knowledge totally outside of religion, metaphysics, ethics, and aesthetics; a reconceptualization that was perceived as necessary during a time of religious wars. The new secular knowledge paradigm was indispensable in re-establishing the certainty that was believed to be necessary to achieving law and order. In Part Three I explain how this association between certainty and law and order came about. Robert Boyle was a key figure in establishing the rules of the scientific experimental method in mid-17th century England. Boyle created the "public laboratory" along with a series of rules to be strictly observed within it. Within a century, Boyle's method became accepted throughout Europe and it is still considered indispensable in the pursuit of science to this day. One of Boyle's rules was the complete separation between the seeker of knowledge and the object of knowledge. In his youth, Boyle had been an occult philosopher, an alchemist. By the mid-17th century alchemy was already tainted with the brush of heresy, since occult philosophers shared the worldview of Anima Mundi with the so-called "witches," a variety of folk healers, many of whom were shamans.

The worldview of Anima Mundi understood the world/cosmos as being completely integrated. Plants, minerals, animals, humans, the planets and the stars, among many other things, were all connected among themselves materially, psychologically, and spiritually, with the whole being pervaded by the divine. However, by 1484, the Pope had declared witches to be heretics and with them most of the occult philosophers also came to be seen as heretics. By Boyle's time, it was necessary for him to make very clear that his public laboratory was the opposite of the occult philosopher's cabinet of experiments, where in his youth he had pursued simultaneously a knowledge of the world and a refinement or purification of his own soul.

This development came on the heels of René Descartes having established the philosophical bases for this new knowledge, what some at the time called "the corpuscular" theory of reality. Today we would replace the word 'corpuscular' with 'atomic' or 'materialist,' perhaps. This new knowledge began much earlier with Copernicus' theory of heliocentrism, published in mid-16th century, and was continued by many others, including Galileo in the early 17th century. Together, these new philosophies completely delegitimated the worldview of Anima Mundi, replacing it with a mechanical, materialist, reductionist worldview that was radically separated from the sacred and the ethical. These new developments opened a chasm between the seekers of knowledge—then known as natural philosophers, today known simply as scientists—and the object of their knowledge, namely nature or the cosmos. Seeking knowledge of the world could no longer be simultaneously a refinement of the seeker's soul/mind. This new philosophical practice quickly came to be known as 'science' *tout court*. It was not seen as one more knowledge system among the many existing in the world, but as the only correct, universal one, totally independent of any religious or cultural or historical tradition. Today it has indeed spread worldwide.

From the point of view of this new scientific knowledge, shamanism is at the antipodes of the mind, meaning the opposite of rationality.[5] Although shamanism was eradicated in Europe during the 17th century,[6] it survived in the Americas, despite laws that were passed at the beginning of the colonial period to eradicate it, especially in the Spanish and Portuguese colonies. Shamanism, and with it the knowledge of psychedelic plants and mushrooms, was preserved by indigenous societies throughout the Americas even in the face of severe persecution. Today, the last glowing embers of this ancient Western fury against shamanism can be recognized in the illegal status of shamanic plants and mushrooms, classified as Schedule I dangerous drugs. This law, passed in 1970 in the US and imitated in many other countries,[7] makes no distinction between destructive, addictive substances such as cocaine, heroin or oxycontin, and non-addictive shamanic plants such as mushrooms and derivative substances like LSD.

In the historic battle between science and shamanism, the latter has recently reemerged as a strongly efficacious remedy for curing a long list of modern mental illnesses, which have acquired epidemic proportions in the more modernized parts of the world. The scientific study of shamanic substances, started in the 1950s and interrupted in 1970 for almost thirty years, has recently resumed, despite the fact that in most parts of the world shamanic substances are still illegal. In various countries and certain U.S. states such as Oregon, these shamanic drugs have now been legalized for therapeutic purposes.[8]

I have included the ecological crisis in the list of the ills of modernity and to introduce this aspect of the healing effect of shamanic substances, I will here turn to the work of a neuroscientist Jill Bolte Taylor, who suffered a massive stroke in 1996 that incapacitated her left brain. It took Taylor eight years to completely heal from her stroke and regain her speech, mobility, balance, and several other faculties controlled by the left hemisphere. In her first book, titled *My Stroke of Insight,* Taylor details how her stroke brought home to her the role of the right hemisphere of the brain. In the minutes following the stroke she perceived her body as not separate from the rest of her environment, a feeling she calls nirvana.[9] In her latest book, she describes how "when my left thinking network went off-line....my ego-self also disappeared.... I could no longer identify the physical boundaries of where I began and where I ended... I perceived myself as a gigantic ball of energy that blended fluidly with the rest of the universe..... My perception of myself bypassed all boundaries and I literally became as big as the universe.[10] Taylor's experience leads her to recognize the importance of both the left and the right brain, and how developing what she calls a 'whole brain' can enable us to foster peace in the world.[11]

What emerges from Jill Taylor's account, as well as from other authors I discuss later, is that Western modernity has denied that we are part of nature and the cosmos, insisting that to think or feel in this ancient way is to be not only heretical in the Catholic and Protestant churches but also labeled false, confused, backward and primitive by science. Science enacts strict rules to separate us from what we study, and insists that this separation is not only necessary for achieving truth, but in fact reflects our actual reality in the world. We, or more precisely our minds, are totally separate from the world *around* us, a condition the Canadian philosopher Charles Taylor has called 'the ontological cleft' between humans and the cosmos.[12]

The ontological cleft meant that this newly minted mechanical, insentient world, totally separate from humans' minds, could be manipulated, extracted from, and used in whatever manner seemed most advantageous to humans. Such extractivism and manipulation did not elicit a feeling of having hurt a part of ourselves, since we perceived ourselves to be wholly other from Nature. To my mind, this is the deep origin of our current disastrous ecological crisis. Although non-Western cultures, where Western science did not arise, have also suffered ecological crises, our current crisis is the only one of planetary proportion, capable of wreaking global destruction.

One of the striking effects of ayahuasca, and psychedelics in general,[13] is that shortly after ingesting them one experiences the dissolving of one's ego-self or mind, which, as Jill Taylor writes, is in the left part of the brain. The implications of an over-reliance on the left hemisphere are made clear by philosopher of religions Christopher Bache:

Our divided and damaged world was created by a species operating out of the egoic level of awareness. For all its many virtues and strengths, the ego is a fragmented consciousness isolated from the underlying fabric of life that binds us together.... If the private ego remains in control of our lives, we will remain a divided people, and if that happens, we will likely perish. The ego of the private self built our divided world and is being consumed by the fires that are consuming this world.[14]

The dominance of the ego over the left hemisphere of our brain is relatively recent and specific to the modern West. My own experience with shamanism in the Peruvian High Amazon has shown me that humans are capable of moving beyond ego-dominance. At the beginning of my ayahuasca experiences I typically experienced an intensely frightening moment where I felt I was dying. With time and more aya-huasca ceremonies I eventually realized that this was the dissolving of my ego-self-mind, which would return fully after the ceremony. The well-known Yanomami shaman Davi Kopenawa, in his autobiography, says that people from his tribe commonly refer to taking their psychedelic as "dying." Kopenawa observes that those he calls "the whites" see this as losing one's mind—which is in fact literally true of one's left-brain mind. Of course, what those whites—i.e., denizens of modernity—do not see is the therapeutic value of a temporary eclipse of our left-brain mind. Jill Taylor also writes about her ego-self disappearing when she had her left-brain stroke. Shamanic psychedelics allow us to safely experience something akin to what happened to Taylor.

The temporary eclipse of our ego-self-mind reveals a completely different landscape, imbued with numinosity. Jill Taylor's choice of the Buddhist word *nirvana* as well as the word 'bliss' is not a coincidence. Those words evoke sacrality and numinosity. The testimony of volunteers dying of cancer confirms that the psychedelic journey is a both numinous experience and a therapeutic one: terminally ill patients lost their acute anxiety about death after a single injection of psylocibin.

With the temporary eclipse of our left brain, which modernity simply calls our mind, comes an immersion in what many of the cancer patient volunteers call God or the Heart or Mind of the Universe. We experience both being an integral part of the universe as well as that universe having a numinous heart/mind. Such an experience is healing. I think it is significant that the experience has never been reported as a communion with a particular being with specific attributes. It is typically spoken of as an experiential immersion in an ineffable numinous reality.

If such an experience were made common in our society, it would be known that we humans are entirely at one with the universe, integral to it. This worldview is common among indigenous societies that practice shamanism today, as it was among the pre-modern European healers and occult philosophers. In a world that is alive, conscious, and numinous, violently extracting things from the Earth or pouring toxic materials into its atmosphere, waters, and soils becomes reprehensible, even sinful, since it ignores the sacrality of the cosmos. With the eradication of shamanism and the takeover of the scientific worldview, the violent use of the planet in pursuit of progress, increased production, and economic gain is seen as rational and applauded, leading us to our current planetary ecological crisis.

My discipline of anthropology has tended to consider shamanism as a form of magic, incapable of affecting reality—be it the world or the human body. The very word 'magic' is a legacy of the longstanding eradication of shamanism in the West. One of the father figures in anthropology, Bronislaw Malinowsky, in his 1935 book on the agriculture of the Trobriand islanders in Melanesia, titled *Coral Gardens and Their Magic,* uses the word 'magic' to refer to actions designed to affect the external material world. He distinguished between practices affecting the material aspect of agriculture and those he declared to be purely symbolic, i.e. 'magic,' with no real effect on the external material world. Magic practices were invocations, chants or dances; agricultural practices were planting a seed in the soil. Such a separation between magical and material actions has been canonical in anthropology until recently.[15]

The modern discipline of anthropology arose in the second half of the 19th century in Europe, initially as a handmaiden to the colonization efforts of England and France. It has typically seen its "object of study" as separate from the personal life and beliefs of the anthropologist. My personal direct experience of ingesting the psychedelic brew ayahuasca over a period of some twenty-five years, combined with my firsthand witnessing of Randy's transformation from a typical materialist secular mestizo into an effective spiritual shaman, has drastically altered the light under which I carry out the anthropological practice of cultural analysis. It has enabled me to see modernity from outside of its basic premises, questioning them in the light of what shamanism and neuroscience has shown me.

The modern university has institutionalized the scientific paradigm. During my 35 years as a professor in American academia, the radical separation between spirituality and intellectual pursuits ultimately became unbearable, leading me to retire from academia early and create a center in the Peruvian Upper Amazon, which I named after the indigenous spirit of the rain forest, Sachamama. One of the breakthroughs I have experienced as I witnessed Randy's transformation is the realization that the varied discarnate entities that continue to appear to him and give him powers are not hallucinations or imaginative beliefs. I have abandoned my erstwhile anthropological view that such entities are the product of the collective cultural "beliefs" of indigenous peoples. Randy has been visited and given powers by entities he did not know but that others around him have been able to identify and that sometimes belong to far-flung cultures. This perspective is quickly dismissed in academia as "New Age" and therefore illegitimate. However, my direct witnessing of Randy's profound transformation, combined with my personal knowledge of him over more than 25 years since he was 15, simply left no other alternative for me.

I first came to Peru in 1994, invited by a Peruvian NGO named PRATEC. This group took me to Lamas in the northern department of San Martin, where eventually I created the Sachamama Center. My hosts requested that I join in their practice of regularly participating in ayahuasca ceremonies. I found that ayahuasca opened extraordinary spiritual horizons for me. I have had deep mystical experiences and been healed mentally and emotionally during difficult periods of my life by this shamanic practice. However, I hasten to add that I was never initiated to be a shaman, nor have I ever received powers to heal others in these ceremonies. I also never formed the notion that I wanted to write about my experiences; they were just too ineffable and too personal. However, this is not the case with Randy, whose initiatory experiences were extremely precise and clear, investing him with highly effective powers to heal others that he not only never possessed before but had never been interested in pursuing.

Randy is a mestizo, a descendant of Europeans and indigenous people; his parents raised him without religion, and they had a negative view of shamanism, which is locally known as *curanderismo*. In the next section, I will offer a brief portrait of shamanism in the Upper Amazon, focusing first on how it is understood among indigenous groups. This will be followed by a portrait of the relationship between the largest local indigenous group, the Kichwa-Lamas, and the mestizos in the department of San Martin. The small colonial town of Lamas has an indigenous sector named Wayku, where originally all the indigenous people were gathered and catechized. The mestizos live in the center of Lamas, although today the separation between the two populations is much less strictly maintained. The last section of Part One introduces the main characters that appear in Randy's story of his initiatory journey, as well as in my own transformation and journey.

This extended introduction will give the reader the necessary background to enter into the very different and strange world of Randy's initiation, and place him—and me as well—in our respective social contexts.

2. SHAMANISM IN THE UPPER AMAZON

Although the region of Lamas with its many Kichwa-Lamas inhabitants[1] has been deeply penetrated by modernity, from the market economy to the modern knowledge taught in the state school system, there is nonetheless a widely distributed vernacular knowledge of the main principles of the indigenous worldview. This worldview is held close to the chest nowadays, mostly by the elderly Kichwa-Lamas. To make such a worldview visible, and especially the role of shamanism in it, I will turn to the writings of the Kichwa community of Sarayaku in Ecuador. These Kichwa people of Ecuador are the same people as the Kichwa-Lamas in the department of San Martin in the Peruvian Upper Amazon, speaking the same variant of Quechua and remembering ancestral ties between them.[2] They used to go on pilgrimage to the same salt mountain together, located in the Cordillera Escalera near Lamas, and have entertained marital relations between these two branches until very recently. I chose the written words from this Kichwa group in Ecuador because I have not yet found any of the local Kichwa-Lamas that had so succinctly and beautifully captured their worldview.

For more than 70 years, the community of Sarayaku suffered the destruction wrought on their territory by oil companies. They won a very lengthy court battle against the State of Ecuador in the Inter-American Court for Human Rights in July of 2012 with a hefty settlement of several million US dollars. With this settlement they began reorganizing their territory, following traditional indigenous core values. The lengthy battle against the oil companies and the State of Ecuador as well as the destruction endured for several decades had prepared them for

15

just this kind of endeavor. They had experienced firsthand the terrible destructive effects of modernity. The following short excerpt from their communal declaration, made public in June 2018, conveys a fundamental aspect of what they call their 'cosmovision':[3]

> For the peoples and nations that inhabit the Amazon basin, the forest is alive, it is **Kawsak Sacha** [Living Forest]. It is inhabited by Protector Beings that carefully secure the equilibrium in the fragile ecosystems and their relationship with human beings. The waterfalls, the lakes, the rivers, the swamps, the wetlands, the salt sources, the great trees, and mountains have their own Protector Beings; they are **Runayuk.** Those places are inhabited by beings who have a life like our own.

> The perpetuity of Kawsak Sacha rests upon the continuous relationship with those Protector Beings, and therefore the maintenance of the diversity of life. This in its turn permits a natural equilibrium and the vital harmony among beings as well as our own continuity as people. The living forest is where the life of the original inhabitants begins and takes place. **Kawsak Sacha** is itself a being with whom the **Yachakkuna** [shamans] communicate to receive and share their knowledge with the people with the support of other wise men and women. All this learning guides and orients the Amazonian people toward the **Sumak Kawsay** [Right/Good/Just Living]. **Kawsak Sacha** is the primordial source of **Sumak Kawsay** and as such offers a living space for its diverse beings and people and revitalizes their emotional, psychological, physical, and spiritual aspects. [my translation]

This excerpt emphasizes the crucial role of shamans (*yachakkuna*[4]) to maintain not only the life of the human

16

community but the life of the forest in its incredible diversity, encompassing not only animals and plants but also waterfalls, lakes, rivers, swamps, wetlands, salt sources and mountains. All these latter have their own protector beings who are all *runayuk*. The root of this word is *runa*, which means 'person.' The human beings, the animals, the trees, and other plants are persons too, as well as the "non-living" parts of the landscape such as rivers and mountains. In other words, the whole of nature (or the cosmos) is not only alive but has sentience and agency, just as humans do.

The human persons who can speak with the non-human beings and translate their knowledge for humans are the *yachakkuna*, the shamans. Their role is central to the wellbeing of both the humans and the non-humans. Among both the Peruvian Kichwa-Lamas and the Sarayaku Kichwa of Ecuador, as well as among many other Indigenous groups of the Amazonian region, shamans prepare a sacred brew from the Amazonian psychotropic plant liana, mixed with the chakruna bush and often other plants as well, a brew known as ayahuasca among the Kichwa, although other groups may use different names for it.[5] It is in the visions and other communications received by shamans during ayahuasca ceremonies that they transmit knowledge, protection, and healing from non-human beings. Shamans hold ayahuasca ceremonies for other humans who can receive healing and/or knowledge. Those ceremonies are key in mediating or communicating between the living forest and its human and nonhuman diverse inhabitants. As the quote above indicates, the living forest teaches how to live rightly and well, and this teaching is conveyed by the shamans ingesting their psychotropic sacred plants. The living forest, through the mediation of shamans, revitalizes the emotional, psychological, physical, and spiritual wellbeing of *all* the beings inhabiting the Kawsak Sacha (Living Forest) and not only the wellbeing of the humans. The non-humans, such as the forest, rivers and mountains, may also stand in need of revitalizing or healing their emotions, their psyche, and their spirits as well as their physical beings.

The visions and words of Davi Kopenawa, a Yanomami shaman[6] from the Brazilian Upper Amazon, were recorded and translated by a French anthropologist who worked for some 30 years with this shaman and is fluent in his language, and who produced an autobiography in French (now translated into English) beautifully capturing this shaman's way of speaking.[7] The Yanomami use the bark of a certain tree called yakoana that, like ayahuasca, contains DMT[8] and is prepared as a snuff blown into the nasal cavities. Kopenawa explicitly contrasts his people's worldview with that of those he calls 'the whites':

> Since the beginning of time, Omama [creator spirit/deity] has been the center of what the white people call **ecology...** For the shamans, these have always been words that came from the spirits to defend the forest...In the forest, we human beings are the 'ecology.' But it is equally the xapiri [spirits], the game, the trees, the rivers, the fish, the sky, the rain, the wind, and the sun! It is everything that isn't surrounded by **fences** yet....
>
> If the forest were dead, we would be as dead as it is! But it is truly alive. The white people may not hear it complain, yet it feels pain just like we humans do.[9]

The worldview expressed by Davi Kopenawa is common to most Amazonian indigenous peoples and certainly to both the Kichwa of Sarayaku in Ecuador and the Kichwa Lamas of Peru. It is a worldview where humans, non-humans, and other-than-humans such as spirits are all part of the same world and are all alive and sentient. Those worlds are not divided into a world of humans and their thoughts and artefacts (what we would call a 'cultural' world) on one side and the natural world on the other, separated from a 'supernatural world' of immaterial and invisible beings above nature. Furthermore, this living world is not only comprised of animals and plants but includes such things as the rain, the wind, the sun, the moon, or the sky. The whole cosmos is alive. The whole cosmos feels like humans do and humans are, as Kopenawa puts it, part of the ecology. When Davi Kopenawa says: "If the forest were dead, we would be as dead as it is!" he is saying that if the non-human world were an insentient, mechanical, dead object, the humans would be as dead as that mechanical insentient world. In other words, for Kopenawa and Amazonian indigenous people, humans are part of the environment, *in and of* it, not just surrounded by it.

When the Europeans first appeared in the Amazon forest, this first contact decimated the indigenous population—9 out of every 10 persons died. In his own lifetime, Kopenawa has seen the survival of his people and the survival of the forest deeply endangered.[10] Kopenawa often wonders why those he calls 'the whites' do not believe in the spirits and thus do not call them. In his own words:

> White people are surprised to look at us become spirits with the yākoana [their sacred psychotropic]. They think that we are losing our minds... Yet, if they understood our language and cared enough to ask...they might understand the words that the xapiri (spirits) bring us from the edges of the earth, the sky's back, and the underworld they come from. But [...] white people prefer to remain deaf because they find themselves too clever with their paper skins, their machines, and their merchandise.[11]

Kopenawa says that white people may not hear the forest complain but the forest feels pain just like humans do. The whites who consider shamanic sessions as "losing one's mind" and thus reject the knowledge the forest brings to humans, are deaf to the forest which for them cannot feel or communicate.

The Sarayaku declaration says that the healing or revitalizing that results from shamans transmitting what the spirits say to them applies to the cosmos or nature as much as it applies to humans. The cosmos has a psyche—or to say it differently, a consciousness or soul (*psyche* in ancient Greek)—just like humans and hence has emotions like we humans do. The delicate equilibrium of the Amazonian ecosystem, which of course includes humans, is protected by the Protector Beings, who make up the cosmos.

3. RELATIONS BETWEEN KICHWA-LAMAS AND MESTIZOS

In Lamas, where our center is located, the penetration of evangelical churches, schooling and modernity in general, have all profoundly eroded the traditional indigenous worldview. In my more than 25 years of regularly visiting Lamas several times a year, I have noticed an increasing internalization on the part of many Kichwa-Lamas of the colonial gaze of the dominant mestizo society. This has been precisely and mercilessly detailed in a lengthy article by a Peruvian anthropologist, Luis Calderón Pacheco, who did fieldwork in Lamas intermittently from 1997 to 2001 on the topic of the relationship between Kichwa-Lamas and Mestizos there.[1] The historical situation of the Kichwa-Lamas is starkly different from that of the Sarayaku Kichwa or the Brazilian Yanomami, whose territories are difficult to access, hence slowing down the penetration of the dominant society. The only way to access the Sarayaku territory is by plane or helicopter or by very lengthy river transportation. Since their court victory against the state of Ecuador and the oil companies, the people of Sarayaku are now completely in control of their borders and no one can come into their territory without the permission of their leadership. Before their victory, the oil companies came to their territory with impunity. Now control of access to their territory by air, water, and land is exclusively in the hands of the Sarayaku leadership; even representatives of the Ecuadorian government require permits to visit.

The colonial town of Lamas was established in 1656 by the conquistador Martin Rivas y Herrera after three military campaigns against the local indigenous people. The Spanish regrouped six distinct subgroups of indigenous peoples and "reduced" them (from the Spanish verb *reducir*) to the status of minors under the guardianship of the Spanish authorities. Entire native populations were hand delivered to the Spanish settlers and were forced to settle in the periphery of the city of Lamas on its Western flank, in the indigenous sector of Wayku. The whites, also known as *criollos*, and the mestizos lived in the center of the city of Lamas, the two sectors keeping separate. The indigenous population was forced to pay tribute to the Spaniards and mestizos of Lamas in the form of cultivated produce or hunted and gathered food. The indigenous population were also forced to provide slave labor to the dominant society. People in Lamas in their 60s and 70s have told me that they grew up in houses with Kichwa slaves, where their fathers copulated with the women to produce more slaves.

The Jesuits established a mission in Lamas that lasted for two centuries, where the Kichwas were indoctrinated in the Catholic religion. The only instruction the Kichwa received was in this mission.[2] Not until the 1970s were indigenous children and youth admitted into schools in Lamas.[3] With the Independence of Peru in 1821, the situation for the indigenous people worsened due to the opening of the Amazon to the mercantile extractive economy, which had a devastating effect on the indigenous Amazonians. Shortly thereafter, in 1824, the new republican government created incentives for highland peoples to migrate to the Upper Amazon. If those migrants deforested and fenced at least a 100 hectares (over 200 acres) of forest, they were given title to the land. The criollos and mestizos continued a feudal-like bondage of the indigenous people even though the new constitution affirmed that Indians were equal to all other Peruvians. From the 17th century well into the 20th century, the dominant society considered the Kichwa-Lamas as beasts of burden to carry goods between the different commercial centers, carrying sacks weighing up to 120 pounds as well as carrying people. Calderon Pacheco includes a photograph of a Kichwa man carrying a white woman on a wooden chair on his back.

Despite 400 years of permanent contact with white criollos and mestizos, the Kichwa-Lamas have preserved a good deal of their culture and their own social organization. In the 1990s the Kichwa-Lamas initiated a process of cultural/ethnic affirmation creating a native organization, bilingual schools, demarcation of indigenous territory, and the regeneration of institutions that had deteriorated due to the ethnocidal practices of the State and the majority society. However, Calderon Pacheco remarks that the cultural regeneration of the Kichwa-Lamas has proved difficult due to environmental changes, particularly the drastic reduction of their ancestral territories, which were either appropriated by the dominant society or transformed into biological reserves. Local experts at the State University of San Martin in Tarapoto assert that for a sustainable use of the indigenous method of slash and burn, a family needs a minimum of 50 hectare of land. Today the average size of Kichwa-Lamas land is between 3 and 10 hectares with a mean of 1 hectare of cultivated land. In such a reduced territory, it is impossible to have long enough rotation periods between clearings to allow a strong enough regeneration of the forest and over a period of between 40 and 50 years, the shortened rotation periods eventually slowly lead to degraded land where the forest no longer regenerates, and nothing grows except weeds. This deforestation and degradation of the land can be clearly seen just driving or walking in the region of Lamas.

All the large landowners are mestizos and most of them raise cattle, a species and practice introduced by the Spaniards and foreign to the indigenous peoples. The mestizos own the better situated lands with better soils, closer to market, whereas the indigenous people must make their *chacras* (cultivated fields) on extremely steep slopes or in old growth forest with difficult access to markets. Calderon Pacheco asserts that the wealthier mestizos push the Kichwa-Lamas to starvation to force them to sell their labor and accept the wages imposed. Beginning in the early 20th century the Kichwa-Lamas began migrating to virgin forested lands in the region for liberty and for hunting. They now live in some 300 communities in the department of San Martin with an estimated population of around 30,000. The Law of Native Communities, passed in 1974 by the revolutionary government of Francisco Velazco (1968-1975), enabled indigenous communities in the Amazonian region to demarcate their territory and run their affairs along traditional parameters. Several Kichwa-Lamas communities in San Martin have begun the process of having their communities recognized.[4]

Poor mestizo farmers, small landholders owning between 3 and 4 hectares of land, maintain close ties of friendship with their Kichwa-Lamas neighbors through exchanges of products for services and carry on a continuous exchange of socio-cultural patterns. Many mestizos speak Quechua, know and respect indigenous traditions, practice native cooking and have recourse to shamanism.

Although today there is a vibrant national indigenous movement fostering a re-appropriation of native categories on their own terms, the local history has deeply marked the Kichwa-Lamas of the region. Many of them have converted to one of the many Evangelical churches, which consider indigenous practices and beliefs as works of the devil. Early on in my efforts to regenerate the pre-Columbian highly fertile human-made (or anthropogenic) soil known as Terra Preta do Indio, one of my earliest Kichwa-Lamas collaborators put me in touch with an organization of Kichwa-Lamas farmers. At a meeting where I showed them a film about this black earth, and used native spiritual terms like Pachamama and Sachamama, I was greeted by snickers from most of them. Shocked by this, I later inquired from my indigenous collaborator and was informed that all of them belonged to Evangelical churches and considered their own indigenous deities/spirits as devils.[5]

The ancestral territories of the Kichwa-Lamas are being prospected by oil companies, timber companies, palm oil companies, and others who often have bought off the indigenous leadership. At the time of the publication of Calderon

Pacheco's essay, there was only one Kichwa-Lamas indigenous cultural organization. Since then, some half a dozen of them have been created. Leaders of such organizations are typically Evangelical. Traditional values are found today mostly among the elder Kichwa-Lamas population, although I have also seen indigenous values in some of the young Kichwa-Lamas who have worked in our center. One such is Don Aquilino Chujandama, the shaman at whose ayahuasca ceremony Randy was initiated, from a native community about half an hour downstream from the small town of Chazuta on the Huallaga River.

The technical staff at our center are Kichwa-Lamas, young and very strongly identified with their Kichwa culture. However, it remains true that the indigenous population of the department of San Martin continues to be considered at the lowest level in the local social hierarchy. Many of my Kichwa-Lamas friends have told me of suffering discrimination in the high school reminiscent of the racism in the US toward African Americans. The first high school in the indigenous sector of Wayku was created in 2011. At the other two high schools in Lamas, Quechua is not taught even though it is mandated by the federal government—Quechua and Spanish are the two official languages of Peru, but most schools and universities in the country use only Spanish.

The process of devaluation of indigenous worldviews began with the enactment of the laws of Extirpation of Idolatry (*extirpación de idolatría*) that were created only a few years after the 1532 arrival of the first Spanish "conquistador" in South America, Francisco Pizzaro. Archbishop Jerónimo de Loayza enacted these laws in 1545, continuing the practice of the Holy Inquisition that was dedicated to eradicating practices considered heretical in Europe. The earliest inquisition in Europe dates from the late 12th century, created to combat the Cathars of Southern France, considered heretics by the Roman Church. The type of inquisition that arrived in Peru in the 16th century originated in Spain, where Ferdinand and Isabella wanted to eradicate Jews and Muslims, as well as those deemed pagan, the "witches." The laws of extirpation of idolatry in South America were aimed at the practices of the native population in what is now Peru. These are the words of Archbishop Loayza:

> ...they will work in order to find out if there are sorcerers [*hechiceros*] or Indians who have communication with the Devil, and speak with him, and in that way enlighten them [and remove] this blindness and stupidity, making them understand the great offence toward God in having communication with the devil and in believing the lies that he tells them...and also they will threaten with the pain and punishment that will be meted out to those who have done so.[6]

As historian Irene Silverblatt has shown, during the transitional period between the last years of the Incan empire and the beginning of the Spanish Conquista, the Spaniards singled out especially women priestesses and shamanesses for persecution, following the familiar practice of their native Spain.[7] A brief historical portrait of the singling out of women by the inquisition is presented by the anthropologist Bonnie Glass-Coffin at the beginning of her ethnography about a northern Peruvian shamaness.[8] Among the few women curanderas I have encountered, there is one who I deeply trust and came to admire when she came to Sachamama Center and led a group of visitors in a series of ceremonies. However, it is also true that in Lamas the only two known curanderas are widely considered to be witches. It is much harder for a woman to become a trusted curandera than for a man.

A telling remnant of this historical legacy resides in the language used by everyone in Lamas and the region: all the native deities and spirits were and are still today called *diablos* or *demonios* (devils). To this day in Lamas, the word *diablo* refers to local spirits or deities and is used by everyone, Kichwa-Lamas and mestizos alike. However, it seems that its heretical edge has been greatly blunted. The Spanish word *diablo* today only identifies a native spirit. Nevertheless, this is not true of the Evangelical churches for whom all native spiritual entities are really considered devils. For most mestizos, as for Randy before his initiation, these spirits simply do not exist and belief in them is considered superstitious. As is evident through strolling in the former Inca city of Cuzco, the Inca temples and deities were destroyed and on their foundations churches and monasteries were erected.

Although the laws of extirpation of idolatry have never been removed from the books in Peru, I am told that they are no longer enforced. With the imposition of Catholicism in colonial Peru, continued after the republican revolution of 1821, the practice among the indigenous peasantry has been to continue their ancestral practices under the façade of Catholicism, its saints, and holy figures. In Lamas, the annual festival in the indigenous section of Wayku in late August is the feast of Santa Rosa. The figure of Santa Rosa, a Catholic Saint, is carried in procession throughout the indigenous neighborhood at the beginning of the festival, after a mass in the small Catholic church in Wayku. However, during the following five days of festivities the dances, costumes, communal feasts, songs, and multiple exchanges are all along traditional indigenous lines. Families from most of the native communities in the region come to Wayku for this indigenous festival. In this mostly oral milieu, the awareness of the difference between certain Catholic figures and indigenous ones is often blurred and the awareness of the historical legacy seems to exist mostly among those educated past the secondary level. In the great majority of Kichwa-Lamas practices, as I have observed them in the past 25 years or so, whether practiced by curanderos or in festivals, the inclusion of Catholic saints and virgins has become part of the local spiritual landscape and is not perceived as alien. Therefore, the term 'façade' is not exactly appropriate since it implies an awareness of the alien status of Catholic elements, an awareness not always or even usually present.

In the public education system, religious instruction is obligatory, as is baptism in Roman Catholicism. Randy told me the only reason he was baptized was that it was a requirement in his school, otherwise his parents would not have had him baptized. Needless, to say the religious instruction is entirely Christian. Since 2012, I have been collaborating with the Lamas state board of education (UGEL, *Unidad de Gestion Educativa Local*) teaching in various primary and secondary schools how to regenerate the pre-Columbian anthropogenic Amazonian soil. I have constantly run across the dominant mestizo attitude toward indigenous practices and knowledge. I have been asked whether my use of indigenous terms has not proved to be an obstacle to communicating my findings in the US, thus making clear to me that for the teachers who made that comment, indigenous terms were perceived as a barrier to acceptance of the practice.

This pre-Columbian human-made soil is full of broken ceramics, which, as my Kichwa collaborators taught me, come from offerings to the spirits of the *chacra*, the cultivated field. I have completely failed in trying to induce schools to perform such offerings. This has been consistently refused as superstitious and against the rules of the school, even in primary schools located in native communities where all the students are indigenous. Although in their own communities and families indigenous people may continue to practice ancestral customs (if they have not become Evangelical) publicly the practice remains Catholic.

It is nevertheless remarkable that there exists in the Andean and Amazonian region a tendency known as Andean Catholicism. I became aware of this during my period of lecturing in PRATEC's course on Andean/Amazonian culture and agriculture from 1994 to 2004. One of their regularly invited lecturers was a Dutch priest who had lived among Andean peasants on the border between Chile and Peru for the past 30 years. He advocated for a fusion of Catholic and Andean practices and was wildly popular with the participants in the course, although PRATEC's own predilection for the rejection of anything

European/Northern/Christian was made noticeably clear to all. PRATEC was not only my host in Peru, having invited me to lecture in their course, but I collaborated with them from 1999 to 2004 in the creation of a non-profit organization in Lamas named Waman Wasi, after the local sacred mountain. Besides my own center, that organization is the only one in Lamas that tries to revalorize and incentivize what PRATEC calls the "affirmation" of Andean-Amazonian indigenous culture. Most other NGOs are to one degree or another beholden to the ideology of development that comes with the Western modern knowledge system and the market economy, in other words with the principal institutions of Western modernity.

I must here mention that the Takiwasi Center in the neighboring commercial city of Tarapoto also works to revalorize the indigenous medical knowledge system. The Catholicism at Takiwasi can be described as a successful hybridization of Catholicism, indigenous medical and spiritual knowledge, and some forms of Western psychotherapies, especially of the Jungian and transpersonal varieties. Takiwasi always has a team of 5 or 6 psychotherapists who themselves attend ayahuasca ceremonies as well as forest retreats and help the interned patients process their recovery. I have never felt any pressure to convert to Catholicism on the part of any member of this organization.

The intended effect of the Inquisition's pursuit of the practice of "extirpating idolatry" was to eradicate indigenous shamanism—a pursuit one can now see as having basically failed in Peru, unlike what happened in Europe. However, the ideology of development is highly valued and quite dominant, strongly advocated by the Peruvian government and taught in most universities. Several years ago, one of my Kichwa staff members asked me to view with a Kichwa friend of his, an *ingeniero* (a university- educated indigenous person), a documentary they had watched but could not decide what to think about. The three of us sat down and watched the film, made by a well-known Peruvian economist named Hernando de Soto.

The documentary was about persuading indigenous leaders to adopt a capitalist economic ideology and practice. In this documentary, de Soto interviews several local Kichwa-Lamas leaders, as well as indigenous leaders from the US and Canada who had created successful enterprises in their territories. The main emphasis was on the necessity for Kichwa-Lamas to own property privately and give up the notion of the commons, which would enable them to take out bank loans to create businesses and thus better their prospects.

Having worked with indigenous leaders from the Six Nations indigenous territories in New York State and Canada for many years, such as the late Professor John Mohawk, I had become aware of the consequences of the historical legacy of the US government pushing private property on the northern indigenous peoples: it resulted in a severe loss of community organization, culture and coherence. This was nowhere mentioned in the documentary. Also absent from de Soto's vision was the recognition that it is almost impossible for indigenous people to secure loans from banks, due to severe discrimination—the banks perceive them as high-risk clients.

To illustrate the foregoing, let me discuss the example of what started out as the indigenous community of Yurilamas, founded by a small group of indigenous families from Wayku in the 1960s. This community is situated to the Northeast of Lamas, some eight hours' walk from the nearest community with a road. One of the indigenous collaborators at my center, Royner Sangama, was born in this community, where his late parents were among the founders. Initially the territory surrounding Yurilamas, densely forested, was treated as a common; in traditional fashion, the elders gave the use of land to each family, according to its needs. Private property did not exist. Today, according to Royner, only two Kichwa-Lamas families remain and the rest of the inhabitants are 'colonos'—mestizos who came in search of land. This colono movement was incentivized by the Peruvian government throughout the 20th century as a convenient way of avoiding the implementation of true land reform. In typical colono fashion, these families cut down the forest, replacing it with pasture to raise cattle, and erecting boundaries between their individual private properties. In recent years, the colonos of Yurilamas have been loudly demanding the building of a road so they can gain better access to markets.

Despite all these incursions by mestizos in indigenous territories and lives, the tradition of shamanism among indigenous Kichwa-Lamas remains strong. Royner participated in several ayahuasca ceremonies led by an indigenous curandero in his native Yurilamas. In Randy's own retelling of his initiation at Don Aquilino's center in Chazuta, as well as his second visit there, this indigenous curandero (Don Aquilino) had a powerful effect on him even though he did not accept his offer to become his apprentice and never returned to him. My own interpretation of Randy's refusal is that his discarnate Ashaninka master was already his *maestro,* his own personal teacher shaman, the one who gave him his *yachay* and who continued to instruct and heal him during his apprenticeship period.

Randy's vision of the woman who turned out to be the Virgin of Guadalupe for me powerfully embodies and represents the contemporary relationship between indigenous shamanism and Catholicism. Randy was ignorant of the identity of this famous Mexican saint and learned of her identity during a session in the office of the French MD, Jacques Mabit, who founded a center in the region to treat drug addicts. Dr. Mabit was doing a sort of exorcism on Randy to ascertain whether his Ashaninka master was a sorcerer or a healing shaman, during which Randy had a vision of his Ashaninka master coming and kneeling in front of a beautiful young woman with dusky skin like his own. Dr. Mabit showed him a picture of the virgin of Guadalupe asking him whether that was the woman in his vison; Randy said that she was.

It is possible that what is being stated in that vision is the indigenous nature of the Virgin of Guadalupe. When Randy and I visited Mexico City in 2018, we went to visit the Virgin's church and learned from maestro Juan Ernesto Arellano that the Virgin of Guadalupe is the pre-Columbian earth goddess Tonanzin. This clearly became very salient and important to Randy, as evidenced by the fact that he inscribed the Virgin's name in the open-air chapel he constructed for her as Tonantzin, Virgen de Guadalupe, giving precedence to her indigenous identity. It is also evidenced by Randy's regular use of the *ikaro* (shamanic chant) in Nahuatl that maestro Juan Ernesto gave him in Mexico. Whatever be the case regarding the identity of the Virgin of Guadalupe, there is no question that she played a fundamental role in Randy's initiatory journey. Randy received from her two kinds of power and was asked by her to construct her image.

Randy also received an extremely strong power from the Waman Wasi mountain sacred to the Kichwa-Lamas, which came to him in the shape of an enormous eagle. He received additional healing and teachings about plants from various plant spirits. The green bird woman is also an indigenous spirit who gave him the power to diagnose patients just by looking at them. At key moments in this initiatory journey, Randy was accompanied by grandmotherly indigenous women rhythmically shaking the *shacapa* (the dried leaves used by shamans in this region). Thus, when Randy refers to the Virgin of Guadalupe, he is simultaneously referring to the Nahuatl pre-Columbian mother goddess Tonantzin.

The indigenous strand introduced Randy to a worldview that was completely foreign to him before his initiation, namely the worldview that my friend and colleague Stefano Varese, the well-known ethnographer of Amazonian and Mesoamerican indigenous peoples, has called cosmocentrism. Cosmocentrism refers to a living cosmos in which diversity and reciprocity are central. This is how Varese defines the term:

Contrasting with the Euro-American anthropocentrism (with an old genealogy in the Judeo-Christian-Islamic and Scientific cultural heritage), indigenous peoples constructed during millennia *cosmocentric* and *polycentric* cosmologies based in the logic of diversity and the logic of reciprocity. This is a diverse cosmos in which there is no privileged center, nor hegemonic singularity.[9]

To illustrate Randy's previous attitude toward a living cosmos I will use a mundane anecdote. Initially, I tried to introduce to the mestizo staff at my center some basic notions of recycling and composting. I asked the staff to create compost by recycling food waste in the main kitchen and leaves, cuttings, and such from the maintenance of the land. I bought two trash bins for the kitchen to separate what was biodegradable and what was not, since there is no recyclable pick-up from the municipality. We also constructed fenced enclosures for the land clippings. My indigenous staff had no problem understanding my request concerning grass and other cuttings and placing them in the right enclosure so they could become compost. However, the kitchen staff, led by Randy's mother Ida and Randy himself, were a completely another matter. It turned out that discriminating between what was biodegrable and what was not was surprisingly difficult to learn and even more difficult to make a habit. It must be noted that the municipality of Lamas has only one category of trash and one machine to pick up the trash weekly. The discrimination between something compostable or recyclable and something that is not, is simply not implemented in Lamas and of course in most of its mainly mestizo inhabitants' households.[10] When Randy and his then-partner Kemy moved into the apartment at the center in January of 2016, the same difficulty was encountered. Kemy simply ignored the requirement and Randy did not insist upon it. Although such a domestic and mundane anecdote may not speak of such a vast theme as people's attitude toward a living non-human world, it nevertheless illustrates a very widespread lack of awareness among the mestizo population of Lamas concerning the destruction wrought on the planet by modern modes of life. This is not helped by the fact that Kichwa-Lamas ideas about the sentience of natural entities are considered by most mestizos to be a silly superstition.

Before his initiation, it would never have occurred to Randy to ask permission of a plant before harvesting it. This is something he demonstrated when we did our first medicinal plants workshop in August of 2017. As I report in the next chapter of this section of the book, Randy never accompanied Royner, me, and the students to harvest mycelium (micro mushrooms) from the forest with a ritual asking permission and then one of gratitude when leaving with our harvested mycelium. He never participated in any ritual involving the non-human world that Royner led us in. But Randy completely changed during his initiatory journey. In the closing ritual for the 2017 workshop, Randy took all of us to a stream where he addressed the water, chanted to it and poured it over each one of us. Randy was profoundly transformed by his initiatory journey and came to hold what I, following Stefano Varese, would call a cosmocentric worldview, abandoning his erstwhile anthropocentric materialist one.

4. SITUATING OURSELVES IN OUR SOCIAL CONTEXTS

To convey the unexpectedness of Randy's initiation I need to draw his portrait and describe what kind of person he was before he was initiated against his will. I also need to sketch the history of our relationship and with others central to the center I eventually created, in which Randy plays an important role. I will sketch a portrait of another staff member in Sachamama Center who is indigenous to highlight the differences.

I first met Randy in 1998 at his parents' home in Lamas, when he was 15 years old. I had visited Peru for the first time in 1994, when I was invited to collaborate with PRATEC.[1] Having decided to abandon the practice of mainstream ethnography (for reasons I discuss in Part Three of this book), I was fascinated by PRATEC's work of rethinking the indigenous cultures of Peru as viable alternatives to Western modernity. PRATEC introduced me to Lamas, and we began offering mini-courses with members of PRATEC in that town, lodging in Randy's parents' home, where his mother ran a bed and breakfast. I quickly discovered that Ida Gonzales Flores, Randy's mother, was a marvelously talented cook and a warm and friendly person.

A few years later Grimaldo Rengifo, the founder and director of PRATEC, decided to buy land in Lamas to construct a community center. He invited me to join him, buy an adjoining piece of land and help him construct the center. When our funds ran dry, I began to run study-abroad courses for my American undergraduate students, to help us complete the newly built but not quite finished center. I knew that Randy's mother, Ida Gonzales, would be the perfect person to take charge of feeding and caring for the students. Ida proved to be key to the success of the study-abroad courses and she remained an indispensable assistant to me, until Randy's fateful initiation.

Around 2000 I invited Randy to join me and an indigenous woman friend in an ayahuasca ceremony led by a local indigenous curandero, one of those regularly invited by PRATEC. Randy had demonstrated a serious passion for painting and drawing, and I thought that taking ayahuasca would deepen his artistic creativity. He indeed produced several beautiful paintings inspired by his visions in that session. However, it was clear that he was not interested in repeating the experience and he evinced no interest in ayahuasca itself. I believe Randy was about 18 when we did this joint ayahuasca ceremony.

Much later, in 2009, after I no longer collaborated with PRATEC, I bought land on the other side of town and with Randy's help I constructed another center, which I named the Sachamama Center for Biocultural Regeneration—Sachamama being the local indigenous name for the spirit of the rain forest. I began to bring US and Canadian students there, with Ida and Randy as my right-hand assistants. This period was difficult personally for me. My older brother, who had raised me, had recently died and my huband of 36 years had just left me for a much younger woman. I decided to do an ayahuasca retreat at Takiwasi center in the nearby city of Tarapoto. I had met its founder, the French medical doctor Jacques Mabit, in 2004 and had started going to ayahuasca ceremonies there. I had been attending ayahuasca ceremonies since around 1994, when the members of PRATEC told me they did this regularly and insisted I participate. Until then, I had never partaken of any psychedelics save for the occasional joint at parties. I had never heard of ayahuasca and had no idea what its effects were. However, I soon discovered that ayahuasca ceremonies opened up for me heretofore unsuspected horizons and I have not stopped this practice since.

Following Jacques Mabit's advice, I did my first retreat in Takiwasi's forest in February 2009, hoping it could help me in this painful period of my life. It profoundly healed me. I took a 'master plant' known as 'the memory of the heart' which taught me things that years of therapy had failed to do. I returned to my center with a new lease on life. That December I would be hosting the first study-abroad course on that land, but the center was unfinished, requiring a new kitchen-dining room and many more rooms to house students. I left Randy in charge of the construction with trepidation. When I returned in the summer, I was stunned by how far along the construction had advanced, and by the time the students arrived end of December everything was ready. It was obvious that Randy was reliable and competent and he had an aesthetic sensibility that matched mine.

During my collaboration with PRATEC I had learned that one of the main challenges for indigenous farmers was their lack of sufficient land; the length of their rotation between clearings in the forest to make food gardens was not long enough for the forest to regenerate robustly. This was leading to the expansion of degraded land where the forest no longer regenerates, and food crops no longer grow. When I created the Sachamama center I was asked by leaders of the indigenous communities where I brought my study-abroad students to help them with their main problem: the rapid spread of deforestation and the increasing inability to practice their method of agriculture, namely slash and burn. I immediately decided that this would become the focus of my center. Meanwhile I had also learned that a series of archaeological excavations throughout the Amazonian basin had shown that one of the most fertile and sustainable anthropogenic soils in the world had been made by the pre-Columbian inhabitants of the region.[2] This meant that we would not be importing some new-fangled foreign technology to help the indigenous farmers, but rather regenerating their own ancestral technology. I immediately set about trying to make this pre-Columbian anthropogenic soil in my center.

I was right away faced with a substantial challenge. Specialized ovens were needed to produce biochar by carbonizing biomass under high temperature with little or no oxygen. This is where Randy revealed his remarkable ingenuity. A quick web search revealed that people were devising affordable backyard biochar ovens all over the world. Randy and I perused the many examples of backyard biochar ovens, and he told me he would continue to investigate while I was back home in Cambridge, Massachusetts. During the months of my absence he designed, constructed and tested a biochar oven based on a combination of two backyard oven models found online.[3] Randy's oven has faithfully produced the biochar we need for our regenerated pre-Columbian Terra Preta do Indio ("Black Earth of the Indians" in Portuguese.)[4]

The other important ingredient in this anthropogenic black soil was mycelium, which attaches to plant roots as mycorrhizal webs.[5] I had heard that there were farmers in Costa Rica who were able to grow food permanently and organically by creating a natural fertilizer using mycelium from the forest floor. However, no one could find the agronomist who had gone to Costa Rica and knew how this was done. I finally decided to go to Costa Rica myself, armed with the name of one of the farmers using this method. There this farmer taught me how to collect mycelium from the forest floor, ferment them, and make a brew that transformed soil into one with a reliable, permanent productivity. The method was simple, and the mycelium were freely accessible in the forest.

A third ingredient found in all the archaeological soil is broken ceramics. Having carefully gone over the published material on this soil there was only one article about a possible provenance of the ceramics, and that referred to ceramics broken and placed in the grave of a woman from the Brazilian Amazon. However, the explanation of broken ceramics in graves—or the idea of ceramic shards coming from middens (trash heaps) could not explain the fact the broken ceramics were found wherever this black soil was discovered. Those shards of ceramics were found regardless of the presence or absence of graves or middens. A much more convincing explanation came from one of my indigenous staff members, Girvan Tuanama, a Kichwa-Lamas. Girvan told me that his grandmother used to always bring broken ceramics to offer to the spirits of her *chacra* (food field).[6]

Discussing the matter with the indigenous communities with whom we collaborated, they all expressed a keen desire to begin making these offerings once more, since the custom had faded under a combination of the forces of modernity and the judgment of the dominant mestizo society. Mestizos have generally identified with their European ancestry, preferring to forget about their indigenous roots or at least not emphasize them. Led by my staff member Royner Sangama, when my students and I visited indigenous communities we began to make offerings of the pre-Columbian corn beer known as chicha, very much still in use today, in ceramic vessels that we then shattered, burying the pieces in the soil.

In my study-abroad classes, entitled "Indigenous Spirituality and Ecology," we not only learned about indigenous spirituality through readings and discussions in seminars but also from our indigenous staff members as well as our hosts in the communities we visited. We would go to a nearby patch of rain forest and collect mycelium from the forest floor as I had been taught. Before entering the forest and leaving it, we always did a brief ritual offering tobacco smoke—the food of the spirits—first asking permission and expressing gratitude before leaving. We did these small rituals in our center's food garden as well. Those rituals were always led by Royner Sangama, who often invoked the spirits in his native Quechua. Royner would often bring along his wife Cindy and together they made invocations in Quechua to the spirits.[7] We also celebrated ritually the full moon when it rose dramatically over our center, glowing orange. We also marked the solstices. In all those ritualistic celebrations, we were led by Royner, who knows the gestures and the words. Royner, an immensely gifted language teacher, would also offer an introductory course in the Quechua language, and would lead us on tours of the many medicinal plants found on our center's land. Royner would give their names, their use and the ritual practices associated with them.

Royner, in other words, became central to my learning about Kichwa-Lamas' spirituality and language, and to my teaching at center Sachamama. He has remained quite close to me and central to both my teaching and my project of regenerating the pre-Columbian anthropogenic black soil—known as Terra Preta internationally and rebaptized by Royner as Yana Allpa, meaning 'black soil' in Quechua. Royner became an expert at making Yana Allpa: ritualistically collecting the mycelium from the forest floor, fermenting them with air (aerobically) and without air (anaerobically) and preparing the brew that was added to the soil. He would lead the offerings of broken ceramics and preparing biochar in the oven constructed by Randy.

Since ayahuasca is classified as a Schedule I drug in the US, and thus illegal, the ingesting of it—or for that matter of any other indigenous medicinal plant—was totally out of bounds in my courses. The colleges and universities where the students came from were categorical about this issue and I of course was extremely rigorous in keeping ayahuasca and shamanism completely out of my students' experience. It should also be pointed out that Royner, although extremely knowledgeable in the traditions of his Kichwa-Lamas indigenous culture, was not himself a curandero (shaman). A knowledge of Amazonian shamanism was not necessary for carrying out the activities of either regenerating the pre-Columbian black soil or leading offering rituals at the time of planting, the full moon, and the solstices. My own practice of participating in ayahuasca ceremonies was carried out for purely personal reasons and never took place during my courses.

Randy never participated in the rituals led by Royner and never accompanied us to the indigenous communities we visited with the students. Randy never expressed any distaste or disapproval for such rituals but he expressed no interest in them and simply never joined us in these indigenous practices. At the communities we would visit, Randy would go in advance to build a waterless composting toilet or to rebuild their kitchen so it could accommodate a greater number of students or to organize the sleeping quarters for the students and teachers. However, he did this before any of us arrived in the community and did not wait for our arrival. Unlike Royner, Randy was not involved in my teaching activities directly, only in providing the necessary infrastructure.

Randy is mestizo; his paternal great-grandfather came from China, hence the patronymic Chung. Though he never displayed the feeling of superiority that many mestizos show toward indigenous peoples, he did evince the secularism of his parents. Ida and her husband did not celebrate Christmas or Easter or even birthdays. They seemed to reject any ritualistic celebration whatsoever. This was surprising in Lamas, where most people were either Catholic or belonged to one of the many Evangelical Protestant churches in town. This unusual secularism was not at all typical in Lamas.

I learned from Randy that his paternal great-grandfather had been sent to Peru by his family in the late 1920s, to escape the Chinese civil war between Chiang Kai-shek and Mao Zedong. Randy told me that his Chinese ancestor was a revolutionary, meaning that he might have adopted some form of anti-religious Maoist ideology. I have surmised that this is the source of Randy's family's anti-religious attitude, passed down the generations on his father's side. Randy's mother, Ida, comes from a rural farming mestizo background and would not originally have shared such an attitude, but as women of her generation typically do, she adopted her husband's views. Both of Randy's parents are retired high school teachers, he in history and she in home economics with a specialization in cooking.

I never tried to convince Randy to participate in the ritual offerings my students and I engaged in, led by Royner. I respected his preferences and did not question them. It was obvious to me that this was not Randy's specialty, and it did not even occurr to me to ask Randy to be present during such ritualistic offerings much less to ask him to lead them. I always relied on

Royner, who was always eager to participate in those rituals and share his culture with the students from abroad, in the process escaping from the generally dismissive and belittling attitude of the dominant mestizo society toward indigenous rituals. As an anthropologist, I generally associated indigenous spirituality with indigenous peoples, though there were exceptions: the Takiwasi center was founded and headed by a French Catholic doctor, and there were also many mestizo curanderos in the region, some of whom had led ayahuasca session in which I had participated. When it comes to ayahuasca, indigenous spirituality was often practiced by non-indigenous people, but this was not the case with offerings for the spirits of the food garden.

Since shamanism is so central to indigenous Amazonian spirituality, I not only had students read anthropological essays about ayahuasca but additionally would bring them for a tour of Takiwasi center in the nearby city of Tarapoto. At Takiwasi we were taken on a tour by one of the psychotherapists working there, who would explain the therapeutic protocol developed in this center for curing drug addiction, through a combination of Western psychotherapy and indigenous Amazonian medicine, including ayahuasca.[8] The tour concluded with a lecture given by Dr. Mabit. Randy never joined me in those tours. He displayed no interest in learning about the use of ayahuasca and other indigenous therapeutics for treating drug addiction, or for any other purpose for that matter. Royner did not accompany us on these tours either, since he already knew about the plants.

Before summing up these sketches of Randy and Royner's role in the center and my activities there, I would be remiss if I did not include one of the main constructions for which Randy was responsible. Three years after founding the Sachamama Center, we realized that the facilities were being used only during a few weeks in December-January and another several weeks from May to August, depending on the number of courses being offered.[9] For the rest of the year the facilities were not being used, but the staff necessary for our main project of regenerating Yana Allpa had to be paid throughout the year. The same is true of the cooking and cleaning staff attending to the needs of students during course offerings; it was impossible to have reliable temporary help, so we had to pay salaries throughout the year. Ida and Randy both suggested that we open the facilities to tourists whenever there were no students using them. This was an obvious solution to the strain on my finances and I adopted it immediately.[10] We decided that the part of the property dedicated to regenerating black soil, namely the food garden and the biochar oven, would be reserved for those activities and the big two-story house, the dining room, kitchen, and bungalows would become an 'Hospedaje" or hostel for tourists during the rest of the year. Ida and Randy decided the hostel part needed its own name for purposes of recognition.

There is in fact a revealing incident around the perceived need of a new name for the hostel. The name of my center: Sachamama, which I chose, refers to the spirit of the rain forest for the local Kichwa-Lamas. It is one of the spirits invoked by Royner during offerings to the chacra. This spirit of the rain forest is represented as an enormous snake. Randy told me that one time as he was picking up students at the airport in Tarapoto, he was holding a sign saying Sachamama Center for the students to identify him. He reported to me that several people, some of whom he knew, snickered and laughed when they saw the name on the sign. I was puzzled but he explained to me that for most mestizos this Quechua word sounds ridiculous, like the rituals that the name implies. Since it was more than likely that many of the hoped-for tourists would be mestizos from Tarapoto it would be much safer to give the hotel a more acceptable name for this possible future clientele, one free of indigenous-identified implications. One of Randy's uncles suggested the name Sangapilla, which is the name of a local plant that flowers in late August with deliciously fragrant blossoms. This flower is named in the Lamas anthem and carries no special indigenous connotations.

So now we had a hotel with a nice, 'safe' name. One German acquaintance of mine came to visit me around that time and said,

"This is a beautiful place. I am staying at a hotel in Tarapoto and paying good money for it and I believe that if you built a swimming pool like that hotel has, you could charge similar rates." Her argument was very persuasive, and I decided we should do that.[11] However, I wanted this pool to be ecological, free of the usual chemicals to which I am allergic, and which furthermore are terrible for the environment. So, Randy and I went back on the Internet to look for models of ecological pools. This was in 2012, and all the models we found required that such pools be encircled by aquatic plants that would clean the water naturally.[12] Before going back to the US, I drew on the dirt the outline of the pool, kidney shaped, in the only flat location available. Randy oversaw its construction. When I returned several months later, I will never forget my reaction at seeing what he had done. I simply gasped in astonishment and wonder at the beauty he had created. The pool was encircled by abundant aquatic plants, surrounded by dwarf palm trees, and Randy had landscaped the surrounding land in a stunningly beautiful fashion, complete with a natural-looking waterfall and more trees and lush plants.

Shortly after the completion of the pool, Randy asked his partner Kemy, a mestizo trained as a junior accountant, to administer the hostel. Randy was brilliant at construction, painting and landscaping but not gifted at accounting and managing. Kemy proved to be extremely good at both these things. Soon enough she had a website made for the hostel, listed in Bookings.com and more. With Randy's construction and landscaping genius and Kemy's managerial gift, the hostel began to be frequented by tourists, mostly from Tarapoto but with the occasional visitors from Lima and even abroad.

It will be clear from this sketch of my closest collaborators that Randy was the mestizo secular specialist in designing and building structures as well as machines, while Royner was the specialist in indigenous Kichwa-Lamas culture and spirituality. I will let Randy's own voice in part II tell of the totally unexpected, unanticipated, and frankly unwanted event that changed Randy's life radically and therefore has also affected my own life, as will be clear in the following pages. Randy never writes anything, but he told me about these events after they happened. The first time I heard his account, shortly after it happened, I was so awestruck that I did not write anything down. Later he and I arranged to find time for him to retell me (in Spanish since he does not know English) what had happened to him, and I wrote down his extraordinary story.

The turning-point event of Randy's experience of being initiated by discarnate beings took place in June 2016 and I played a key role. My insistence on his accompanying me to Don Aquilino Chujandama's center in Chazuta that fateful day in June of 2016 was atypical. I have often wondered why I behaved as I did then, given what transpired, but the only reason that keeps surfacing is simply that I did not want to be alone with people I knew very slightly during a long overnight trip. We went to that center at the request of a couple from the US; the woman was required by her doctoral program to do a two-week field study of Amazonian medicinal plants and Randy suggested that a friend of his, Carlos, teach her. Royner was unavailable since he was occupied with our Yana Allpa project. Since I barely knew the couple or Carlos, I asked Randy to accompany us on the two-day journey to do an ayahuasca session at the center where Carlos was apprenticing to become a curandero. When I asked Randy to accompany me, he flatly refused. I insisted and finally he reluctantly agreed.

This was the first time I had ever insisted that Randy accompany me to my ayahuasca sessions or to the indigenous communities that we visited for a few days and with whom we participated in ritual offerings to the spirits of the *chacra*. My forcing him to accompany us on this fateful visit to Don Aquilino's center was totally unusual. There is of course always the possibility that I unconsciously wanted him to do an ayahuasca ceremony. The possibility of an unconscious desire on my part to have Randy be initiated must be discarded since I had never heard of such an occurrence; the idea that Randy would be initiated was one of the most unlikely and far-fetched scenarios for me, for Carlos, and of course for Randy himself and it did not occur to any of us. All the curanderos we had known had sought out living teachers to initiate them on that path. In other words, we were—all of us—totally shocked to learn what had happened to Randy that fateful day in Chazuta. What Randy says in Part Two about what the spirits told him on the first night of initiation concerning my role in this event came to me as a surprise, but it is nevertheless extremely intriguing since it shows that my role was crucial.

When I later asked Randy to tell Dr. Jacques Mabit about his experience at Don Aquilino's, he said that he had heard of something like that only once or twice in his more that 35 years of living and working in Peru. Jacques was utterly taken aback by Randy's story, as was his wife, the medical doctor Rosa Giove, who exclaimed "This kind of thing never happens!" However, several of the themes in Randy's initiation are well known in the anthropological literature. In his classic book on shamanism, Mircea Eliade describes terrifying and gruesome examples from many cultures of dismemberment, flaying, decapitation, and other horrible ordeals undergone by novice shamans, in comparison with which Randy's severe beating begin to look mild.[13] Joan Halifax's *Shaman: The Wounded Healer* similarly gives many such cross-cultural examples of initiatory torture and death at the hands of spirits who violently transform the novice's body into a shaman.[14] But at the time of Randy's initiation I had not yet explored the relevant literature, so I had no awareness of the classic nature of shamanic initiatory torture and death.

Since the June 2016 turning point event, Randy continued to tell me details of his initiatory journey whenever I was in town. We scheduled several special times when we were both free and in a calm environment, so he could retell me what happened to him slowly enough so I could write it all down.[15] His narrative is related in Part Two of this book.

I realize that I should also briefly give some background as to my own spiritual upbringing and current inclinations since spirituality is at the very core of this book. I was raised in my father's Alsatian religion of Lutheran Protestantism.[16] In my late adolescence I strongly rejected this upbringing and became an ardent secularist of a revolutionary bent. A few years after World War II, when I was quite small, my parents moved from Strasbourg in France to Tangiers in Morocco where I was raised and went through the French school system. Eventually, under the influence of my best friend, the son of a Moroccan Muslim politician who fought against French rule, as well as from my high school philosophy teacher, a Communist, I realized that my parents were typical colonizers in their attitude, ideology, and politics. This resulted in my rejecting rather forcefully my religious upbringing as well as my parents' politics.

My father was a doctor, and he moved to the US where my mother, little sister and I followed him after I finished the lycée. My older brother was doing his engineering studies in Switzerland at the time. It was only after more than a decade in the US that I discovered the deeply buried secret that my father had been tried in France after the war for collaboration with the Nazis and forced to emigrate. I had known for a while that his politics were extreme right but the discovery that he had adhered to the Nazi party was a seismic brutal shock. This discovery was extremely difficult for me to digest and understand; as a result, I have been in some form of psychotherapy for a great deal of my life·

I married young, not long after arriving in the US, basically to escape my parents. My first husband took me to India, where he did his PhD research in economics. I began studying Indian classical dance, something I pursued also during our second stay in India. When we returned to the US we divorced and I began graduate work in cultural anthropology and married my second husband, also an economist. Later I did my first anthropological doctoral fieldwork in a famous pilgrimage center in the eastern state of Odisha in India, focusing on the women temple dancers whose form of dance, Odissi, I had studied. India cured me of my secularism and enriched and transformed me profoundly. I did fieldwork in India over many years. However, by the early 1990s I could no longer carry out any fieldwork, feeling that I had no way to reciprocate for the profound spiritual gifts I had been given. I decided that if I were ever to go to a country that had been colonized by Europeans I would only do so if I were invited because my hosts desired something I could offer. This happened in 1992, at an international conference on alternatives to development, where I met Grimaldo Rengifo, the founder of the Peruvian NGO, PRATEC, who was saying things that I found entrancing. My then-husband and I invited this organization to join our international research group focused on alternatives to development.

This story of my spiritual journey continues with my second child, a daughter, Jessica. I had had a son with my first husband when quite young whom I raised in his father's and (at the time) my own secular tradition. Having been spiritually awakened by my Indian experience, my second husband and I decided to raise this second child in her father's religious tradition, Judaism. When Jessica was confirmed by the rabbi of our congregation at age 16, she chose mystical Judaism as the theme for the year-long study with her rabbi. Jessica wrote a paper for her confirmation giving a Jewish mystical interpretation of the Schema, the fundamental profession of Jewish faith. Two weeks after reading this essay I was in this rabbi's office telling her I wanted to convert. This woman rabbi first asked me to tell her of my spiritual journey. After hearing of it, she told me not to abandon any of my Hindu and Dzogchen (Tibetan Buddhist) practices[17] but to consider this new path another initiation. This I have done. After an initial two-year of study of the mystical Jewish tradition I underwent a traditional conversion ritual, complete with total immersion in a mikveh (traditional Jewish bath), converting to what is known as the Jewish Renewal brand of Judaism, a renewal of the very ancient Jewish mystical tradition created by the late Zalman Schachter Salomi. This rabbi learned from not only

Sufism, Buddhism, Hinduism, mystical Christianity but also took ayahuasca and participated in other shamanic practices. This neo-Jewish mysticism has incorporated many features of other traditions, changing the gender language of the prayer book, and promoting a spirituality-suffused ecology. Following my wise rabbi's advice, I have never given up any of the spiritual practices I have acquired in my life, to which now must be added Amazonian shamanism.

PART II

INITIATED BY THE SPIRITS:
RANDY'S VOICE AND ILLUSTRATIONS

INTRODUCTORY REMARKS
by Frédérique Apffel-Marglin

This section consists of twenty-two chapters, nineteen of them Randy's words and three of them written by me but relating events affecting both of us, directly relevant to Randy's three-and-a-half-year initiatory journey as well as to my own transformation. Randy was willing to tell me about the major events in his initiation but preferred me to write those that happened in what he calls this worldly (*terrenal* in Spanish) realm, in which we were both involved.

To this day, Randy's parents have not accepted the change in him and have sadly almost totally cut off communication with him and his new partner Karen, who was selected for him by the spirits. When Randy approached Karen at the end of his initiatory journey, he separated from his former partner, who his parents much preferred.

The overwhelming majority of shamans in the upper Amazonian regions have voluntarily sought to apprentice with elder shamans. Although initiation by discarnate beings is well known in the general anthropological literature about shamanism, in my more than 25 years of regularly participating in ayahuasca ceremonies in Peru, I had never heard of such a thing.

For at least a year and a half after his initial initiation, Randy lived a somewhat divided existence between his worldly life and his shamanic experiences. He could not doubt the reality of the latter but integrating those into his everyday life took some time. He suffered from depression for about four months, the first and only episode of depression in his life. He almost gave up the initiatory path altogether after he experienced being pierced by a magical (i.e. invisible) dart that was intensely painful and frightening. The turning point was his session with Grimaldo on December 12, 2017, when the Virgin of Guadalupe appeared to him, giving him two kinds of power, and asking him to build her image. For me it is of momentous import that this turning-point event fortuitously happened on the Virgin of Guadalupe's festival day—which neither of us knew at the time.

Both Randy and I have been deeply affected and transformed by these events, as is evidenced by our 2018 joint pilgrimage to Tepeyac, Mexico, where the Virgin first appeared to a Nahuatl peasant in 1531. Now the image of Tonantzin is next to that of the virgin of Guadalupe on my altar along with several other images, displaying the spiritual diversity advocated by the founder of Jewish Renewal, which I have gratefully embraced.[1]

1. THE INITIAL SESSION AT DON AQUILINO CHUJANDAMA'S CENTER

June 2016[1]

You, doctora[2] came in May to teach a course with Jeremy Caradonna of the University of Victoria. The course finished at the end of May 2016. In June, a psychotherapist from New York with a Peruvian husband arrived to do a two-week field study about medicinal plants for her doctorate in Mind-Body medicine. I called Carlos to teach her. They wanted to take ayahuasca. Carlos decided to take them to his master Aquilino Chujandama in Chazuta. I did not want to go; I had no interest whatsoever in ayahuasca. I thought Carlos would take them, and you would go with them. I expected that you all would go but you, the day of going there, came looking for me. I did not want to go but you became insistent and obliged me to go. We went in the black car; it was an hour and a half of suffering; my stomach was getting loose and I was sweating. I suffered until I was in the session. I did not want to be there. We drank [the potion] and the initiation voyage began.

The first vision was of an egg and a sperm that entered the egg. Afterwards they showed me[3] my childhood with my brother and my parents, nice things and not so nice things, but simple, no traumas. After that, my bad things: playing with women, vices, beer, billiard. I never beat the women, but I played with them.

Then about ten men began to beat me, to take from me all these bad things. They kicked me, hoisting my body above the ground and throwing me down all battered. And I remembered

55

a book, *Don Tuno: The Lord of the Astral Bodies* [a shaman from the North] which said you can protect youself by saying: "with me you will not be able." Saying this helped me to withstand the beating. They stopped kicking me and two others came and took me by my arms to a room where there was a large table and four elegant [discarnate] elders with long white beards. They wore a single robe with brilliant thread embroidery. The place looked like a judicial court. The old ones began to speak to me: "We have selected you; you have passed this first test of the beating. We are giving you a wisdom, a gift to help people." I did not want to receive this and kept saying: "Why me?" They did not answer me. I was asking for explanations: "Why choose me?" They made me understand that it was not a coincidence that you [F.A.M.] forced me to come to Chazuta.

Then I had another vision. You grabbed my hand and took me flying. We flew along the whole route from Sangapilla to the tambo[4] of Don Aquilino. We saw the whole trajectory: the road, the Huallaga River, the small stream, everything. At that moment I accepted that it had to be that way. You let go of my hand and said to me: "Continue! It gives me great calm and security that you will look after me." And then I accepted.

Then there was another type of test: two paths. I was walking on a path and suddenly I was faced with a fork in the road. The first path was taking me to a place with a radiantly sunny sky, a beautiful valley with gorgeous trees and many-colored flowers, and there was a fence that separated a garden. A fragrant pleasant breeze also reached that place. Next to the fence were two men in armor like those in medieval times, each of them mounted on his horse. One of the horsemen said to me: "Come this way. You will have everything: health, knowledge, money, jewels, women." In one instant, I had the memory of my whole life with my family. Faced with this situation, my parents' teachings influenced my decision quite a lot. Although I was tempted, I did not choose that path. The second path led me to an obscure dark valley, where a humble and divine voice said to me: "Come this way." I decided to go on this second path. When I accepted, another scene immediately arose: a street with goats, carts drawn by horses, children, women, and old people, many people walking—it was like a pilgrimage in an antique time. I was walking in the middle of this multitude and, I was hearing music, like the sound of the flute used in India to enchant snakes. I did not know where I was going. We were all going on a single road. I just walked and observed. Suddenly the scene changed and I found myself in a different place. I was sitting on a tree trunk on the ground. Everything was calm. And there, in front of me, I was looking at the Amazon River; it was dusk; and one could not see the other bank. I saw an immense ship with a black hull. I raised my eyes and I saw what was in that ship: a celebration of the New Year. The music in this feast was strident and there was a feast with many sailors, waiters bringing alcohol, men with bare torsos, men with much jewelry on their bodies, and prostitutes. And I was wondering about my visions within my visions.

I came back to reality. I needed to go to the bathroom, and I said aloud that someone should take me there. I was not even able to stand up because I was in a deep trance. Carlos helped me and took me to the bathroom, where I had diffuse visions at first. I was seated there, destroyed, bent over. I raised my eyes and saw three lights, placed vertically, in the form of lozenges of different sizes: the biggest one was in the upper part and the smallest one in the lower part. In that moment I understood that these three lights were everything: the unique God. The creator of the whole universe. The light was so strong that I could not withstand it. Twice I raised my head. While this was going on, I saw three grandmothers with their hair held up in a bun, each of them playing their *shacapa* [shamanic leaf rhythm beater]; they were ancient shamanesses. The vision ended.

I stood up and Carlos took me back to my seat. I was destroyed. The light was turned on. You, doctora, they took you to rest, and I was unable to react. I was worried. With a tender smile, Don Aquilino said to Carlos: "Take the *tigrillo*." To call someone a '*tigrillo*' [small jaguar] means that this person can bear beatings, that he perseveres.

The visions came again. They showed me scenes of my life at high speed, as if in a film. I saw from my conception, with the ovule and the sperm, until my death. I felt like an old man of 80 or 85; I was on my deathbed and during some three seconds I was dead. I heard the song of Don Aquilino and this song was as if two hummingbirds came out of his mouth and came toward me. I could feel the vibration of their little wings close to my chest as if those two birds were performing an operation on my heart, and after this I began to revive. I was calm and I was alive. I opened my eyes; my body could not move, and I saw a white cloud at about a meter and a half above my eyes. And from that cloud emerged a hand holding out to me a lance made of gold, of about a meter and half long. With my last strength, I lifted my left hand and took hold of the lance and my arm fell to the ground, holding it. Immediately I felt a great peace and calm.

Vision #1: Vision with ayahuasca. Members of the "tribunal" wherre Randy was taken after his beating. "We have selected you; you have passed the test of the beating."

Vision #2: Vision with ayahuasca. "Ancient curanderas plying the *shacapa*."

2. RANDY RECEIVES SHAMANIC KNOWLEDGE/POWER FROM A DISCARNATE MASTER

June 2016

We returned to Lamas [the day following the first initiatory session]. Everything was quiet for a week. I was assimilating all that had happened, somewhat confused and afraid. I would go out every night with my friends to forget and live my worldly life, but I did not drink any alcohol since I was in *dieta* [the period after an ayahuasca session when you have to abstain from alcohol, among other things]. On the fourth or fifth day I returned to Sangapilla around midnight, bathed and came into our bedroom and turned out the lights. Kemy was sleeping. After about fifteen minutes in bed, I saw a winged white horse flying in circles above me. In a moment, the master [i.e., his discarnate indigenous master] appeared to me for the first time.

The master had the face of a man of about 80 years old, wearing a cushma[1] with blue lines and a necklace of pearls that looked like a rosary but without a cross. He carried a cotton talega,[2] with a cap with a wide border like a chumbe[3] that covered his head. He was levitating above me. At that moment my body became cold; my heart was beating hard, and I remained observing, afraid. The master took something like a plant out of his talega and offered it to my mouth.[4] I woke Kemy up and asked her if she saw anyone in the room. "Nobody," she said and then she went back to sleep. As I had not accepted what had been offered, everything disappeared.

The next day, concerned, I went out at nine in the evening to ask someone knowledgeable in those things and the only one I knew was Carlos. I related to him the things I had experienced, and he told me in an aggressive manner: "You are a good one to become a sorcerer."

"Why do you tell me this, since I harm no one?" I replied.

His whole attitude calmed down and he said to me: "Receive; it is a *mariri*[5] that they are giving you."

I felt that Carlos seemed to be jealous. Full of fear, I returned to Sangapilla around one in the morning, thinking that this master would not come back. I bathed and went to bed. After a few minutes, the winged horse reappeared and so did the master. He took a green liquid out of his mouth and poured it into his hands. He then poured this liquid into my mouth. I felt that it penetrated my throat like energy, like air, like something entering in me. Near the wall on my right, a branchlet of snakes like ferns [appeared]. The master smoked a *mapacho*[6] and blew the smoke on my face. When the smoke was near my face it transformed itself into a small dragon, made of this white smoke. After that he smudged me [by blowing tobacco smoke] from the feet up to my head and disappeared.

Vision #3: Vision without ayahuasca. A winged horse flying in circles above Randy just before the apparition of his discarnate master.

\

Vision #4: Vision without ayahuasca. The discarnate master giving Randy his 'yachay.'

3. RANDY'S FIRST VISIT AND CEREMONY AT TAKIWASI DRUG-ADDICTION TREATMENT CENTER

July 2016

When I told you, doctora, all that had happened to me, you took me to see Dr. Jacques. You asked me to tell Dr Jacques all that had happened to me. Dr Jacques listened to my narrative and told me that such a type of initiation was extremely rare; that he had heard of it happening only once or twice. Afterwards Dr. Rosa arrived, and Dr Jacques told her quickly [what I had told him] and she exclaimed: "This is extremely rare. It never happens!"

A week later you took me to an ayahuasca session at Takiwasi. In that session, I was frightened by the first ikaro[1] of Dr Jacques, very fast and strong. When I looked at him, I saw him holding a whip of seven cords, each of a different loud and luminous color, as if he held a rainbow in his hands. He was lashing me hard on my back. I felt the pain of it and could hear the crack of the whip. I thought "What have I done?" It made me want to throw up.[2] I could feel the taste of the plant that rose in my throat. At that moment, in my trance, I heard an authoritative voice like your own, doctora, that said: "Don't throw up!" This voice told me not to worry—he would take care of all of this, and would protect me; he was on my right; he was my master.

At that moment I had a feeling of egotism. I had brought a shawl for the session, and I threw it over my chest with pride.

The *ikaros* of Dr Jacques did not affect me. Though I was saying to myself "Don't fool around; he will punish you," I felt secure and protected. I was not in trance, but I had visions. I saw myself at about age 45, seated in an armchair in a living room. Immediately about fifteen women with long flowered dresses entered the living room. The women were dancing with each other, and the master pointed with his hand to the dancing group and the circle of women opens and Karen appeared, clothed all in white; she was the only one in white. Pointing at Karen, the master said: "She will be your wife and you will have a child with her." This left me thoughtful, but I did not give this vision much importance.

At the end [of the ayahuasca session] Dr Jacques called me to come near him. I went somewhat still in trance. He smudged my back, as everyone—Dr. Jacques, Jaime, Fabienne, Dr Rosa, the priest—all of them together sang the *ikaro* "authentic little curandero..." Suddenly a strong trance came over me. A vision appeared: I was seated under a waterfall with a great deal of vegetation all around it and a whole tribe in front of me was singing this *ikaro*. I calmed down. It felt like an initiation.

When the session ended, Dr Jacques came to me and asked me how it had been for me and I was annoyed as I said to him: "Good." And then you, doctora, came close to me and we talked.

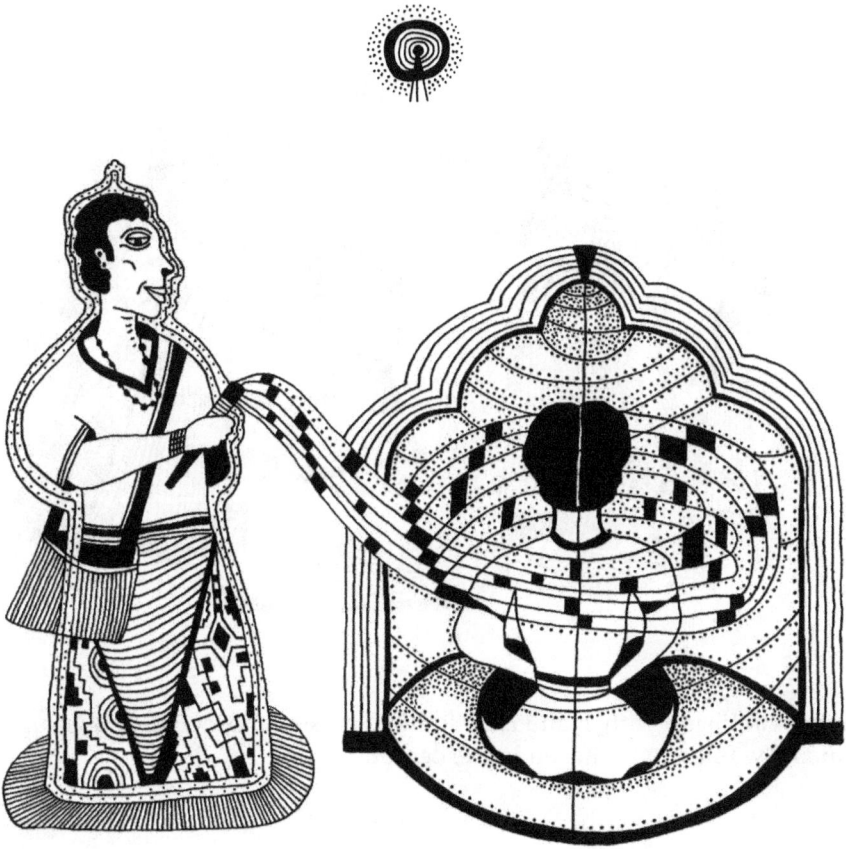

Vision #5: Vision with ayahuasca. Jacques giving Randy lashes.

Vision #6: Vision with ayahuasca. Randy's master shows Randy a group of dancing women, with Karen in the center.

4. A SHATTERING EVENT

Report by Frédérique Apffel-Marglin, August 2016

This section is not in Randy's voice since it is not about a vision or a session of Randy's, but it is about what he was shown in the previous ayahuasca session and about what his master told him then. It describes an event that happened that same summer while I was in Peru. This event in normal reality reverberated in a frightening way with Randy's previous vision, where he was shown a woman by the name of Karen who was to be his wife. Karen is the sister of Randy's best friend. At the time, she was married to a well-known dentist in Lamas and had two daughters. Shortly before my return to the US at the end of August, we received the news that Karen's husband had just died in a motorcycle accident. I will never forget the feeling that possessed me when I got the news of his death. A terror seized my heart. When Randy's discarnate master showed him Karen emerging from a group of dancing women, and told him that she was going to be his wife and the mother of his child, Karen's husband was alive. That is probably why Randy gave no importance to that vision then, since such a future seemed totally impossible. Both Randy and I were terrified by the news. I admonished Randy not to breathe a word of his vision of Karen and of what his master had said. I need not have worried; Randy did not share his ayahuasca experiences with anyone, and he was as spooked as I was. Given how widespread sorcery is in Lamas and Wayku, people would most likely have accused him of having arranged the accident by hiring a sorcerer. Of course, at the time Randy was happily ensconced in a longterm relationship with Kemy and was not remotely interested in Karen. We will see how this developed over the next three years and in the process realize that the spirits' designs are much more powerful than our own.

5. RANDY RECEIVES MENTORING FROM DR. JACQUES AND A VISION
July and August 2016

D r Jacques told me to come back the next day at 6 pm to talk. Although I had some doubts about telling him all that had happened to me, he was able to bring out my trust and I told him that he had lashed me and that my master had appeared to me during the session. He told me that he thought the *yachay*[1] could be from a sorcerer and that was why he had acted in that way: wanting to make me throw up. He performed a sort of exorcism on me. He took a book out from a drawer in one hand and placed his other hand on my head. He read as if it were a prayer but in a different language. And suddenly, a vision appeared. My whole field of vision became red. Afterwards, a woman appeared, covered with a mantle, with brown skin, tender, very beautiful, with an angelic smile and two dimples in her cheeks. She wore a pearl necklace and pearl earrings. Her hands were placed one over the other on her heart and she looked at me with her head slightly inclined forward. As I described all that I was seeing to Dr Jacques, he stopped his prayers and exclaimed: "It is a Virgin!" From afar I saw my master coming. He knelt in front of the woman. I told all of this to Dr Jacques. He immediately put down his book, removed his hand from my head and sat down in his armchair with a satisfied smile. Pointing at me with his finger he told me: "Your master is not a sorcerer!"

After this I saw many hands coming close to me. I asked Dr Jacques what this meant, and he told me that many people would come to me. He showed me a portrait of the Virgin of Guadalupe and asked me: "Is it her?" Yes, I said, she is the same as in my vision, but in my vision, the look in her eyes was of an incredible sweetness.

Then we began to talk about the nature of this path. He told me: "If the '*mariri*' was black or red it was from a sorcerer, but if it was white or green it was from a genuine shaman." He also told me that I had to settle my life: root myself and consolidate my life with my partner. Finally he smudged me, placing his face very near mine. He looked at my throat and placed there a lighted '*mapacho*'. In that moment I felt he was a great master and a deep respect for him welled up in me. It was as if he had done a purification, but only he knows what he did to me.

Dr. Jacques said to me: "The *yachay* is in the throat."

Vision #7: Vision without ayahuasca. Randy's master kneels in front of the virgin.

6. RANDY'S FIRST ENCOUNTER WITH SORCERY/BRUJERIA

September 2016

After you returned to the US at the end of August, doctora, I felt that I needed to go again to Takiwasi. I went in September. When my trance began, I was seated and suddenly I saw Oscar and the sorcery that was being done to him by another person who was interested in his wife. In the vision I saw the sorcerer and conversed with him. The sorcerer opened the door and invited me to come in, and I asked him: "Why are you doing this to Oscar? Who paid you, and how much?" But I already knew who had paid the sorcerer for the work. In the vision I asked Dr Jacques to teach me what to do in such a situation, and he replied that the knowledge was in me. That made me angry, but now I realize that he was right.

I had a second session in Takiwasi in September, and in the vision I was told that I had to go to Chazuta with some friends: Oscar, Rafael, Paul, Adler, and Teddy. I was thinking that if Oscar went to Chazuta, he would see the sorcery done to him. After the trance in that second session I called Kemy around 3 am and told her everything. I made the decision to bring Oscar to Chazuta to see whether what I had seen was true. I was somewhat incredulous about this plant, the ayahuasca. The next week I offered to take Oscar to Chazuta.

SECOND SESSION WITH DON AQUILINO IN CHAZUTA

Randy Acquires More Tools and Powers
September 2016

I went to Chazuta in September with the five friends I was told about in the second session in Takiwasi. The session began at 8 pm. When we arrived, we were received by Don Aquilino's son, who is following in his father's footsteps, and accompanied us in that session. When the trance began and Don Aquilino began to sing, my trance was not of visions. Instead, without being aware of doing so, I was imitating his songs. Adler told me this the next day. At the same time, in the trance, I was conscious of the people that I had brought to this session. Oscar was on my left and Paul on my right. In the middle of my trance, I came close to Oscar and asked him in his ear, softly, what he was seeing. He was in a deep trance and told me that a person came close to him with a human body and the mask of a horse, with a renaco tree behind, who was promising him that in exchange for his wife he would give him a car and that his business would go well. Oscar desperately wanted a car.

I asked him: "Do you see your wife's betrayal?" and he said: "No, but they are offering me this."

I told him: "Don't worry, I will take care of you. Be careful—if you accept this offer you will ruin your life."

And he responded: "No. What? Am I going to abandon my little daughters?"

I became more conscious of the plant; I was happy about what I had verified. I returned to my seat.

Paul began to shout; he was crying, calling for his father and his mother. The curandero in me came out and I began to visualize the nature of his problem. I began a conversation with Don Aquilino: "I am seeing a man from Huancayo [a city in the Peruvian Andes] who is doing sorcery to Paul."

Yes, Don Aquilino said. I began to sing *ikaros* from the highlands, and the man from Huancayo was surprised. The *ikaros* from Huancayo are different from the ones from here. And I told him: "I am going to kill you. I am going to kill you! I am going to kill you! Get lost!"

Then I say to Don Aquilino: "He has already left." Don Aquilino was only listening and observing.

After a while, the man from Huancayo appeared again. Then knowledge came to me. I heard sounds of wind, of birds, and I was making the sound of chattering teeth. It was as if I had known those tools from before. I began with very vulgar words: "Son of a whore, your mother's cunt, get lost, I am going to kill you!" He did not want to leave, protecting his work with Paul.

I said to Don Aquilino: "Don Aquilino, do I kill him?" He responded: "Don't kill him."

He stood up and came near me and put a big piece of cinnamon bark in my mouth and said: "Don't kill him, make him blind."[1] He sat down and said to me: "Tomorrow I will give you a secret."

Paul began to calm down. He called me to his side and embraced me, telling me that he loved me, that I should take care of him. I left him calm and returned to my seat and an extraordinarily strong surge of egotism emerged from me along with a vision: I was flying like a bird, making bird sounds. looking down on an Amazonian valley floor. I saw the tallest tree that stood above that plain. I landed on the tip of the tree. I had the body of a human, but with wings and a beak. I was naked, and I was singing a song of victory.

And then this vision disappeared. I beat my chest with pride and said: "I am a master!" And Don Aquilino told me: "You are not a master, only a little master."

After hearing what Don Aquilino said, I asked forgiveness. I am not like that; I am humble, and I accepted what he said. Don Aquilino called us, smudged each of us and we all went out of the *maloca* to urinate, but not in trance.

When we returned to the *maloca*, we were all grabbed by a trance once again, a strong one. Don Aquilino noticed, and he sent us away to go and sleep, and I said: "No! We are not going; the work is not yet done." Don Aquilino stayed impassive, but he got up and left with his son. They left us. And I began again making sounds and songs of birds, blowing air, making gestures.

Rafael got up, went to Don Aquilino's altar, and grabbed a *mapacho* from there. He sat down, lit it and smoked it. After doing that, he felt that this smoke was affecting his body and, frightened, he said to me: "I am not feeling well ever since I lit up this *mapacho*." He gave me the *mapacho* and as I took it I felt as if it were a wild horse. I took it with the lit end pointing up and I began blowing air and making sounds on it. I was conversing with the spirit of tobacco that was working with Don Aquilino. I wanted it to also work for me and be my ally. It transformed itself into a little girl and I began to speak to her nicely: "You are going to be my little girl, from now on you will work with me when I need you." I placed the *mapacho* on the ground, saying, "Rest little daughter, rest." And I sang her an *ikaro* that I do not remember, an *ikaro* offered as a gift. I smoked it and I felt that it had accepted me, and I left it on the floor.

After that I felt that the spirit of the water was calling me. I asked to be brought water. Adler and Rafael brought a jar of water around three in the morning from Aquilino's kitchen. I placed the jar and a glass in front of me. I asked permission of the water, blowing air and bird sounds. I felt the energy of the water, very strong. I called my friends one by one. I gave them the water. They drank and went to their seat. And there the session ended, around 4 in the morning.

The next day I woke up early and went looking for Don Aquilino with ego but healthy, not arrogant, and somewhat angry because he had left us. I wanted to ask him what the secret was. He smiled, lowered his head, and said to me: "You have to come here in order to learn and take *floripondio*."[2] I felt that he was not my master and responded that I did not have the time.

Vision #8. Vision with ayahuasca. Randy transforms into a therianthrope. *"I had a human body but with wings and a beak, I was naked, and I sang victory songs."*

8. RANDY RECEIVES MENTORING FROM DR. JACQUES MABIT

September to December 2016

Dr. Jacques told me that I should draw all my visions and send the drawings to him via email and later he would give me a time to see him and discuss those visions. We had about four or five sessions until December, in which Dr. Jacques served as a guide when I was confused. I had accepted the spiritual plane; but on the earthly plane I was disoriented, frightened, and confused. The meetings with Dr. Jacques calmed me and guided me a great deal. His words were key. He opened doors to that world, counseling me about what I should and should not do. I was reassured. There was a similarity in our paths: everything that happened to me had happened to him as well. He said to me: "I don't know what mission the spirits will give you; to me in the path they told me: 'We will give you all the knowledge and in exchange you must heal drug addicts.'"[1]

What served me quite a bit were the two paths; I was clear that I needed to pursue the path of the good. Dr. Jacques told me very clearly: "Always maintain humility and control the ego; don't be egocentric. Because if you let the ego control you, the spirits will take away all the knowledge and it will be as if you were 100 meters from the shore of the sea without knowing what to do." Those words guided me to continue in the path of healing and of the good. Dr. Jacques also awakened my devotion and faith in the Virgin.

I felt that he was the right master for my mission; he fit my situation exactly.

Dr. Jacques envisioned what would happen: that temptations would come; that I would have to change my life in society; take care of my diet and change my habits with beer and women; that I would have to root myself and establish a home with a woman. At that time, I was in a hurry to learn how to prepare the ayahuasca brew; he explained to me that I had to have patience. I was very anxious to begin in this path.

Dr. Jacques suggested that I do a '*dieta*'[2] with the bark of seven different trees, to strengthen me. The visions would arrive when I returned around midnight to Sangapilla, after an evening of conversing with my friends.

One night, there in my bedroom, a vision came to me. First the master appeared to me and afterwards a bald man with a tunic. Next to them was an Amazonian indigenous woman with her back to me, dressed in the traditional indigenous manner. I had those three beings in front of me. Two of them were observing me, only the woman turned her back to me. I drew my vision and sent it to Dr. Jacques. We got together in the afternoon, and he explained to me that it was Saint Benedict and explained who he was: the one who straightens out sorcerers with his cross. He gave me a medallion of St Benedict on a little cord.

A week later I had set up my own room with an altar. One afternoon I went there and closed the door, lighted a candle and started listening to a cassette recording of the ikaros of Dr. Jacques. I was thinking about everything that was happening. Almost immediately I had visions: a furry being appeared to me with the snout of a wolf, with big ears, red eyes, and enormous horns twisted like those of a goat. It was coming towards me and I was very afraid. Then on my right side appeared the Virgin and my master, as if observing the scene. They gave me a great confidence and right away, I was no longer afraid. Suddenly two angels appeared; they grabbed the creature by each of its arms and walked it to my feet. A chasm opened, and they threw it down there. The Virgin, the master and the angels disappeared and when I looked at the ceiling of the room, I saw a cupola with stained glass with red, blue, light blue, and yellow colors and a white light that bathed my body. Almost immediately the cupola disappeared, and a basket arrived like those woven by Don Simeon;[3] it covered me and inside it the white light reappeared.

It was an incredible vision, this one! I was calm, peaceful, and happy. I had no idea what these visions signified. I drew the whole scene and sent it to Dr. Jacques. He replied: "The cupola is the protection of the Virgin, and the basket refers to your master."

A few days later, around midnight, lying in my bed, I had another vision. An indigenous woman appeared with a pale green face, with a shining crown of white feathers. Along her arms, from her shoulders down to her hands, feathers came out of her body. Suddenly she took my head in both her hands, raised it, and brought it close to her face. She sent lights in circles from her eyes and mouth to me; I felt a soft energy penetrating in my eyes and mouth. I drew that drawing the next day, but did not send it to Dr. Jacques. That day Carlos arrived, and I showed him my drawing of the woman with feathers. When I told him that I was going to send it to Dr. Jacques, he immediately said: "Don't show him your drawing. This is a knowledge that they are giving you; just by looking you can know what sorcery or problems people have."

Vision #9: Vision without ayahuasca. The apparition of a 'devil,' angels, his discarnate master, and the Virgin.

Vision #10: Vision without ayahuasca. Randy underneath a cupola of protection of the Virgin.

Vision #11*:* Vision without ayahuasca. Randy underneath the basket-protection of the Ashaninka master.

Vision #12: Vision without ayahuasca. Randy receives more knowledge/ Powers from the bird-woman.

9. RANDY'S FIRST DIETA IN TAKIWASI IN FEBRUARY 2017, FOLLOWED BY FOUR MONTHS OF DEPRESSION

The retreat in Takiwasi took place in February 2017. I was afraid. At times I did not want to go and be alone in the forest. But you, doctora, pushed me to go to this *dieta*. First, I purged[1] in Takiwasi with milk of magnesia and the next day taking a plant called *sauco,* which purged me from below like never before. I went to the bathroom some fifteen times! The next day, a Thursday, we did an ayahuasca session in Takiwasi, but I don't recall much of it. I only remember that there were vibrations in my body, and I felt that the earth was vibrating; but I had no visions. I was only a spectator. That evening in the session there were a priest, two nuns and patients from Chile and Spain.

On Friday we went up to the Takiwasi forest in the morning and they assigned me to my *tambo*. It was raining when we arrived. In the afternoon I was calm, getting used to the place. At dusk came the worry. I was fighting with my fear—the snakes, the ghosts—I did not go outside even to urinate. I didn't sleep at all the first night. The next day I told myself to give myself up to this forest, to conquer my fear.

On the third day they started giving us the purges: seven tree barks (*bolaquiro, chuchuwasha, bobinsana, cocobolo, renaquillo, renaco, came*) plus liquefied coca leaves. Around 4 in the afternoon an unbearable pain in the kidneys took hold of me. That night I could not sleep, and I had a vision. My master appeared. The *tambo* disappeared and only my bed was left, with the forest around it. The master placed himself next to me; in his right hand he was holding a clay jar and in his left a *pate* [a natural cup made from a tree fruit]. He filled the *pate*, put the jar to one side and with his hand he sprinkled my whole body with the liquid in his *pate*. At that moment I felt a heat in my whole body and the master left. The image of a cosmos, a universe appeared to me and from the depth of this cosmos appeared a bird with a long tail. It flew closer and closer to me until I could see that it was the phoenix bird, and it landed on my arm. Then a big black boa snake appeared at my side, and after that an eagle and some ugly, diabolic sirens. I looked at them without fear, like a spectator, enjoying the visions. Afterwards a little bird appeared, which ever since my initiation, in my worldly life, always sings beautifully at night, but does not let itself be seen. But he came in that vision because I heard his song. I woke up the next morning renewed and well, without pain.

On the fifth day they gave me concentrated tobacco juice and my brain did not stop thinking. Everything was intense. I was thinking about my life, about everything that was happening. I tried to draw a diagram organizing my life on paper. I would begin to cry, then calm down, and then be happy, then a headache would come, I could not sleep, and it went on like that, I was unstable. At night I clearly heard *ikaros* that came from far away. I thought that they came from a tribe.

The next day I asked Edgardo, the person who gave me the purges, if he had sung ikaros the previous night and he said to me: "No. It is the plant." I told him that I had not been able to sleep ever since I arrived, and he said: "Why did you not let me know?" He gave me a plant bath, smudged me, and gave me a valerian pill. On that night I slept peacefully. The next day they cut our dieta[2] at noon and gave us a chicken soup around 4 pm. I was anxious to eat and leave. We returned to Takiwasi the next day.

From that time on, I no longer had any communications with Dr Jacques. For the next three or four months I was like an idiot. Everything bothered me. I was seriously depressed. This had never happened to me before. I called Edgardo and he recommended that I should take cinnamon bark, which helped quite a bit. I was smoking a lot of mapachos to calm my depression. That depression lasted through May. You arrived on June 13 during Pat and Peter's course[3] and you taught your course until the middle of August. In July I prepared my first ayahuasca in Sangapilla with Adler.

Vision #13: Vision without ayahuasca. The discarnate master heals him during Randy's retreat in the forest.

10. RANDY LEARNS HOW TO PREPARE AYAHUASCA
July 2017

What was missing for me was to learn how to prepare ayahuasca. No one wanted to teach me. They are jealous of their medicines. I wanted to make my medicine of the same strength as the one in Chazuta. I looked and looked with a great desire. Around that time, the people from Uruguay arrived with the man from Argentina, bringing patients with addiction to do a retreat in Sangapilla. Mario, the one from Argentina, knew something about medicinal plants. I met Daniel, the man from Uruguay, a psychologist, eight years ago. Daniel used to come to Winston's center to do retreats and he also brought people for Winston. Winston's center is called Situlli and is near Chazuta. This time Winston was going to come to Sangapilla to give ayahuasca, but he asked a very steep price and the man from Uruguay decided to give ayahuasca himself to the whole group. Daniel went to Tarapoto looking for someone who might know about preparing ayahuasca and whether there was another option. In the craft market very near the central plaza in Tarapoto, Daniel met Napoleon who told him that he knew a young man to whom he sold craft and who also was in the world of ayahuasca. The Uruguayan contacted him, and they made a time to meet in the craft market. The young man told them that he gave ayahuasca to foreigners and that his grandfather had taught him and that he knew this and that. The young man was from Iquitos. They decided to try him out in a session

89

of ayahuasca in Sangapilla, alone with Daniel and Mario. Later they decided against it. Conversing with the young man they asked him if he could procure for them ayahuasca with chakruna. He said that yes, that he knew a man who grew ayahuasca and chakruna in Sauce.[1] Mario and Daniel decided to buy it and that they themselves would prepare the ayahuasca. For five years they had done retreats in Winston's center and observed how he prepared the ayahuasca brew. But on this occasion, in the workshop in Lamas, they decided to fly with their own wings. That same afternoon, when they returned to Sangapilla they told me everything and I became interested in taking them to Tarapoto with the car to collect the ayahuasca and the chakruna. The three of us went down at 2pm: Mario, Daniel, and me. We looked for the young man in his room. He lived in a hostel for backpackers. We arrived, but the young man was not there. No one knew anything about him, and he did not answer his cell phone. We left him a note on the door with my phone number.

Half-way on the return trip to Lamas, he called me saying that he had the plants. We turned around and met with him at the bus stand in Tarapoto, where he was waiting for us with four sacks: two of ayahuasca and two of chakruna. They bought a total of 80kg of ayahuasca and 40 kg of chakruna. I took this opportunity to chat with the young man who told me he got the ingredients from a man called Joaquin, who grew ayahuasca and chakruna in Sauce. From the young man I also got Joaquin's phone number and this contact served me later to get the ingredients for preparing my own ayahuasca.

Daniel invited us for a pizza and he was complaining, annoyed at all the difficulties we had in picking up what they had ordered. The young man, surprisingly, pointing his finger to Daniel's forehead and told him sharply: "One thing you need to learn is patience." This surprised Daniel. The young man said that ayahuasca is prepared like a hamburger: always more ayahuasca and less chakruna. He also told us that he knew of a place where there was a lot of mukura, and explained how it is prepared and how it is given. You must pick the *mukura* near a stream, he said.[2]

We came back to Sangapilla around 8 in the evening and rejoined the rest of the Uruguayans, about 12 or 13 people. The next day they invited me to participate in the preparation of the ayahuasca. I accompanied them, singing and praying. I stayed up two nights to look after the cooking of the plants. You cannot leave the ayahuasca alone. My role was that of a guardian and observer. I learned to make a refined brew and to try it with a spoon to know when the ayahuasca is good. The next evening, when the ayahuasca was ready, Mario and Daniel gave the brew to their people and we were satisfied. I had learned what I wanted to learn. A few months later, I wrote them a note of thanks.

11. RANDY LEADS HIS FIRST AYAHUASCA SESSION AND HIS FIRST WORKSHOP
August 14–26, 2017

After your summer course ended in the middle of August, you did a workshop about medicinal plants with me during the last two weeks of August, and you said that I had done marvelously well. It went so well that you decided to no longer teach courses but rather do this with me. Everyone wanted to take ayahuasca during the workshop [they had all graduated from the university or were older]. Adler was my assistant. I taught the group how to harvest and prepare the purge with the plant *rosa sisa* and tobacco. The first session took place in the *tambo* in Sangapilla. About half an hour after taking the brew, I began to sing. I felt that something was happening with you. You were turning around. I came next to you and sang the *ikaro* of the Little Red Dragon and I smudged the crown of your head and your back, but you were getting worse, and I decided to lay you down on the ground. Then you lost consciousness but your whole body was still vibrating.

I went back to my seat and began to sing. My spirits came near me, dancing with the *shacapa*. There were five of them, tall with white beards and embroidered robes, dancing elegantly as they looked at me. Meanwhile, you were not reacting, and I began to worry. The others were almost all calm: Angelina was a little bit afraid; Maisie was calm; and David was as if nothing was happening (because he had been taking drugs since the age of 19). But you were not reacting, and a great fear possessed me. I lit the candles, not letting my worry show; I stood up and began singing and suddenly you woke up, happy. For me it was an incredible relief. I came near you, and you looked at me fixedly and later described to me that you saw me with geometric designs painted on my face in light green, with small prongs over my eyebrows and on my ears, with an earring in one ear. My face was more angular, and this vision you had of me lasted a long time.

Noah began to wake up and said: "I can't bear it! I want to get out of this! Please make me come out of this!" And you went to him on all fours, like a mother, calming him and you singing a song in Hebrew about Shalom.

In the second session three days later, David and Noah did not participate. You felt extraordinarily strong pains that came and went and the voice of a woman who was saying to you: "This is a cosmic energy that cannot be measured, that can never be quantified."

Erin had asked in her intention to be shown her ancestors by ayahuasca. In her vision she saw that some white hands were giving blankets infested with the smallpox virus to brown hands.[1] And she was told that she needed to return to her culture, to know her roots better, and to decolonize herself. Maisie said that she was working with you, helping you in this incarnation to give birth to the new Earth. At the very end you saw Erin as the Mother of Corn.

In the last days of the workshop, we made extract of plants and I took everyone to Chumbakiwi to bathe them with rue on the bank of the stream.

12. RANDY DECIDES TO ABANDON THE PATH OF CURANDISMO; SESSION WITH GRIMALDO ON DECEMBER 8, 2017

The session with Don Grimaldo took place in the Waman Wasi center, in his bedroom located in the lower level, underneath a living room, which could only be entered through the back of the house. The session was only between the two of us. I began with the Ganesh *ikaro*[1] and the one of *suy suy*.[2] I stood up, looking straight at Grimaldo; from each side of his body shadows of dark persons were coming out, as if they were escaping. Then, from the center of his chest came a tall, thin man, with pale skin; he held a curved samurai sword. I thought this entity was part of Don Grimaldo, his protection, or the spirit of some plant that he had taken. I stopped singing and asked Grimaldo if he was testing or challenging me. He reacted in a loud voice: "*Carajo*! [expletive] Do you think that at my age I am going to do something like that!" A doubt entered me, but what he was telling me was true. Guidance from Dr Jacques came to my mind, that in such cases one must sing *ikaros* invoking sanctified entities such as Jesus and St Benedict, and that is what I did. The entity disappeared for a moment, and I turned around to return to my seat. I felt a slight twinge in my left kidney. We closed the session. Afterwards I wanted to urinate in the bathroom, but I could not. I suspected that I had received a *virote* [magical dart].

The next day, at home, I woke up around 9 and an hour later I began to feel a pain in my left kidney. "This is a bad sign," I thought. The pain increased as time passed until I could no longer bear it; it was an unbearable pain. I was sure it was a *virote*. I became desperate. This was the first time that such a thing happened to me, and I did not know how to cure myself or who could do it. I called Don Alberto [another curandero in the region] and after I explained everything to him, he told me to drink two liters of malva [a medicinal plant] and to sit naked in a basin with malva. I did that but without any result. The pain was getting worse. It was bad. I went to bed and called my mother, but she did not know what to do. I called Edgardo, who told me to drink mineral water with a lot of sugar. I did this immediately, but nothing happened. I thought that I needed a medical doctor or to go to a hospital. However, I remembered what had happened to a woman of 26 in the hospital. The nurse gave her an injection and the girl died. I thought of calling Dr. Benzaquen [his mother's doctor], but I was conflicted because I could die. At that moment words of vengeance come out of my mouth directed at the one who sent me the magical dart. I needed something to take away the pain; in my mind I was asking for morphine. With Kemy, I went by car to Dr. Benzaquen and I told him about my symptons. He concluded that I had kidney stones and prescribed an injection for the pain. I got in the car and drove home; Kemy went to buy the injection and bring a nurse to administer it.

While I was waiting at home, I recalled Doña Alberta, the lady who reads cards, and out of deperation I called her, not expecting her to have a solution. When I told her what happened, she began by scolding me, telling me I shouldn't be taking ayahuasca. I pleaded with her to give me a remedy, and she calmed down and told me: "Cut a lime, heat it in a frying pan and massage yourself with it where it hurts; squeeze the hot lime juice there." I did what she told me and within minutes the pain disappeared. Then I went to the bathroom and urinated.

The next day I went down to a clinic in Tarapoto where they do ultrasounds, to clear up my doubts. They checked my kidneys, my pancreas, my liver—everything was fine. I returned to Dr. Benzaquen with the proofs and the only thing he told me authoritatively was: "I diagnosed you with what I had learned. I don't know what else it could be."

It was Saturday and we had a session that Sunday. I called Don Grimaldo and told him everything and he told me to rest. He was sure it was a magical dart and we decided to do our next session on Tuesday. Sunday and Monday I did an internal preparation. I brought my whole altar, all my tools, all my musical instruments and my cinnamon stick.[3] I told myself: 'I am not going to be vanquished, but if I must die, I will do it fighting.' A rage of vengeance took hold of me. I was furious that I had been hit. Although I was not afraid, I felt strongly that the path of shamanism was not for me. It was much too dangerous, and I did not want to feel again the pain that this entity had caused me with its magical dart. It was the 12th of December. I went to the second session with Don Grimaldo with the intention that this would be my last session.

Vision #14: Vision with ayahuasca. An evil entity holding a sword gives Randy a *virote*.

13. RANDY'S TURNING POINT ON DECEMBER 12, 2017: THE VIRGIN OF GUADALUPE EMPOWERS HIM

I set out my altar. Having taken my decision that this would be my last ayahuasca session, I brought all my musical instruments and all my tools, taking great care in the preparation of my altar. I placed on it the Virgin's candle. I also made a circle of white rose petals around the altar, and Don Grimaldo and I later sat ourselves inside that circle. When the time came to take the ayahuasca brew, we did not want to drink a full cup, we only took a half of the little cup. We drank and waited about 20 minutes for the effects to begin. Then I began to sing, my voice breaking. I only went into a light trance. I took the drum, but I felt that its sound did not connect with me; nothing was happening. I decided to let go of the drum and I began to whistle. Still nothing. I had the feeling of being a novice who didn't know what he was doing. Perhaps Don Grimaldo was thinking the same thing. I was worried.

Ganesh came to my mind. I thought of his invocation and when I sang it the trance began and I felt the path opening. My body began to connect with the plant and with Ganesh, whose image was on my altar. This was the first time that I had felt a connection with Ganesh, and I began to feel more confident.

When I finished singing, I began to see a little old man kneeling in front of me with *floripondio* flowers coming out of his forehead, shoulders, and chest: it is the deity of that plant. After that I saw two women and a man. They were also deities, spirits of plants. Feeling somewhat calmed, I told

Grimaldo what I was seeing, and he said: "They are looking after you and protecting you." Protecting me from what, I did not know. I observed them quietly, without singing, staying calm and focused. When I raised my head, I began to see a blurred image of the Virgin. I was recounting everything to Don Grimaldo in the moment, as it happened. I begin to sing *ikaros* that I had learned.

Suddenly, the same guy with the sword appeared again, the very same entity I had seen before. I was not afraid. I thought to myself: "I will not disrespect my altar, the Virgin, or the circle by fighting here." I decided to get up. I became very sure, and I said to Don Grimaldo: "That entity has arrived, and I am going to the bathroom." I went to the bathroom as if I had not seen it, ignoring it. I sat down in the bathroom, feigning as if I were about to move my bowels. I began to blow air like my master, the Ashaninka who always visits me. I was doing the blowing that he had taught me. I sang, also, but I do not remember what those songs were. I was not cowardly. I had an incredible strength. I had no fear at all, none. I was making bird sounds and with my hands was agitating the air. And I grabbed the entity and sank him into the earth. Don Grimaldo knew what was happening with that entity and was saying to me encouragingly: "Grab him! Blow on this shit! He is a coward!!"

I got up with my chest out like a victorious rooster, and came out of the bathroom, saying to Don Grimaldo: "Now you know who I am." For me, the session had ended. And this was also the end of my shamanic path. I had decided to renounce this path; it was too difficult and dangerous for me. I intensely desired to return to a simple life without complications.

I walked back to my seat and lit a candle. I sat down, in a bit of a trance. I raised my eyes and saw the Virgin: she was tall, as high as the ceiling, shining with a resplendent white light. In that moment I felt such a strong trance that I was unable to control it; never had I felt something like that. I said to Don Grimaldo: "Please smudge my head and my back."

Don Grimaldo got up, smudged me and at that moment a second trance entered him as well. He went back to his seat in a deep trance. I said to him: "Don Grimaldo, I do not feel my body."

He was worried, saying to me: "If you collapse, who will look after you?"

"Don Grimaldo, don't worry," I said to him. "The only thing we need to do now is to let ourselves be carried by the trance. We are well protected. No-one can enter here."

I fell to the ground, and heard a woman's soft, celestial voice saying to me: "Now I will teach you songs and I do not want you to sing any other songs."

More visions came. I saw myself in a fetal position. I saw a tiny factory with tiny men, little elves; they were working on a machine that makes music. Then the little men began to come into my body. I felt vibrations, as if energy was arranging itself in my body. I was telling Don Grimaldo everything that was happening.

The Virgin said to me: "I will place knowledge in you, in order for you to help people in need."

Again, there was this sensation of vibration. I looked at my body and it was entirely entwined with snakes of intense, psychedelic, phosphorescent colors: green, orange, blue. The snakes were all over my body: on my chest, entwined around my arms, around my neck. My skin was like quicksand and slowly those snakes sank into my body. I felt an energy like a vibration enter my body and then I felt as if my bones were contorting.

My trance came down a bit. The Virgin said to me: "Stand up and heal this man."

I stood up and went to Don Grimaldo's side, bringing the shacapa[1] and the agua florida.[2] I blew agua florida on his head and down his back. Then, moving the shacapa a few centimeters above his head, I began singing him ikaros. At that moment he began to throw up. After vomiting he felt a great relief and calm. During my healing he was seeing flower petals falling on his head.

When I felt that everything was done, I went and sat down on my seat and sprinkled *agua florida* on my *shacapa*, passing it all over my body. Lastly, I sprinkled *agua florida* on the part of my body where I had received the *virote*. I did not want any signs of it left. Afterwards I felt a great happiness and joy and desire to continue in this path.

As we lay down to sleep, the room totally dark, I saw the spring of Sasima [name of a spring in Lamas] and a voice told me: "Here is where I want you to make my image." I saw a great number of people coming down to that place, and the Virgin let me know that I had to make her shrine next to the water.

Vision #15: The deity/spirit of the *floripondio* flower.

Vision #16. Vision with ayahuasca. The apparition of the Virgin in the second sesion with Grimaldo.

14. RANDY FULFILLS THE VIRGIN'S WISH

Reported by Frédérique Apffel-Marglin
December 2017–April 2018

This was Randy's third powerful vision of the Virgin of Guadalupe since he had first seen her in Dr. Mabit's office more than a year previously, but it was the first time she spoke to him and gave him powers. Randy commited himself completely to the curandero path and began building the Virgin's image in the place she had shown him, by the spring at Sasima. He later learned that the 12th of December—the date of this second session with Grimaldo—was the date when the Virgin of Guadalupe appeared to Juan Diego in 1531 on the hill of Tepeyac, today part of Mexico City. As is so well known, especially in Latin America, the Virgin of Guadalupe spoke to Juan Diego in his native tongue, Nahuatl.

Here I want to tell the story of how Randy went about constructing the Virgin's image at Sasima. The spring of Sasima is remarkably close to our center, in the Lamas neighborhood called Suchiche. Randy first gathered the Suchiche neighborhood association and proposed to its members to build this shrine. He told me he did not want to tell anyone about his vision since it would be interpreted as a boast and a lie hiding ulterior motives of political ambition. This surprised me but he insisted he knew the Lamas people and that telling them of his vision would ruin the project. He created a collective neighborhood project for the shrine and asked people to contribute according to their means. He contacted a sculptor friend, Juan, who moved into Randy's apartment in Sangapilla to make the statue of the Virgin, a process which lasted almost four months. I witnessed this creation and how everybody donated something to it. Randy also organized donations for the purchase of a separate statue of the Virgin of Guadalupe for the main Catholic church in Lamas, where there had never been one. He also organized the blessing and dedication of the Sasima statue by the priest of the main Catholic church in Lamas. This took place on Sunday April 29, 2018, while I was back in the US, but Royner filmed the celebration so I could see it. The celebration began with a mass in the main church and continued with a procession to Suchiche with the image of the Virgin of Guadalupe that had been purchased for the church, everyone carrying a white rose, the symbol of the Virgin. This procession was part of Randy's vision at the end of the session with Grimaldo and he organized it. The church image was left at the dead-end street above the Sasima spring, and the procession went down to the spring and the new shrine there, where the priest blessed the image with holy water and Jacques Mabit made a beautiful speech explaining the genealogy of this Virgin who had appeared at the site of an ancient temple of the pre-Columbian earth goddess Tonantzin. Jacques did not mention Randy's vision of the Virgin, since I had explained to him about Randy's wish that this remain private. Randy told me that in his vision he had seen the statue standing on an existing natural rock, which is where he had it installed. The dedication of the small shrine with the statue of the virgin of Guadalupe at the Sasima spring was attended by a great crowd of some 100 people. Randy and the Suchiche neighborhood organization have been celebrating that Virgin on December 12 ever since.

15. PROPHETIC SESSION WITH KAREN AND THE VIRGIN
December 15, 2017

Not long after the last session, we had a session in Karen's house, for her and two of her women friends. At the beginning, energetically speaking, the session was dark; it was disagreeable for everyone. The patients cried and were afraid. I was standing and began to sing *ikaros* invoking Jesus and St Benedict to purify the session, so that it could become calmer. I went and sat at my place. As I sang other *ikaros*, Karen started singing as well. I noted something strange in her; her voice had the sound of an older person. I began to listen to her and a trance I could not control came upon me. And this song of hers was influencing her women friends, who began to vomit. Karen was emitting the sobbing song of an old woman, a melodious, mystical wail. I stood up and went to the bathroom. I could not bear the sound of that song. I came out of the bathroom and came near her and asked her not to sing. Then I returned to my seat. But whenever I stopped singing, she sang. It was like a string of songs. I realized that she has a gift. This was her very first session of ayahuasca.

I lit the candles and saw that one of the women had fallen asleep. I came out of trance for a moment, but then it began again, for Karen and for me. I grabbed the long necklace *shacapa* in my hands[1] and when I lifted my head the Virgin appeared to me with her blue mantle. It was something magical and special, I could feel the positive energies of a being in synchrony, peaceful and calm. I gazed at the Virgin, no longer seeing the other two women. Everything all around was like luminous, dynamic stained-glass windows. At this point I heard the song of the Virgin for the first time:

Dear Virgin, dear Virgin, dear dark one, miraculous one, healer;

Dear Virgin, dear Virgin, dear brown one, miraculous one, heal, heal dear little body;

Dear Virgin, dear Virgin, dear brown one, heal, heal the spirit.

I saw the Virgin in front of me on an altar. Karen and I were kneeling in adoration. Karen began to sing the same song. Our two voices merged, and it became a single song. I became quiet and said to the Virgin: "We are your dear children, protect us and take care of us." And then I completed the *ikaro*:

"Dear Virgin, dear Virgin, illuminate her path, illuminate her destiny."

The Virgin was in front of us and we felt the incredible power of this song. We all became quiet and happy, the women happy like little girls. At the end, all of us were surprised. For me it was one more manifestation of the Virgin, as in my previous sessions. Later Karen told me that she had been a devotee of the virgin of Guadalupe.

16. PRELUDE TO RECEIVING POWERS FROM THE SACRED MOUNTAIN

February 16, 2018

There were 8 patients, men and women in Urkumamanwasi.[1] The night was clear. It was a normal, calm session. I was singing to the Virgin. When a type of vibration comes upon me, I know it is the Virgin. Before the session, the mountain Waman Wasi caught my eye: it was cloudless. Almost at the end of the session, around 1 am, I saw the mountain from my seat, and I began to call it mentally, asking it to come near me. Immediately a trance entered me, and I had a vision as if I were at the foot of the mountain: there were flowers and trees. A fresh breeze brought the scent of the forest. It was the first time that I had seen the mountain Waman Wasi up close. I was left thinking about this vision. I ended the session amazed. I had heard on some occasion the experience of Don Julio Valladolid with Apus in the highlands, and I also heard about Don Grimaldo's experience.[2] Joy and happiness took hold of me as I remembered my experience with Waman Wasi.[3]

The day after, I called Don Grimaldo and told him what had happened in the session. He was a bit surprised because he had never heard of Amazonian rain forest curanderos having experiences with Apu mountains. Don Grimaldo said to me: "How long has it been since anyone made an offering to this mountain? We must make a ritual for this mountain." As I did not know anything about such rituals, I was at the mercy of Don Grimaldo. So, we organized an ayahuasca session and he told me what to bring.

17. THE SACRED MOUNTAIN COMES TO RANDY AND GIVES HIM POWERS
February 23, 2018

Before going to Urkumamanwasi I bought mangos, grapes, pineapples, caramels, two bottles of wine, and red and white roses. We prepared the altar with the offerings, two of each of the things I had bought.[1] I had also brought my musical instruments and tools. Don Grimaldo suggested that I orient the altar in relation to the cardinal directions. He had a great deal of experience with mountains, and I was his assistant. I was clear that the session was specifically for me to contact the mountain Waman Wasi. Don Grimaldo said: "Tonight we will do a vigil for the mountain. This session is for the mountain."

I drank the first cup of ayahuasca and then served another one for Don Grimaldo. Immediately I was in trance. This greatly surprised me. In my mind I was thinking: "I don't know what is going to happen tonight." I was a bit afraid. In the middle of my trance, I said to Don Grimaldo: "You will sing this night."

In a serious voice, he answered: "Randy, calm down; calm down, Randy." And I calmed down.

Then a strong trance possessed me. I lowered my head and then raised my eyes and saw aerial ships in the form of bells, with a silvery metallic shine, floating in the sky near the mountain Waman Wasi. The whole structure of the *maloca* had disappeared. I described to Don Grimaldo everything I was seeing. I saw a large eagle with its wings spread out, flying towards me from the mountain. Then, on the flank of the mountain, a giant was lying down looking up towards the sky, like the *pinchudos* from Chachapoyas.[2] Don Grimaldo said he was the guardian of the mountain. The strangest thing happened afterward: suddenly my body was dragged toward the altar, and I began making gestures and bird sounds, blowing air. It was all a ritual, as if I were introducing myself to the mountain.

I looked at the altar with the offerings, and suddenly the whole altar became a city. I saw the city from above, as if I were flying. The sky was red. I was looking at many constructions: forms of truncated pyramids, colored lead that ended in a square base on the roof. While I was looking fixedly at a pyramid, I saw the construction of a woman's face on one of its sides. From her shoulder to the top of her head there was a crown or a veil, like Nefertiti. When I described her to Grimaldo, he said: "It is showing you other worlds." The images of the city and the face of the woman appeared and disappeared, alternating like that several times.

Then, from the city, something like an arm came towards me, moving like a snake. In its hand, it had something it was offering me. My hands involuntarily joined together to receive what this arm was offering me, and I drank it. After drinking, I felt as though my body—my muscles and bones—were contorting themselves. It was extremely painful. The vibration was intense. It was its *mariri*. I said to Grimaldo: "I can't bear it any longer!" Grimaldo told me: "Bear it, you cunt! Bear it! This is not for just anyone!" This was a sensation stronger than when the snakes of the Virgin entered in my body.

For me, this moment was like a key—a portal to be able to enter the world of the Apu. I returned to my seat and sat down. I began to sing, but then I felt as if the mountain did not like my song, and I became silent. After a while I sang another song, but the mountain did not like that one either. The mountain is demanding. The third song he liked. We synchronized and I became happy. Then I stayed in silence. I requested the mountain to take care of and protect all the persons I love. I expressed my gratitude to the mountain, and I began singing the song of the mountain: "Beautiful, beautiful is my dear mountain..." I stood up and the mountain made me dance softly, slowly, like an old man, side to side. And then I returned to my seat and closed the session.

Don Grimaldo said to me: "It is your initiation to the rituals. Do you realize, you can no longer smell the mango? The mountain likes it. How long ago did you wake up the mountain? It was hungry. Now you have the mountain and the Virgin inside you, and along the path you will discover how you will be able to heal people with them."

Vision #17: Vision with ayahuasca. The spirit of the mountain Waman Wasi (house of the Eagle, behind the Eagle) *"I see a great Eagle with its wings open that is flying towards me from the mountain."*

18. RANDY LEARNS TO EXORCISE A POSSESSION
April–May 2018

B. is the illegitimate son of a relative of mine. He had been wanting to take ayahuasca for quite a while. Previously he had gone to see Don Abilio[1] and told me that he found no answer there. Disappointed in Abilio, he called me, wanting to take ayahuasca.

We did the first session with B. in Urkumamanwasi. On that occasion, I had eight patients, both men and women. In his trance, B. exhibited rather strange behavior: many extravagant gestures and a rather abnormal, demoniacal look; the expression on his face was challenging me. His laughter as well was not his own; it was a mocking laughter that frightened the others. I thought: "Something strange is happening here." His presence in the session made me uneasy. When the session was coming to an end, I did not realize that there was an entity in him. At the beginning I thought it was a psychological issue, perhaps because his father did not recognize him as his son.

With B. we did a total of six sessions. In each session, his behavior got worse. He showed a certain aggressivity towards me. His energy was ruining the sessions; the other patients were afraid of his demoniacal gestures. After the fifth session, I was almost sure that B. was possessed by a demonic entity. Normally he is timid, quiet, not very social. But in the trance, he showed anger. He looked at me, blew on me, and sang. After the session I talked to him, telling him that he has something serious: an entity has possessed him. I told him that the next session would be for just three of us: him, myself, and Paul.

We did that session in May. Although I had never encountered such a situation before, I knew what I was facing. I was curious and wanted to learn from it. I asked the plant, Jesus, and the Virgin to help me with this case. When the trance started, B. began to laugh mockingly and blew on me aggressively with a challenging look. I could not see what he had in his body. The session ended and I was unable to see anything. I stood up, went next to him, put my hand on his head and recited the prayer of the Blood of Christ that Dr. Jacques gave me. When I finished this prayer, a trance came on all of us, like at the beginning. I took my hand away from B.'s head and he began to throw up. When B. entered in trance, I felt that this was the propitious moment to sing and resolve this situation once and for all.

I had a vision: everything became light and green, and I could see everything. I kneeled in front of the painting of the Virgin and began to sing her *ikaro*. As I was singing, B. put himself in a strange position, crouching and resting with his arms on the ground like a crab. In the vision he was black with red eyes. The entity manifested in his body: thin, with hands like sharp needles and an elongated face. His face transformed into a demonic one and he spoke in an unknown language, looking at me with anger. Paul heard what he was saying but he did not see anything.

I kept singing to the virgin while looking at B: "Dear Virgin, Dear brown one, ding, ding, ding, dong, dong, dong." I sang this line 3 times, my voice rising when I sang the part of the bells: "ding, ding, ding; dong, dong, dong." This was the first time this *ikaro* had come to me.

The entity disappeared. Surprised, I stood up and said to B: "This is the power of the Virgin."

There was fear in B's face. He entered in trance, lifting his arms as if he were receiving something and then gave it to me saying: "Thank you, Master Randy." He did this whole simulation several times. Later B. told me that in his vision he was seeing a light in the sky and a white woman who was giving him doves and was saying to him: "Give them to Randy so they can protect him." After giving them to me, B. did 'namaste' with his hands at the height of his forehead, bending low in gratitude. With the Virgin, I felt quite secure, without fear, supported.

19. RANDY IS HEALED BY PLANT SPIRITS AND RECEIVES A PROTECTION FROM THE VIRGIN
June 5, 2018

This session took place in Don Grimaldo's room. Each of us drank half a cup. That was enough. I was feeling very relaxed that evening, given to the plant, feeling peaceful. In this session each of us danced with his own scarf, meaning each of us was concerned with himself. I felt I only had to sing a few *ikaros*.

In previous sessions, a terrible cold had entered in my left leg, something strange. The curanderos, to make it clear it is a case of sorcery, say: "they made you step on it." In this session, I wanted to see what was happening with my leg. I drank a glass of water and then began singing to the water. I raised my eyes and saw that the whole space of the room had become a forest. Slowly spirits appeared in human form; but they were taller, with longer arms and legs, white skin, wide shoulders, and small waists, wearing loin cloths. There were about five of them: long-haired, all looking the same as if they were one clan of a tribe. These men and women organized themselves to pick leaves from a tree and passed those leaves from one to another until they reached my hands. I received the leaves and rubbed them on my left leg. Instantly, I was healed of the cold.

I began to thank them for their concern and the goodness they showed towards me. I was very thankful. Little by little the vision disappeared. I began singing to the Virgin, asking her to look after me, to protect my back. When I ended my song, I got up to walk and I felt as if armor was being placed on me, first on my back, then on my chest, and afterwards on my arms and legs. I said to Don Grimaldo: "I think they are putting a protective armor on me. "And he said: "Yes because you were asking for that in your song." Then Don Grimaldo looked at me and said: "You look tall."

I tried to walk, and my body felt very heavy. I was able to sit down again, and I sang an *ikaro*; then suddenly I had a vision of a palace or temple courtyard. There was a wall on the left and several columns on the right. On the floor was a red carpet of about 50 meters long and four meters wide. From between the adjacent columns, the head of a dragon looked out. It turned its head and stared directly into my eyes.

I remembered that Dr Jacques had told me, because I had seen dragons, that I controlled the four elements. For me it was a very interesting session, increasing my trust in the Virgin.

20. PILGRIMAGE TO TEPEYAC IN MEXICO AND THE VIRGIN OF GUADALUPE

Reported by Frédérique Apffel-Marglin, September 2018

I returned to Boston at the end of August 2018 and after only a few days took a plane to Mexico City where I was speaking at a conference. I had decided to invite Randy to meet me there so we could go and visit the shrine of the Virgin of Guadalupe. Randy's close friend Paul accompanied him from Tarapoto to Lima and then on a plane to Mexico. Randy had healed Paul of a years-long gaming addiction and the horrors, financial and otherwise, that it had created. Because of his cure Paul had become a devotee of the Virgin. I was immensely relieved that they would be traveling together since I knew that Randy was afraid of planes and had never traveled in one or gone abroad. This way, he could travel with a close friend, which I knew would calm his fears. We met up in the hotel in Mexico City and I was able to arrange a visit to Tepeyac—the site of Juan Diego's vision of the Virgin of Guadalupe in 1531—with a former psychotherapist from Takiwasi living now in Mexico City, named Jesús Gonzales Mariscal. At the conference, totally fortuitously, I made the acquaintance of Juan Ernesto Arellano, a traditional healer who had been brought there by a Mexican anthropologist. Arellano was the guardian of the volcano Popocatepetl. I asked him and his anthropologist friend whether they could accompany us to Tepeyac. They were delighted to do so and one morning we all went to Tepeyac in a large SUV.

For Randy and me, this was our very first visit to the most famous pilgrimage site in all Latin America, the shrine of the Virgin of Guadalupe. Master Juan Ernesto first took us to the main modern basilica, a very imposing and large structure with an immense domed roof and a vast esplanade in front of it. When we entered the basilica, we realized that an important mass was taking place. The place was filled, and many robed religious figures surrounded the altar. There were lots of enormous lit candles, incense, and a singing choir. We knelt briefly and made our way behind the altar, under the famous framed mantle of Juan Diego with the image of the Virgin imprinted upon it. Maestro Juan Ernesto recounted the story of the place where the Virgin had appeared in 1531, only a few years after the arrival of the Spanish conquistador Cortez, to a simple Nahuatl peasant whose Catholic name was Juan Diego. The original site was situated on a nearby hill, and Master Juan Ernesto took us there after our viewing of the mantle. At that place, Juan Diego suddenly saw the figure of a woman surrounded by light, with copper colored skin and a long starry mantle, who spoke to him in his native tongue, Nahuatl. The Lady asked him to go to the top of the hill and gather flowers. Juan Diego told her that he was hurrying to the home of his uncle who was dying. She told him not to worry. When Juan Diego was able to visit his uncle later, he found him completely restored to health and knew that the Virgin had accomplished this miracle.

The Virgin told Juan Diego to put the roses she had asked him to gather up on the hill into his own mantle and take it to the bishop in the city. Roses are not indigenous to Mexico but to Europe and at the top of the hill in that time of year, specifically the 12th of December, no flowers bloom in this region. The bishop or his servants had refused twice already to see Juan Diego but on the third visit, his insistence was such that he was allowed in the presence of the bishop who earlier had asked for proof of what Juan Diego was telling him. When Juan Diego opened his mantle and the flowers tumbled out, they all saw the image of the Virgin as Juan Diego had seen her, imprinted on the mantle. This convinced the bishop of the truth of Juan Diego's report of his conversations with the Virgin, in which she had requested that the bishop build her a shrine at the hill where she had appeared to Juan Diego. When the chapel on top of the original hill became too small to accommodate the growing number of pilgrims, a second much larger church was built, which has now been replaced by the huge current cathedral, where the framed original mantle with the Virgin's image imprinted on it is worshipped by enormous crowds of pilgrims. The mantle has been subjected to multiple scientific tests and the fiber out of which it is made, as well as the colors of the image, have all been dated to 1531. Furthermore, the stars adorning the Virgin's mantle are in the position of the constellations that were in place on the day and year of the vision, as has been verified by astronomers.

Master Juan Ernesto led us through the park, up many stairs and through gardens, stopping on the way at a waterfall for a picture. Maestro Juan Ernesto arranged us in a hieratic pose, with me between himself and Randy. We continued up the hill until we reached a small chapel at the place of Juan Diego's vision. The frescoes completely covering the inside walls of the chapel showed throngs of indigenous Nahuatl people coming to this place to worship the Virgin—men and women, young and old, children, babies, all kinds of people, some highborn and some peasants. Dr. Jacques had told me that the Virgin appeared at the site of the famous temple of the pre-Columbian mother goddess Tonantzin, and that afterwards the rate of conversions to Catholicism shot upward. What for me was unknown was what Maestro Juan Ernesto told us: "We call her Tonantzin-Maria." Clearly, the identification between the Earth/mother goddess Tonantzin and the Virgin of Guadalupe is alive and well after 500 years. When we exited the small chapel, Maestro Juan Ernesto asked us to form a circle and join arms, and he led us in a ritual of welcome, protection and blessing, mostly in Nahuatl.

Maestro Juan Ernesto later taught Randy a song in Nahuatl invoking and praising Tonantzin-Maria, which Randy has made one of his *ikaros*. After returning from our Mexican pilgrimage, Randy inscribed the full name of the Virgin at the small shrine he had built for her by the Sasima Spring: The Virgin of Sasima, Tonantzin Maria Guadalupe.

Later in this trip, we decided to visit the famous Tenochtitlan complex of temples and pyramids some half an hour outside of Mexico City. Once there, we climbed to the top of the pyramid. Randy had brought his sacred shamanic necklaces with him. Once on the top he lay down flat on the very center of the small square there, placing all his necklaces on it and performing a private invocation, explaining to me later he wanted to gather the power of the pyramid into himself and into his necklaces.

Close to the day of our departure we went to a small store, part of an ongoing archaeological excavation within Mexico City and there I was able to purchase a small statue of Tonantzin, made of a black stone, with a serpent skirt and a skull in the middle of her body. This statue of Tonantzin bore for me an unmistakable resemblance to the Goddess Kali of India: both emanating the power of generation, degeneration, death, and regeneration.

21. RANDY IS BLINDED BY A JEALOUS CURANDERO, MARCH 2019; AND SECOND DIETA IN TAKIWASI, APRIL 2019

One day, in my living room, I did a session alone with my relative B. I began singing *ikaros* and after some two hours I felt tired, and I asked B. to sing. I stretched out on the sofa and fell asleep. After a moment, a vision came to me: I traveled to a large *maloca* and immediately I found myself in front of a *shipibo* master.[1] He was tall and imposing; and I, looking at him from below, was very small. I saw the skeleton of a snake coming out of his hip, moving in spirals, descending towards me. In that instant the scene was so real that I was very scared. I wanted to leave that place, but I could not move. I began to invoke the Virgin with a song asking her to protect me. The guy was showing me that he had an immense power in the world of shamanism; he was imposing, sure of himself. I asked the Virgin to take me out of this situation and again, I suddenly found myself back in my living room where we had drunk the potion.

A bit later I felt as though a lance had pierced my back. I was amazed at the journey of the body and soul that brought me to that place, and I did not know why. Maybe this master had brought me to his *maloca* to do sorcery on me? I had always heard from other curanderos that they would come out of their bodies. For me, this was the first time I experienced such a thing; I hadn't wanted it, and it had not been pleasant. I did not know who the guy was.

Later, I drew the scene and sent it to Dr. Jacques, who told me that this person was a famous sorcerer. "Why did he do this to me?" I asked. Dr. Jacques responded that this person wanted to be the strongest shaman in the whole Amazonian region. Don Grimaldo also told me: "Sometimes, certain curanderos don't want to do retreats and they steal others' *yachay.*"

Afterwards, I did several ayahuasca sessions, but I had no visions at all despite having drunk two cups of ayahuasca.[2] The visions did not arrive, nor any trance. I made an appointment with Dr. Jacques. In my meeting with him, he worked on my forehead with songs. He sucked on my back and spit out yellow phlegm. He recommended that I do a session with B. to find out whether the visions would return. This is what I did and the first thing I saw was the Virgin in profile with a white moon behind her head. I was happy because I had regained the ability to have visions. It was as if she had placed her hand on my back, as if she were cleaning it. This magical dart was so strong that it had required two hands to remove it: first the hand of Dr. Jacques and then the hand of the Virgin.

The pain disappeared but there remained some vibration, which meant that the work was not finished. Dr. Jacques recommended that I do a retreat at Takiwasi, taking the master plant named Ushpa Washa. This I did in April of 2019. During that *dieta* in the forest of Takiwasi, the Virgin came and sat down at my side on my cot and cleaned my body with a wet cloth; afterwards she put her hand on my forehead and said to me: "Go to sleep," and immediately I fell asleep. After this, the pain and the vibration have disappeared.

Vision #18: Vision with ayahuasca. Randy finds himself in the presence of a powerful and jealous sorcerer.

22. RANDY HAS A BEAUTIFUL VISION
Late Spring 2019

After the retreat in Takiwasi, I did a session in the *maloca* at Urkumamanwasi. There were four of us, but Karito[1] was not present on that occasion. In the vision I saw myself going outside of the *maloca* into a very dense forest. I walked some 20 meters towards a gigantic, imposing tree that I suppose was a *lupuna*, the tallest tree in the forest. I was dressed all in white.[2] When I arrived at the foot of the tree I began to levitate slowly until I reached the bower of the *lupuna*.

Right away the branches opened, and I went inside the bower—it was like a nest, and Karito was seated inside it, legs crossed, all dressed in white. The whole space was bathed in a bluish violet mist. When she realized that I was there, she immediately stood up and I walked towards her. Then she opened and stretched her arms out as if asking to clasp my hands. I took her hands and we kissed.

This falling in love was the first one in the spiritual realm. Later, around the middle of December of 2019, we fell in love in the worldly realm.[3] The people in Lamas say that I made her fall in love with me with sorcery, with love potions (*pusanga*). But that is not true.

Vision #19: Vision with ayahuasca. Randy with Karen in a 'nest' in the bower of a lupuna tree.

CONCLUDING REMARKS ON PART II
By Frédérique Apffel-Marglin

The turning point for Randy, when he fully embraced the shamanic path, was on the day that he had decided to abandon it. The moment he was about to leave what he thought would be his last ayahuasca session, the Virgin of Guadalupe appeared to him, gave him two kinds of powers, and asked him to build her image, showing him where to do it. Just two months later, he received powers from the sacred mountain Waman Wasi. These events are extraordinary because they are unheard of in the region. Together with the mentorship of Jacques Mabit and two retreats in Takiwasi's forest, Randy finally became a full-fledged curandero, having completely resolved his ambivalence and doubts. Even though Randy's reputation as a curandero has been steadily growing in Lamas and Tarapoto, the fact that a famous curandero tried to blind him to eliminate him as a rival is a signal that Randy might be fated to become much more well-known.

For Randy, the fact that he has been cured by his discarnate Ashaninka master and by the Virgin, as well as receiving strong protections from them, has also greatly contributed to his fully embracing this path. In Karen he has finally—three and a half years after the spirits told him she would be his wife—fallen in love with the soulmate the spirits have intended for him. This resulted in his leaving his former companion, who belonged to his materialist secular past but no longer fit in his new life.[1] All these transformations have come at the cost of the approval of his parents. After Kemy left Sangapilla in January of 2020, Randy's parents stopped communicating with him.

For me a major turning point was the medicinal plants workshop I asked Randy to lead in August of 2017, including two ayahuasca sessions, both described by Randy. I recognized that in those activities I was fully able to integrate spirituality, intellectual pursuits, and activism. I decided that I would stop leading my own courses, replacing them with leading these kinds of workshops together with Randy. This was the moment I became fully conscious of the extent of my transformation, which is also due to my witnessing Randy's transformation.

I want to close these remarks with mentioning the issue of sorcery, *brujería* in Spanish. This is a widespread practice in the region and Randy has suffered from it. It almost succeeded in derailing his initiatory journey. In his first initiation session at Don Aquilino's he was shown two different paths and he chose the humble modest one. He was told that if he had chosen the one offered by two brilliantly attired horsemen inviting him on a brightly lit path promising him women and riches, he would have become a *brujo,* a sorcerer. The historical and ethnographic evidence clearly confirms that shamanic powers can be used to dispense either harm or healing. Clearly the Catholic church, as well as Protestant ones during the Burning Times, simply decided that shamanism itself was the problem making no distinction between those who healed and those who harmed.[2] This led to the eradication of shamanism in Europe. In part III I will come back to the thorny issue involving a culture or religion's attitude towards good and evil. In Randy's case, his initial choice placed him solidly on the side of pursuing healing and forsaking revenge or harm altogether. However, he has himself acutely felt the powerful destructive efficacy of sorcery; he knows it is real and deadly effective. He has become well-known for his ability to diagnose sorcery and remedy it.

CODA: A FEW OF RANDY'S FUGITIVE VISIONS

Vision #20: Vision with ayahuasca. A "fugitive vision" that happened in other ayahuasca sessions. Such visions last a very short time. Here is a therianthrope with the head of a dog riding on a bird resembling a huge parrot.

Vision #21: Fugitive vision with ayahuasca. Yoruba Orisha of the Deep Sea: Olokun

Vision #22. Fugitive vision with ayahuasca: the Kundalini snake, entwined around Randy's spine.

Vision #23. Vision with ayahuasca. A therianthrope man-dog.

Vision #24. Vision with ayahuasca. A woman's face.

PART III

REFLECTIONS ON THE ERADICATION OF SHAMANISM IN THE WEST

By Frédérique Apffel-Marglin

1. THE OLDEST DESTRUCTIONS OF COSMOCENTRIC WORLDVIEWS IN THE WEST

This chapter focuses on the demise of cosmocentrism in Europe and the efforts by various ancient civilizations, including early Christianity, to devalue and eventually ban the use of psychedelics, the rituals of shamanism. In the next chapter I focus on the final eradication of cosmocentrism in the West with what is referred to as "the Burning Times," a period that overlapped with the scientific revolution and was intimately linked with it. It must be underlined that this devaluation of Earth-based, goddess-based spiritualities never happened in non-Western parts of the world. My early work took place in a pilgrimage center in eastern India, in the state of Odisha, where goddess worship remains predominant. I focused on temple rituals by women dancers, embodiments of the Goddess, incarnating the power of life and death.[1] I was even initiated into the Shakta tradition, which is closely related to ancient Western Asian goddess cults.[2]

In 391 CE, the Christian Emperor Theodosius had all 'pagan' temples closed, especially those dedicated to goddesses.[3] He put an end to the centuries-old initiatory complex in Greece, dedicated to the Eleusinian mysteries with its temple of Demeter and her daughter Persephone. The Eleusinian mysteries were profoundly influential in both ancient and later Classical Greek cultural life; initiates came from all walks of life during almost two millennia. Greek philosophers and poets such as Pindar, Plato and Sophocles were initiated there, as were the Romans Cicero, Nero, and others. Although the initiates were sworn to secrecy under pain of death, the mycologist

Gordon Wasson was able to identify the psychotropic plant that the initiates imbibed at the culminating moment of their initiation.[4] Because of its secrecy, knowledge of the ritual almost completely disappeared with the closing of Demeter's and Persephone's temple.

Classical Greece is widely recognized for gifting the Western world with rationality. However, we have forgotten that this civilization owed as much to the Eleusinian mysteries as to its rational philosophy—the latter were deeply entwined with the development and spread of alphabetic writing giving rise to the Classical period.[5] Unfortunately, the Greek legacy to the West lost the Eleusinian mysteries and with them one surmises, the wholeness—what Jill Taylor calls 'a whole brain'—that an equal emphasis on both rationality and the mysteries and their psychedelic initiation delivered. We inherited a lopsided emphasis on rationality.

The initiates were sworn to secrecy and the secret has been kept for almost two thousand years. However, more recent research has been able to identify the psychotropic plant used in the ritual as ergot, a fungus that grows on barley. Barley was cultivated on the plain adjacent to the temple of Demeter and Persephone and the rituals resonated with the transition from hunting and gathering to agriculture and the cultivation of grains. Agriculture, the planting of the seed in the earth, foregrounds the mystery of life, growth, degeneration, death, and rebirth.

Brian Muraresku, a scholar of Classics and Sanskrit, has pursued the thesis first expounded in the 1978 book *The Road to Eleusis,* a thesis that almost cost co-author Carl Ruck his career. In the wake of the controversy, Muraresku set out to find chemical proof of a psychedelic in a cup found in a ritual archaeological setting. Over a period of twelve years, Muraresku pursued archaeological, archaeo-chemical, textual, and other kinds of evidence to ascertain whether psychedelics were part of the Eleusinian mysteries as well as the Dionysian festivals, and the paleo-Christian eucharist, among other traditions.

The evidence detailed in his book convinced him of the existence of a "prehistoric ritual that survived for millennia, in the total absence of the written word, before finding a good home among the Greeks."[6]

In his 2007 book *Supernatural: Meetings with the Ancient Teachers of Mankind,* Graham Hancock reviews the scholarship on paleolithic cave painting, particularly focusing on the work of the French paleologist Jean Clottes and his South African colleague David Lewis-Williams. Paleolithic cave paintings, dating from 20,000 to 40,000 years ago, have been found in many parts of the world, typically placed in remote parts of caves, deep in the recesses of the Earth. In these paintings, two themes regularly appear: the presence of therianthropic figures (part-animal, part-human) and figures of a wounded human pierced by arrows, darts, or lances. Many scholars have come to agree with Lewis-Williams and Clottes that these paintings represent shamanic experiences. Lewis-Williams and Clottes, following Mircea Eliade, posit that caves played a role in shamanic initiation because they are "concrete symbols of passage into another world, or a descent to the underworld."[7]

> The neuropsychological and ethnographic evidence… strongly suggests that, in these subterranean images, we have an ancient and unusually explicit expression of a complex shamanic experience that is informed by altered states of consciousness. That experience comprised isolation and sensory deprivation by entrance into an underground real, "death" by a painful ordeal of hallucinatory multiple piercing, and emergence from those dark regions of an inspired, reborn shaman.[8]

In their 2007 joint book *Les Chamanes de la Préhistoire,* Clottes and Lewis-Williams write:

> The way a great number of images were created and evoked from the rocky surfaces suggests that the "artists"

recreated—or in a certain manner, re-dreamt—their visions and fixated them on the rocky wall considered as the membrane they had to traverse in order to materialize. A cave rich in paintings, therefore, did not simply enclose a certain number of mental images: it was the receptacle of many visions made manifest and tangible by lines either painted or engraved.[9]

As can be seen from the way Randy experienced death and piercings from magical darts (*virotes*) during his initiatory journey, as well as seeing or himself becoming a therianthrope, the classical shamanic experiences depicted in the Paleolithic cave paintings continue to be experienced today.

There is also reason to believe that psychedelics were used in the rituals that produced the Paleolithic cave paintings. The psychedelic mushroom *Psilocybe semilanceata* has been con-firmed as native to Europe;[10] other mushrooms such as the *Amanita muscaria* so pervasive in European folklore could also have been used, or another psychotropic plant. As Muraresku has shown, there is evidence of the use of psychedelic plants or mushrooms throughout European and Middle Eastern history, from the site in south-eastern Turkey known as Göbekli Tepe and the site known as the Raqefet cave in Palestine/Israel dating between 13,000- and 9,000-years BCE to the much later Eleusinian Mysteries. Both Paleolithic sites are associated with funeral rituals, barley fields and the fermentation of beer, as well as, presumably, the harvesting of barley's psychedelic fungus, ergot. Even though Muraresku could not prove the exis-tence of psychedelics in the brewed beer at Göbekli Tepe, it is quite possible that the beer of Göbekli Tepe and the Raqefet cave was spiked, as it was later in Eleusis.

In the temple of Demeter and Persephone at Eleusis, priestesses prepared the psychedelic potion known as the *kykeon,* which gave the initiates a vision that brought with it the certainty that death was not a final endpoint. Muraresku found evidence of this psychedelic in a Greek colony of the Demeter/ Persephone mysteries on the coast of Catalonia, as well as in the catacombs under the Vatican where paintings of funeral or ancestor worship ceremonies during the early years of the current era are difficult to distinguish from eucharistic suppers during the early centuries when Christianity was an unlawful cult in Rome.[11] In all such rituals, women were central; they were the ones who prepared the psychedelic potions, "an experience where women and drugs seem to be the driving force."[12]

The preparation for the pilgrimage to the Eleusinian mysteries was long and arduous, lasting more than a year; the last leg, from Athens to the temple, had to be done on foot. Muraresku emphasizes that the liberation that the initiates experienced at the culmination of this pilgrimage was not only individual salvation but something much more portentous: "It was *only* the Mysteries that could guarantee a sustainable future for the human species on the planet. According to Praetextatus, the temple of Demeter housed something indispensable that was utterly lacking in the Christian faith."[13]

Vettius Agorius Praetextatus was a 4th century CE consul and hierophant in the Roman Empire who, like Cicero and Marcus Aurelius before him, was initiated into the Mysteries. According to the Greek historian Zosimus, Praetextatus in 364 CE successfully convinced the Christian Roman emperor Valentinian to relent on abolishing the Mysteries, stating that doing so would make the life of the Greeks unlivable. He is also credited with saying that Eleusis is the one place that "hold[s] the whole human race together."[14]

What Muraresku says of the Mysteries concerning women is based on impressive scholarship. The Earth goddess Demeter was an adult woman and the mother of Persephone. At the climax of the Mysteries, Persephone gives birth to the Holy Child named Iacchus. This Iacchus, understood as a form of Dionysius by Sophocles in the 5th century BCE, is the god who led the procession to Eleusis. This birth closed the Mysteries in the temple of Demeter and transformed her into a grand-mother and the archetype of the crone.[15] The archetype of the crone disappears with the advent of Christianity, although it is retained in the person of the 'witch,' the old shamaness who knows how to brew phychotropic potions. The archetype of the grandmother appears in Randy's initiatory journey in the form of what he calls 'indigenous grandmothers playing the *shacapa*.' I believe that this recurring theme in Randy's initiatory journey is a significant, living connection to the past, persisting in con-temporary indigenous shamanism.

When the mysteries were proclaimed illegal and the temple of Eleusis was closed in 395 CE, the spiritual legacy it guarded for some two millennia vanished and was replaced by Christianity in the Western world. The dominant Christian view of the Mysteries rewrote that legacy into a satanic, evil tradition. Muraresku shows the continuity between the Dionysian psy-chedelic-infused rituals and the psychedelic-infused eucharist during the three centuries of Christianity's illegal, persecuted—and sometimes literally underground—existence during the Roman empire. Toward the end of the 4th century CE, women were excluded from the Christian mass and its priesthood, and the ritual use of psychedelics was abandoned:

> Like loyal subjects, the parishioners lined the pews to witness the consecration of very ordinary bread and wine by very ordinary men with no particular pharmacological expertise. In a mix of misinterpreted Greek philosophy and shameful Biblical reasoning, Saint Augustine (AD 354-430) and others blamed the passions and appetites of the female body for distancing women from the religious life. Free of the chains of the menstrual cycle, childbirth, and breast-feeding, only men could properly control and tap into the rational aspect of the soul that liberated the male species from their own irrational physicality, connecting them to a spiritual heaven.[16]

The maleness of the Christian priesthood, free from the menstrual cycle and other embodied life-giving female powers, enables the soul to escape the 'irrationality' of the body and thereby access "a spiritual heaven." However, this irrational physicality that plagues women is in fact what enables cycles of birth, growth, degeneration, and regeneration happen. The 'spiritual heaven' that rationality opens to the male soul seems to short-circuit continuous cycles of birth, death, and new life; it lands humans in the linear trajectory of the modern Western anthropocentric worldview, separating us from the cycles of the natural and cosmic world. This worldview gave rise, in what is now Peru, to the laws of the "extirpation of idolatry" in 1545, along with the condemnation of the cosmocentrism of indigenous peoples as an irrational, silly superstition.

The themes of generation, growth, decline, and death are also present in the Christian story of the death and resurrection of Christ. However, the Christian story minimizes links to the cycles of birth, growth, degeneration, death, and rebirth, characteristic of indigenous cosmovisions and most evidently perceived in the menstrual cycle. Instead, Christian thought propounds a more linear development from birth, growth, and death to resurrection, where resurrection is seen less as the return of life but rather as the emergence into a timeless eternity, a freedom from "irrational physicality." In the lunar cycle, the new moon appears out of three days of total darkness and invisibility akin to Persephone's abduction by Hades to the underworld, invisible, dark, like the disappearance of the moon. With the suppression of the lunar cycle, the link between human life and the life of the Earth and the wider cosmos, what we generally refer to as 'Nature,' was drastically dimmed, if not outright extinguished. Women, who through their menstruation are aligned with the lunar cycle, are integral to the cycles of birth, growth, degeneration, death, and rebirth of life on Earth, exactly the drama played out in the Eleusinian Mysteries. The Christian myth did not retain the ancient connection with these natural cycles.

Many small-scale societies have rituals where all the women menstruate in synchrony with each other and with the dark of the moon.[17] As an essay by Fredrick Lamp on several African societies shows, in natural conditions women ovulate in the full moon and menstruate during the dark of the moon.[18] In some north American indigenous societies, when women fall out of synchrony with the moon, they enact a ritual where they spend nights in a special site exposing themselves to the light of the full moon, thereby re-synchronizing themselves.[19] With the rise of Christianity in the West, the view of life as a sacred cycle, with the feminine and her cycles as its very embodiment, was lost.[20]

Among the Kichwa Lamas in the region of Lamas, agricultural activities are performed according to the phases of the moon. Menstruating women are not allowed to enter the *chacra* (cultivated field) and it was explained to me that during the women's 'flowers' (their menstruation [21]) if they should enter the *chacra*, nothing would flourish and grow since menstruation and the dark of the moon are fallow times, when the moon exerts no pull on the sap of plants and thus things do not grow. Menstruating women are also not allowed to attend protective rituals or ayahuasca ceremonies. However, without menstruation and the dark of the moon, there would be no regeneration of life in people or in plants.[22]

With the suppression of the Eleusinian mysteries, the cycles of the cosmos, of Nature, and of women eventually came to be viewed as disorderly, chaotic, and in need of being controlled. This control came to be understood as masculine and rational, whereas Nature eventually came to signify animality, chaos, and a lower form of human life. As Carolyn Merchant phrases it in her classic book *The Death of Nature:*[23]

> At the root of the identification of women and animality with a lower form of human life lies the distinction between nature and culture fundamental to humanistic disciplines such as history, literature, and anthropology, which accept that distinction as an unquestioned assumption.

Nature-culture dualism is a key factor in Western civilization's advance at the expense of nature.

It seems to me necessary here, before proceeding further, to comment briefly on the poststructuralist critique of the category 'woman'. One of its most influential voices has been that of Judith Butler who for all intents and purposes has declared that 'woman' does not exist and all talk of menstruation, the goddesses, the witches, reinforces an essentialist biologically determinist view of 'woman.' She asserts that it would be better to think of gender as a performance.[24] Recognizing that the biologization of woman and the body has brought along with it a host of real and serious problems, let me briefly argue for a more nuanced position between the 'either' of the biologically determined body and the 'or' of a fluid, culturally constructed body. I am here turning to the work of philosopher Carol Bigwood. Bigwood speaks of a body 'connatural' with the world. To my mind the coincidence and significance of the menstrual cycle with the lunar cycle is one of those aspects of woman's body being connatural with the cosmos. Menstruation and the moon are only the most visible aspects of this connaturalness between woman and cosmos or Nature, experienced and practiced in many different variations cross-culturally. Bigwood writes:

> Our connatural body is an indeterminate constancy, not an a priori closed to historical change and cultural variation but an a priori that continually opens us to them.... We are always already situated in an intersubjective (and thus already cultural) spatiotemporal, fleshy (and thus already natural) world before we creatively adopt a personal position in it. Moreover, nothing determines us from the outside or the inside because we are from the start outside ourselves, thrown open to our surroundings in a *semideterministic but constant coition with things*, there is only this incarnate communication, this natural-cultural momentum of existence, this "unmotivated upsurge of

being" of which the body and the environment are only an abstract moment....Our human manners of existing maintain a fidelity to a certain enduring bodyliness that coheres from culture to culture without ever being identical. [my emphasis][25]

Bigwood's phrase "thrown open to our surroundings in a *semideterministic but constant coition with things*" can be mapped onto Jill Bolte Taylor's view that the state of being thrown open to our surroundings is our inherent state when our right hemisphere is not completely muted by the supposedly 'dominant' left hemisphere. Taylor experienced this firsthand immediately after the stroke in her left hemisphere.

This somatophobia of post-structuralism, this rejection in an either/or fashion of our bodily existence, is related to the oppression of women, peoples of color and to the exploitation of the Earth. It is characteristic of the mainstream metaphysical tradition, from the Greeks and Romans to Descartes and the scientific revolution, positing the rational human subject as the stable relational center of reality.

In his book *A World without Women*, David Noble gives us the history of the Western male-dominated church, rooted in a warrior culture where the Crusades were both a religious and a political endeavor.[26] This warrior culture devalued the female body and the Earth. Women were barred from the cathedral schools and universities, where the churchmen had a monopoly of knowledge and education, a banishment of the feminine that continued in the secular autonomous university system well into the 20th century. Although the universities opened their doors to women around the mid-20th century, the centrality of the rational human (in fact masculine) subject continued, with women permitted to participate in the culture to the extent that they take up its masculine structures, living and working according to the methodologies, institutions and the somatophobic foundations on which those are based.[27]

2. THE BURNING TIMES AS A FOUNDATION FOR THE SCIENTIFIC REVOLUTION

In my view one of the deep-seated obstacles that hinders most of us modern folks from really hearing and understanding shamanism is a lack of awareness of the significance of the final eradication in Europe of the shamanic, psychedelic "religion without a name," which had been in place since Paleolithic times.[1] This last eradication took place during what is often referred to as "the Burning Times," spanning roughly from the 14th to the 17th centuries in Western Europe,[2] when the so-called witches, male healers and occult philosophers were persecuted for their worldview, known as Anima Mundi or *hylozoism,* a word derived from ancient Greek meaning 'living matter.' The Burning Times predated the beginning of the scientific revolution, which began in the mid-1500s with the publication of Copernicus' thesis about the then-revolutionary assertion that the sun, not the Earth, was the center of the cosmos. In this chapter I argue that without the successful eradication of the religion-without-a-name, otherwise known as hylozoism, Anima Mundi, or cosmocentrism,[3] what is known as "the scientific revolution" could not have taken place.[4]

Anima Mundi was the sacred, living and communally bonded universe of medieval and Renaissance Europe, heir to the much older 'religion without a name.' Those who lived within this universe were occult philosophers, as well as the wise women and men, the latter constituted by a variety of healers, shamanesses and shamans belonging to the oral culture of the European peasantry.[5] The Anima Mundi worldview was a version of cosmocentrism, in which everything was related to everything else and all of it was sacred, had agency, and was pervaded by the divinity. Furthermore, the Anima Mundi was thought of as female and often represented as a nude woman.

Those whose worldview it was—all lumped under the umbrella term and invective of witches—were declared heretics by Pope Innocent VIII in 1484,[6] though persecution began earlier, with the first Inquisition. The first Inquisition, created in the 12th century, successfully eradicated the Cathar or Albigensis "heresy" in the Southwest of France—by the 14th century the Cathars had been thoroughly destroyed and had disappeared. However, remnants of 'paganism,' namely pre-Christian practices, were also part of the heresies to be extirpated.[7] Many of the peasant healers were shamanesses and shamans who used various European psychotropic plants such as belladonna, mandragora, mushrooms, ergot, or cannabis. There is no doubt that some among them practiced black magic, harming others, as is the case in Lamas and its region today and common in shamanism in general. There is also no doubt that many of them were genuine healers, as are many of the shamans, both mestizo and indigenous, in the Peruvian Upper Amazon as well as in Mexico today.[8]

During the seventeenth century, the fathers of Western modernity and science, such as René Descartes, Robert Boyle, and Isaac Newton, actively argued against the older hylozoic view. Descartes established the philosophical basis for the new science, arguing against hylozoism:

> There exist no occult forces in stones or plants. There are no amazing and marvelous sympathies and antipathies, in fact there exists nothing in the whole of nature which cannot be explained in terms of purely corporeal causes totally devoid of mind and thought.[9]

This statement was aimed at delegitimizing the views expressed by the literate occult philosophers, who practiced shamanic rituals considered magical by Christians. In contrast to Descartes, the fifteenth century occult philosopher Picco de la Mirandola declared:

> All this great body of the world is a soul, full of the intellect of God, who fills it within and without and vivifies the All ....The world is alive, all matter is full of life .... Matter and bodies or substances ... are energies of God. In the All there is nothing which is not God.[10]

Paracelsus, a famous sixteenth century physician and occult philosopher, saw God as the prime matter, the invisible substance that sustains all things. He held that God is immanent to the world and that the human soul is divine. For Paracelsus, each planet crowned a hierarchy of people, animals, plants, minerals, and elements, all of them being bound together so that the action of one affected all the others. All things—be they natural, human, or made by humans—were connected through the Anima Mundi and were sacred and alive since divinity pervaded everything. In other words, for Paracelsus the cosmos was not divided into a profane this-worldly realm and a sacred other-worldly one. It was the opposite of the view held by Descartes, who sought to explain nature through "purely corporeal causes totally devoid of mind and thought." The word 'corporeal,' widely used by natural philosophers at the time, today would be replaced by the word "material"; Descartes' argument is evidence of the persistence in Europe of a cosmocentric vision, against which the fathers of Western modernity—who were originally called natural philosophers and later simply scientists—marshaled their arguments.

It is crucial to place these arguments within the political and religious context of the times. The campaign against Anima Mundi was not a mere sideshow, a minor issue for the fathers of Western modernity; it was at the heart of the emergent worldview they were championing. A living and sacred cosmos had to be effectively annulled, through the murder of those holding the cosmocentric worldview, so that Descartes' vision of a mindless, purely material cosmos could take its place.

Almost immediately after Martin Luther's expulsion from the Catholic church in 1521, conflicts erupted between these two branches of Christianity.[11] The need to destroy Anima Mundi was perhaps the only issue on which Protestants and Catholics agreed. The worldview of Anima Mundi clashed powerfully with the belief shared by both Protestants and Catholics that God transcended this world, that he was outside of His Creation. The immanence—as well as the femininity—of Anima Mundi was too clearly related to paganism and nature worship. The sixteenth century saw eight civil wars in France, and the conflicts between Catholics and Protestants led to the Thirty-year War that engulfed Western Europe during the first half of the seventeenth century, when 35% of the people perished. It resulted in the expulsion from France of all Protestants (known as Huguenots), as well as all Jews.

There was only one issue on which Catholics and Protestants agreed: the need to eradicate the occult philosophers and their peasant allies, the so-called witches.[12] The eradication of hylozoism and the 'witches' was carried out by the Inquisition of the Catholic Church and a similar Protestant organization during the sixteenth and seventeenth centuries, the period of "the Burning Times."[13] The mystical Jewish Kabbalah and its Christian version, Cabala, was also targeted by the Inquisition, having influenced occult philosophers such as Pico della Mirandola, Marsilio Ficino, and others.[14] Ever since the Roman Empire's embrace of Christianity in the fourth century CE, these traditions had been considered in need of eradication so the One True faith could flourish and be protected from infection.

By the mid-seventeenth century, the notion of Anima Mundi had become thoroughly tainted by the allegations of heresy and superstition. Today it is relegated to the status of quaint notions of an earlier unenlightened European age and gets dismissed along with the allegedly exotic and superseded spiritual beliefs of societies deemed to be primitive, backward, and undeveloped—like those of the indigenous peoples of the Americas. Premodern hylozoism and medieval Anima Mundi were numinous phenomena, steeped in sacrality. They spoke of an enchanted world, harboring no nature/culture dualism in its breast, including the earth and everything in, on, or around it: animals, plants, rocks and minerals, human-made things, planets, and constellations as well as a plethora of spirits, elves, and fairies.

Anima Mundi succumbed to the overwhelming combination of stronger forces triggered by the hostility between the Protestant and Catholic churches, aided later by the emerging capitalist economy. However, as Stephen Toulmin has argued, the need to re-establish certainty also played a fundamental role in the search by the fathers of modernity for a knowledge system that rested on a foundation outside of the religious conflicts consuming Europe at the time.[15] In his 1990 book on Descartes, Toulmin argues that Descartes' life was dominated by the conflicts of the time, which led to a breakdown of law and order that generated a breakdown of certainty. Remember that education and the production of knowledge were controlled by the Church: what was certain and what was true had been certified by the Church for centuries. With the emergence of a rival Christian movement that claimed the Catholics were engaged in magical pursuits with their eucharist and its 'magical' transformation of the wine and the bread into the blood and body of Christ, the certainty that Roman Catholic Europe had delivered for centuries was profoundly and irremediably fractured. The total breakdown of law and order that occurred, simultaneously led to the widespread notion that the two were causally related.

In the 16th century, Western Europe became an aggregate of separate Protestant or Catholic polities, all pervaded by the idea that law and order, homogeneity and One Truth went hand in hand. The issue of certainty in the intellectual domain was another matter, however, and it was handled differently. We did not see Protestant and Catholic universities emerging, each producing different kinds of knowledges. However, what did emerge around the mid-17th century were independent academies in England, France, and Italy, dedicated to creating new knowledge outside the control of religious authorities: The Royal Society in England, l'Académie Française in Paris and the Academia dei Lincei in Bologna.

Descartes' radical and famous separation between *res cogitans* and *res extensa* (the thinking thing and the extended thing) transformed the human body—along with the bodies of every earthly and cosmic rock, plant, and animal—into an inert mechanism without sentience, without agency, without mind. Rationality became the distinguishing, defining characteristic of humans, as well as the divine. Thus, certainy was re-established on the foundation of a nature and cosmos thoroughly cleansed of any traces of numinosity, divinity, and mind, as well as of anything labeled "metaphysical." This purely material nature was to be the "object of study" of a group of learned men who were to gather in a new space called "the laboratory." This was a public space not in the sense that it was open to anyone but, rather, in the sense that it was the opposite of the occult philosophers' cabinet of experiments, which were private and even secret, hence the label "occult." In this new space, this new material nature was to be interrogated through experiments involving the use of measuring devices and other types of apparatus. The rules of behavior in that space were strictly enunciated to protect it from any potential conflict arising from political or religious disputes.

Robert Boyle's invention of the public laboratory and the scientific experimental method in mid-seventeenth century England has enshrined the complete separation of the sacred or metaphysical from a nature that came to be viewed as purely material, enforcing a division between a supposedly inert, mechanical nature and anything reminiscent of the mind or emotion—in other words, of the soul, the psyche. Boyle's experimental scientific method and the public laboratory where it is practiced enact the radical separation that Descartes posited between the mind and nature.[16] This new worldview of a world and a cosmos totally devoid of mind, life, and sacrality was able to accommodate itself to a Western Christian understanding of divinity as transcending creation. It fit well with a Christian view of the inferiority of the earthly plane, as can be seen in these words of Boyle: "The veneration wherewith men are imbued for what they call nature has been a discouraging impediment to the empire of man over the inferior creatures of God."[17] This mechanistic worldview ultimately led to the current extractivist, brutal exploitation of the Earth, its waters, and its atmosphere by humans.

Robert Boyle drew on his own alchemical past to invent the laboratory. Alchemy, one of several occult philosophy movements, was practiced in secret cabinets where the philosopher inquired into nature using a variety of instruments. By the mid seventeenth century when Boyle invents his public laboratory, alchemy and occult philosophy in general were already severely tainted by the brush of heresy and Boyle needed to clearly differentiate his laboratory from his alchemical past. Therefore, he called his laboratory a public one. It was not public in the sense that anyone could enter it, but in the sense of not being secret. Only educated men could participate in this new laboratory. In Shapin and Schaffer's classic work on Boyle, they meticulously delineate the rules of behavior that Boyle created in his new public laboratory. Foremost among those rules were those protecting this space from the religio-political conflicts that had been raging in Europe. Talk of religion and politics was absolutely forbidden in the laboratory, along with *ad hominem* criticisms. The personality and personal life of the natural philosopher had to be clearly and visibly separate from his pursuits in the public laboratory. This was quite different from the approach of the occult philosopher, who considered his soul, his psyche, and his behavior as inseparable from a cosmos where everything was interrelated, and thus an integral part of what he was studying. But the natural philosophers, starting with Descartes, "banished the astral linking of universal harmony, cutting off at the roots the connections of the psyche with the cosmos. This appeased the witch hunters and made the world safe for Descartes..."[18]

The new knowledge Boyle was inventing in his public laboratory was completely different from the worldview that the occult philosophers and the 'witches' shared with most indigenous peoples, as well as the initiates of the ancient Greek Eleusinian Mysteries. The older Anima Mundi worldview is one in which ethics and knowledge are integrally enmeshed. The knowledge that Boyle and other natural philosophers invented was radically different, one that not only completely separated humans and their minds from the cosmos/nature but one that invented a purely mechanical, insentient, and non-living cosmos/nature that was totally separate from the ethical concerns in the life of the natural philosopher, now coming to be known as the scientist.

Seeking to steer clear of the conflict between Protestants and Catholics while also re-establishing certainty, Boyle also banished from his public laboratory any involvement with metaphysics—that is, knowledge considered to be incorporeal, supernatural, or based on speculative reasoning. However, to Boyle's dismay, the metaphysical suddenly made its appearance *within* the protected new space of his public laboratory, in connection with a dispute over one of the experiments. One of Boyle's experimental tools consisted of a pump that could take the air out of a glass globe placed atop of it. Once the air pump had seemingly taken all the air out of the glass globe— as evidenced by the fact that the pump could no longer be activated—the natural philosophers gathered in the public laboratory disagreed about what was inside the glass globe, in a disagreement that came to be known as the argument between the vacuists and the plenists. Vacuists asserted that when the pump had taken all the air out of the glass globe, nothing remained in it—it was a vacuum. Plenists asserted that there remained in the globe an extremely subtle substance named *aether* that filled the glass globe but was invisible.

Boyle himself did not try to take sides in the conflict; he

simply asserted that he could not pronounce upon what might remain or not in the glass globe, since the question could not be resolved experimentally. According to Shapin and Schafer, Boyle "made the controversy concerning the vacuum a metaphysical one... 'which therefore we shall no longer debate.'" [19]

Boyle declared that metaphysical issues were outside the bounds of what soon came to be known as the scientific experimental method and of science more generally,[20] leading to the view that whatever could not be established experimentally to exist in the public space of the laboratory simply did not exist in nature. But Boyle could not prove that there did not exist some invisible, extremely subtle substance in the globe after all the air was pumped out, and he openly acknowledged this fact. His declaration that this was a metaphysical issue that had no place in his laboratory was wholly motivated by his desire to protect this space from conflict and to re-establish certainty on a new basis, free of both religion and metaphysics.

This obscure episode set the stage for the later establishment of firmly separate domains for Religion and Science. Religion could claim authority over people's beliefs and inner lives, but Science had authority over nature, a nature cleansed of anything remotely metaphysical or invisible. This dividing up of the turf into what Stephen Jay Gould has named "non-overlapping magisteria," or NOMA,[21] was a diplomatic and safe way of defusing the potential tensions between those two domains. In the new dispensation, the supernaturals, considered to be non-empirical entities, were consigned to a non-real metaphysical and purely religious domain.

The indispensable work of Shapin and Schaffer and Elizabeth Potter has shown that Boyle's boundary between the experimentally verifiable, and the 'metaphysical' was not a separation that emerged consensually from experimental practice. It was instead Boyle's strategic way of protecting his new space, the public laboratory, from the conflicts that raged outside of it. It is perhaps not incidental that women were also excluded from the public laboratory, on the grounds of their insuffient 'modesty.' The requirement that natural philosophers refrain from criticizing each other's personal behavior and life was referred to as the requirement of 'modesty.' The modest man witnessed the experiment and attested to what had occurred in and during it. In general, women were considered incapable of such modesty since it was believed that their modesty resided in their bodies and not in their minds.[22]

The 'immodesty' of women is described in a now-famous anecdote about the visit to the public laboratory of Boyle's sister, Lady Ranelagh, and some of her friends. They could not be kept out since they were in great part responsible for financing the Royal Society. The experiment that day involved placing a living bird in the glass globe and then removing the air in it with the pump to see what would happen. After the air was pumped out, the little bird began to show signs of imminent demise and the assembled ladies exclaimed in horror, asking that the bird be immediately freed to save its life. This compassionate female reaction, with its extremely long pedigree of women priestesses, healers, and shamanesses inhabiting an integral and interrelated cosmos, proved to Boyle their inability to be a modest witness—ie, an emotionless witness—and resulted in their being banished from the laboratory forever more, or at least until the mid-twentieth century. Here we see, yet again, how the "scientific revolution" was built upon centuries of erasure of female practices and knowledges.

In these turbulent and precarious times, when the Church's monopoly on education and knowledge was challenged by the Protestants, who also claimed to possess the One Truth, Boyle's achievement was his ability to create a neutral space in the laboratory, where talk of religion, politics, and metaphysics were strictly forbidden. It was crucial to the success of Boyle's endeavor that his budding experimental scientific method allow disagreement in the laboratory over what had happened in the experiment. This decision was crucial to the robustness of the findings as well as one that avoided the dogmatism of many Church pronouncements. But disagreements were to be kept strictly within the bounds of the neutral space of the laboratory and its rules, a space thoroughly cleansed from any potentially divisive and thus dangerous elements. Boyle, quite arbitrarily, labelled those 'metaphysical.' If there was to be agreement about a scientific fact, it had to be built on a foundation that could be totally separated from those domains where conflicts raged—the ones where the metaphysical was central. Boyle worked hard to make his experimental method the one everyone agreed upon. This general agreement did not happen quickly or easily: he was challenged on several fronts and the final defeat of rival methods took close to a century. His method has dominated the scientific and cultural scene down to our time.

Coda

I want to close this chapter with something I learned during a visit to Sami friends in the north of Sweden. The Samis are perhaps the last European indigenous peoples, and they live above the circumpolar circle in Scandinavia and Russia. I had befriended a Sami couple, Sturre and Aina Nilsson, when I invited them to a conference on Indigenous Knowledge that I had co-organized with Professor John Mohawk at Smith College. They invited me in return to visit them in Sweden, which I did with my family in the early 1990s. We landed from Finland by boat in Umea and drove up north with Sturre and Aina. In what turned out to be an unforgettable experience, they took us to participate in the once-yearly branding of the reindeer, herded by the Samis. The reindeer are left to forage freely in the forest for most of the year but in the summer they are gathered in a corral, lassoed and branded by nicking one of their ears. By the corral was a tepee which, as was explained to me, was the original sauna: heated stones were placed in a hollow in the center of the tepee, and water poured on them to generate steam. My daughter, who was nine at the time, sat with some Samis who taught her how to carve wood with a knife. After this exhilarating event, my hosts wanted to show us a museum of Sami history, which their community had created. I had no idea what was waiting for me there.

The museum recorded graphically the extermination of shamanism among the Samis, which had been carried out in brutal and systematic fashion from the mid-18th into the 19th century by the Protestant Lutheran church, the dominant religion of Sweden. This is how Christianity was introduced to these European indigenous peoples and it was horrifying. I was surprised at how recently these last embers of the Burning Times were still inflamed, much later than I had known. It was still painfully fresh in the memory of the contemporary Sami people. Sturre and Aina explained to us that the Sami shamans were the most famous in all of Europe and that before the extermination, people from all over Europe came in pilgrimage to the circumpolar north to participate in their ceremonies.

What came to my mind then and afterwards were so many of the illustrations of the Alsatian children's books that my father used to read to us, with elves and fairies always shown sitting on red mushrooms with white spots. Much later I learned that this standard image in European folklore shows the *Amanita muscaria, a* psychedelic mushroom. I did not dare ask Sturre and Aina at the time whether the Sami shamans used this mushroom because the whole topic was still painful for them. I did not want to poke my nose in this tender memory, especially since I felt that my Lutheran antecedents somehow implicated me personally. It is also true that this happened a few years before I drank my first ayahuasca brew and many more years before I had ever heard of psychedelic mushrooms.

3. THE ENCLOSURE OF LAND IN EUROPE THEN AND IN SOUTH AMERICA NOW

During the 14th and 15th centuries, the medieval economic-political system known as feudalism—or the manorial system—was crumbling. The economic viability of the manor, the property of an aristocratic lord, was in decline and the aristocracy and richer merchant classes were looking for new sources of revenue to boost their preferred mode of life. One of the ways they achieved this was by forcibly fencing lands that had been held in common among the people and claiming exclusive ownership to them. This *enclosure movement* lasted many centuries in Europe and is widely recognized as playing a crucial role in the birth of what eventually became capitalism and modernity. Less emphasized is that it was also pivotal in the birth of a disenchanted view of nature as being totally devoid of sentience and agency.

The enclosure movement continues unabated today in indigenous communities in South America. To tell that story, I draw not only on a great deal of scholarship on the movement in Europe, but also on the knowledge and perspective I gained through collaborating with indigenous communities in the Peruvian High Amazon, who currently face high rates of deforestation and environmental degradation, as well as ongoing efforts to enclose their common forests.

For the Kichwa-Lamas the rain forest is a common where anyone can go to collect salt, gather medicinal plants, fuel, fruits and other useful plants, hunt, fish, or seclude oneself for extended periods to acquire the help of the spirits for healing oneself and others. The Kichwa-Lamas often refer to the forest as their home, or as their market, a "mercado" where they can get everything they need. For them it is also a sacred place, where beings or spirits reside on whom the continuity of the web of life depends. Humans are part of this web and relate to those beings as elder relatives to whom one must show respect and with whom one must reciprocate to ensure the continuation of the cycles of life.

The common of the indigenous peoples of Amazonia is severely threatened today, not only in Peru but in all the countries of the Amazon basin. The Peruvian government is committed to globalization and is giving away in concession most of its Amazonian people's ancestral common lands. Multinational and national companies are extracting oil, minerals, timber, and medicinal plants from these commons with very little of the profits trickling down to the indigenous inhabitants. On the contrary, their home, their market, their sacred place—the rain forest, and its thousands of rivers—are being severely polluted, making survival often impossible for the indigenous people. This continues a brutal history of colonization, enslavement, and ethnocide. It is also an assault on the global environmental equilibrium since the Amazonian rain forest plays a crucial role in stabilizing the planet's climate. In South America, the forces of enclosure continue to do what the original European movement did, namely enrich the powerful and destabilize and diminish both the cultural and biological—namely the *biocultural*—mega-diversity of this region.

The giving in concession of most of the Amazonian Forest to multinational companies is not spoken of as an enclosure of the commons in the media or the government, although it is recognized as such by critics of globalization. Officially, those lands are defined as belonging to the nation state, the reasoning being that the indigenous inhabitants are not making productive use of them and therefore those forested lands devolve by right to the state. By political sleight of hand, the original inhabitants were discovered to have no legal title to those lands, and therefore no right to them. Both the notions of "productive use" as well as the legal status of titled land are realities created by the original enclosure movement in Europe and exported to the Americas by its colonizers.

To illustrate the violent, criminal nature of this contemporary enclosure of the commons, it is worth recalling an event that happened in Peru in June of 2009 during the presidency of Alan García, after he signed a Free Trade Agreement (FTA) in 2007 with former US president George W. Bush. This event was covered by the international press and gave rise to protests in many countries including the US. Alan García's government had promulgated hundreds of legislative decrees to implement the FTA with the US and open wide some 75% of the Peruvian territory, most of it in Amazonia, to multinational companies, transnational capital, and neo-liberalization. Many of the new laws allowed García's government to sell, give in concession, or promise indigenous territories to these multinational companies. This was done without consulting the indigenous groups concerned, as was required by older Peruvian laws and international decrees. With left-wing guerilla movements such as Shining Path largely defeated, Alan García's government justified his repressive measures in the name of a struggle against drug trafficking and international terrorism.[1]

García also justified his policies in the name of a progress that would benefit all Peruvians and castigated the Amazonian indigenous people for selfishly sitting on vast resources that by right belong to everyone in Peru. According to García, the opening of the Peruvian Amazon to transnational capital would bring prosperity to all Peruvians, not only to a few Amazonian indigenous groups. García repeatedly reiterated that indigenous people formed only a small minority of the national population.

These promises sounded hollow to the indigenous inhabitants of the Amazon, however. In my center in Lamas, on June 5, 2009, I sat glued to the radio, listening in shock and disbelief to reports of the violent repression of a group of indigenous people at a roadblock in the town of Bagua, located only a few hours by car from Lamas. The government sent in helicopters with policemen armed with sub-machine guns, who opened fire on indigenous people armed only with lances, stones, bows and arrows. A group of indigenous men had taken possession of an oil refinery and were holding about a dozen guards hostage there. My shock was intensified by the tone of the reportage that whole day. Nakedly racist language was used by Alan García and members of his government, as well as by the reporters themselves, who parroted Garcías' characterization of the social and indigenous movements that had been protesting his policies since the signing of the FTA as "extortionists." These extortionists, the media claimed, behaved like the "dog of the gardener" (*perro del hortelano*) "who is not hungry but prevents others from eating" by owning millions of hectares of unproductive lands which could only be made profitable by privatizing them through selling or giving them in concession to transnational companies.

Indigenous people were, in this way, characterized as being 'primitive and ignorant savages' standing in the way of progress for all Peruvians.[2] In this 2009 incident, the official government death toll was announced at 14 policemen and 11 indigenous people. However, communiqués and videos made by various indigenous people, social movements, and organizations, reported that protesters in Bagua were 'disappeared' by being thrown into rivers from helicopters or by having their corpses burnt. These sources estimate the number of 'disappeared' at anywhere from 200 to 500.[3]

Shortly after these events, I organized a meeting of local indigenous leaders to voice their opinions of the Bagua 'massacres' for an article that the magazine *Cultural Survival* asked me to write.[4] I reproduce below one of these leaders' remarks:

Since the strike until now the government has done little or nothing, rather it gives in concession native territories. Those are our markets, our house because there we find everything: medicines, comestible and medicinal plants and animals, materials for construction, and the forest is also a sacred place where we pray and ask permission and do rituals. One does not enter the forest just like that; one needs to take certain plants to purge and purify oneself to be in contact with animals and be able to see the spirits.

We are struggling to become united as organizations and form a single fist and say enough to the abuses of the government...They say that we are criminals and that we destroy the forest. But it is the reverse: the enterprises destroy hectares of forest while an indigenous person destroys one hectare to make a chacra [food field] using it for 4 or 5 years and then it is abandoned and left for the forest to regenerate. The cutting of the forest that way is not permanent.

—Lisardo Sangama Salas, Apu of the native community of Solo

This event is far from being unusual or unique. Similar policies have been enacted by other Latin American governments in the name of progress and development, resulting in the enclosing of their indigenous populations' commons. Such moves only further enrich the already rich and powerful.[5]

The original enclosure movement in Europe lasted for several centuries, roughly from the 14th to the 18th centuries. A combination of the economic non-viability of the manorial system and the rise in the price of wool cloth in what had become a world trade were the incentives that pushed wealthier men to enclose formerly common lands. Seeking to graze sheep to create wool cloth to sell in this expanding world market, they grabbed common lands, fenced them, landscaped them to improve grazing and transformed them into pasturage for their sheep. Forcibly excluding all the people who until then had used those commons, the encloser treated the fenced land as his exclusive property and used it as an investment in the pursuit of his individual financial goals, thereby severing his ties to the local community and to what economic historians have called "the moral economy," in which all, regardless of status or ability, were provided for.[6] The European peasants protested and resisted the enclosure of their commons but the wealthier classes, both aristocrats and merchants, were able to prevail in the courts to make their claim stick. This created terrible suffering among the displaced peasants, with many dying of starvation. So miserable were conditions in Ireland that Jonathan Swift suggested, in his satirical *Modest Proposal*, that the noble classes should butcher and eat the year-old infants of the peasantry, adding, "I grant this food will be somewhat dear, and therefore very *proper for Landlords*—who, as they have already devoured most of the Parents, seem to have the best Title to the Children."[7]

A beautiful film by historian Pamela Berger, "The Sorceress," set in southern France in the mid-13th century, captures the first glimmers of the enclosure movements and concomitant Burning Times. In this film, a monk comes to a remote village to ferret out heretics. The village priest tries to deflect the monk and protect his parishioners, including the herbalist forest woman whom the monk tries to condemn as a witch. Meanwhile, the local lord of the manor, a bullying aristocrat, floods the common land where the peasants grew their crops to grow fish to sell for his personal gain. When one of the peasants opens the dam and drains the artificial pond, he is imprisoned and condemned to death. During the monk's inquest to search out heretics, the wife of the imprisoned villager tells the monk that the local lord is the heretic, because he is preventing the villagers from planting their seeds by converting their commons into a fishpond for his private use. The monk tells her that what the lord has done is neither heretical nor a sin, because he is an aristocrat, with more rights to the land than the villagers. She responds, "My husband says the Count can never steal away our right to sow the seed. It's like the rain or the rays of the sun, it can't be taken." These words poetically capture the sense of the people and the land being one, with no exclusive owner, except perhaps for God or the king of France, who owned all the land as God's representative. This concept of divine ownership is far removed from the later concept of an exclusive title to a piece of land, where land has become a commodity in the market. Land as a commodity that could be bought and sold emerged only because of the enclosure movement and the rise of mercantilism, the precursor of capitalism.

The Church, in allying itself with the powerful, focused its inquisitorial attention on those who had an intimate knowledge of the forest. The film beautifully portrays the forest woman, to whom the monk explains that true knowledge can only be found in Church books. The forest woman is part of the oral peasantry and cannot read. She is depicted as having deep and precise knowledge of the plants in the forest, including their properties, their use, and preparation. She attends to the illnesses of the villagers and her potions are often administered as part of rituals deriving from ancient, pre-Christian traditions. The villagers are shown participating in a maypole dance, carrying branches, flowers, and other greenery, under the tolerant gaze of their beloved parish priest.

The following excerpt from an English eyewitness account of such peasant celebrations, dating from 1583 gives us a vivid glimpse into such rituals:

Towards May...every parish, town, and village gets together, both men and women and children, old and young...they run to the bushes and woods, hills and mountains, where they spend all the night in pleasant pastimes, and in the morning they return bringing home birch bows and branches of trees...(T)he chiefest jewel they bring home is their maypole, which they bring home with great veneration...then they fall to banquet and feast, to leap and dance about it, as heathen people did at the dedication of their idols.[8]

By 1583, a century after the Pope had declared that witches were to be burned at the stake as heretics, a parish priest could no longer look upon his villagers' age-old festivities with affectionate tolerance. Such peasant rituals as the Maypole were now identified as heathen and idolatrous.

The maypole is an instance of a worldwide practice involving a pole or tree. The scholarly term for such poles is *axis mundi*, 'world axis.' Such trees connect the underworld through their roots, the terrestrial world through their trunks and the heavens through their highest branches and leaves. Historians tell us that midwives in many parts of Europe used to fetch the souls of unborn children at such trees. Some were called 'tree mothers' others 'wilderness women' and yet others 'forest woman.' Herbalism was not only pursued by women but also by some men. A text in German dating from 1668, said that "The forestman, or the one who digs for roots and herbs, is said to talk or converse often with Rübezahl,"[9] Rübezahl being an elf or fairy, considered a master herbalist.

This piece of historical evidence is strikingly like the contemporary view of Apu Lisardo Sangama Salas, quoted above: "one needs to take certain plants to purge and purify oneself so as to be in contact with animals and be able to see the spirits." In premodern Europe herbalist women and men were often also shaman and shamanesses, as is the case in indigenous Amazonia. They used psychotropic plants that altered consciousness, such as belladonna, mandragora, ergot, cannabis, and psychoactive mushrooms.[10] These plants, ingested under the proper ritual conditions, enabled those women and men to learn directly from the spirits of the plants—called in Europe 'elves or fairies'—how to heal people, how to confer children, how to safely deliver them and much more. Shamans and shamanesses in Amazonia today, such as Randy, learn from 'conversations' with the spirits of the plants themselves what the diagnosis is, and how to cure a particular affliction.

Shamanism, whether in pre-modern Europe or in Amazonia today, needs the commons and especially the forest. The herbalists and other healers could not acquire their knowledge without being in the forest, the prairies, the riverbanks and all those places where one could gather and learn about and from plants. Many such places were commons whose access became more and more difficult in Europe. Just like today in Amazonia, the accelerating rate of deforestation in pre-modern Europe made access to many healing and psychotropic plants more and more difficult.

During the time of these transformations in Western Europe—the Burning Times and the enclosure of the commons—the period of European expansion began with the slave trade and the colonization of the Americas, followed by globalization. The expansion of the modern Western materialist anthropocentric worldview continues apace through the hegemony of its type of education, its form of production, its global financial system, its consumerism, and its technological wizardry.

Varieties of shamanic and other related practices are viewed as ignorant and superstitious, in the same way that the so-called witches were viewed in Europe. The Burning Times started before the slave trade and the invasion of the Americas, profoundly coloring the perception and evaluation of shamanic practices in Africa and indigenous America, both historically and today, as the historian of science Isabelle Stengers trenchantly declares:

> I received this word "reclaiming" as a gift from neo-pagan contemporary witches and other U.S. activists. I also received the shocking cry of neo-pagan Starhawk: "The smoke of the burned witches still hangs in our nostrils." Certainly, the witch hunters are no longer among us, and we no longer take seriously the accusation of devil worshipping that was once leveled at witches. Rather, our milieu is defined by the modern pride in being able to interpret both witchery and witch hunting in terms of social, linguistic, cultural, or political constructs and beliefs. What this pride ignores, however, is that we are the heirs of an operation

of cultural and social eradication—the forerunner of what was committed elsewhere in the name of civilization and reason .... In this sense, our pride in our critical power to "know better" than both the witches and the witch hunters makes us the heirs of witch-hunting.[11]

In South America, the 16th century laws of Extirpation of Idolatry, accompanied by a brutal campaign by the Inquisition to exterminate shamanism, resulted in the dominant *mestizo* and *criollo* society overwhelmingly viewing indigenous spirituality as primitive and backward, steeped in superstition. In my work with several high schools through the local provincial school board, I have regularly encountered such prejudices. However, many non-indigenous denizens of the Amazon continue to seek a shaman either to heal or to do sorcery against an enemy.

This history is also at the root of contemporary resistance to changing the dominant materialist reductionist anthropocentric paradigm, which underlies all the institutions of modernity, including education.[12] This legacy is still very much with us. We have all been colonized by the dominant version of history born in Western Europe. Coloniality—the colonizing mind-set—was born in Europe itself and first trained onto its own "heretics," later spreading around the world. The healing and shamanic practices Europeans encountered in Africa and indigenous America through the slave trade and the invasion of the Americas were similar to the practices and worldview of the supposed heretics of Europe and treated as mercilessly in the New World as in the Old. Robert Boyle's comment that respect for Nature "has been a discouraging impediment to the empire of man over the inferior creatures of God"[13] opened the door to the current unfettered extraction of what are called "natural resources."

Natural resources are not feeling beings with psyches and spirits, but rather insentient matter, available for human extraction and consumption in ways that are taken for granted and seemingly self-evident. However, in indigenous cosmovisions as well as in the pre-modern European cosmovision of Anima Mundi, there were no "natural resources"—instead, there were non-human beings with psyches and feelings with whom humans need to communicate and reciprocate appropriately. This communication between humans and non-humans, both in pre-modern Europe and in Indigenous Amazonia, happened through shamans and shamanesses using psychotropic plants. When humans nurture an equilibrium with the non-human realm, the continuity of the wellbeing not only of humans but of the world/cosmos is assured, as the Sarayaku proclamation articulates so powerfully.

In contrast, the European colonizers developed a violent logic of extractivism, seen for example in the way the Spaniards went about extracting silver from the mines in what is today Bolivia, such as Potosi. Such violent extractivism quickly led to the destruction of the spirit of that mountain—a revered mountain spirit or Apu to the indigenous peoples—as well as the death of an enormous number of indigenous laborers in the death-camp-like mines.[14] It also led to a profoundly new type of global economy.

4. THE ENCLOSURE OF THE SELF AND COSMOCENTRIC RECIPROCITY

A profound transformation of the person took place along-side the enclosure of land in Europe. The historian Karl Polanyi in his classic work on the beginnings of capitalism has famously argued that the heart of capitalism consisted in the transformation of land, labor, and capital into commodities for purchase and sale.[1] The transformation of labor into a commodity affected people's understanding of their relationship to the human social landscape, but their embeddedness in the natural world receded so far into the background as to become invisible, alienating the laborer from nature and making the other-than-humans invisible and mute.

The medieval peasant and the land he/she worked formed a single natural whole, with the activities of sowing or reaping considered as natural as the rain falling or the sun shining. Once the land became the private property of an individual who hired laborers to work that land, the relationship between livelihood and work on the land was severed, since what was grown on the land no longer directly fed the worker. The relationship between land and work became mediated by money, and the enclosed land was transformed into an object to be used for the sole benefit of the encloser. This also had the effect of leaving the land disenchanted, that is bereft of its spirits.

In the world of Anima Mundi, before enclosure, everything was alive, integrated, and numinous. With the profoundly efficacious extermination during the Burning Times of those who lived in such a world, and the creation of land and labor as commodities, it is difficult to recall such a world. It has migrated into European folklore and lost its worldly moorings. The creation of labor as a commodity separated the self from the web of relations not only with other humans but also with non-humans, the normally invisible beings who could take human or animal-human, plant-human or elemental-human features. This other-than-human world of spirits and supernaturals is typically seen by us moderns as mere beliefs, products of the human imagination or hallucinations. Randy, having been raised by non-indigenous secular parents, was initially taken aback by his sudden experiences with spirits, elements, the Virgin of Guadalupe, the mountain Waman Wasi and other discarnate beings. It took him a good year and a half to completely agree to walk the path of curanderismo. Despite his strong initial reluctance to embrace this path, the nature of his visions and experiences were so compellingly *real* that sometimes he could not be sure whether they took place in what he calls the *terrenal* world of ordinary reality or the spiritual world.

Typically, the discipline of anthropology explains shamanism in terms of the collective *beliefs* in shamanic culture. However, Randy did not inherit a worldview in which spirits were believed in. And the tangible effects of the discarnate beings who visit him are real for everyone to see.[2] To give a sense of what such an integrated, numinous world looks and feels like, I will discuss the daily behavior of Kichwa-Lamas I have engaged with in my work at my center in Lamas, which reveals their worldview.

Growing food among the Kichwa-Lamas

Girvan Tuanama, an indigenous former staff member at Sachamama Center, said to me: "My grandmother and the elders used to offer pieces of broken ceramics in their *chacras* to Mama Allpa (spirit of the earth/soil). Now most people no longer do that." Since broken ceramics have been found in all the pre-Columbian anthropogenic black earth, Girvan's information was a revelation for me. In the extensive scholarly publications about this black earth, I had never read anything about these broken ceramics coming from offerings.[3]

So, when we went to his native community, at the time of the *mikuna*—communal meal—we went to his grandmother's house to eat. The little old lady sat on the threshold welcoming everyone in. After everyone had eaten and left, Girvan, his grandmother and I stayed in the now-quiet room. Carmen Tapullima Salas seemed to me to be in her nineties, frail but lucid. Girvan said he did not know her age since she did not have a birth certificate. After some chatter to make us comfortable with each other, Carmen was asked about the offerings in the *chacra* and she said, "Yes, I used to always bring my *shaño* with me and give it to Mama Allpa.[4] That is what we used to do then." Girvan explained:

> It is the *ingenieros* [literally 'engineers,' but meaning all university-educated people] who made us ashamed of this practice by telling us it was a silly superstition. So now only a few of the old ones still do it but, in many communities, this *pago* (offering) is no longer done.[5] But you yourself heard the comuneros of Shukshuyaku yesterday tell you that they keep finding pieces of ceramics in the old *chacras*. That tells them that their ancestors used to offer them to Mama Allpa.

Earlier we had gone to Shukshuyaku, a native community with whom we have created a permanent communal *chacra*, for the first planting of the June agricultural season.[6] Since the ancient *yana allpa* that we are recreating in our center had been discovered by archaeologists to be full of ceramic shards, the *comuneros* (members of a native community) were enthusiastic about remembering their ancestors' practice of offering broken ceramics to the soil before planting.

According to the literature on Amazonian Dark Earth (ADE), popularly known in Brazil as *terra preta do indio* (black earth of the Indians), most of the authors consider that the many pieces of broken ceramics found in ADE come from middens. A few are found in conjunction with burials; one anthropologist studying the ceramics of the contemporary Asurini do Xingu peoples in Brazil reports that at the death of a woman (who like among the Kichwa-Lamas are the potters of the community) her ceramics are broken.[7]

The only archaeologist to have speculated that the broken ceramics found in *terra preta* come from offerings to the deities/ spirits is Alfredo Narváez Vargas, a Peruvian archaeologist and anthropologist who has excavated Kuelap, one of the major archaeological sites of Chachapoyas. Dr. Narváez told me, during a 2012 conversation in Lamas, that when he excavated a few archaeological agricultural terraces near Kuelap, he typically found a dense layer of black organic soil that was easily differentiated from the yellow color of the geological layers. In the black layer he found fragments of ceramics he considered to be remnants of offerings.[8] His findings correspond closely to the descriptions by archaeologists of *terra preta* sites in the low Amazon. Lamas is situated at the eastern edge of the Chachapoyas pre-Colombian culture area. However, to my knowledge no one has reported on the practice of the Kichwa-Lamas of offering pieces of broken ceramics to the various spirits of the *chakra,* including Mama Allpa, the soil/earth; Yakumama, the rain/water; Mama Qilla, the moon, Tayta Inti, the sun, and Sachamama, the spirit of the rain forest. Many of the Kichwa women elders keep some pieces of ceramics for offerings. They also make offerings of corn beer (*chicha*), the traditional pre-Colombian offering.

Offerings of pieces of ceramics are made before planting and at harvest in each of the two major agricultural seasons. Since agriculture is the principal activity of the Kichwa-Lamas, most everyone used to do this. However, the seductions of modernity, combined with the scornful attitude of the dominant mestizos towards such practices, have deeply eroded it. Although poor mestizo farmers practice the same agricultural techniques as the Kichwa-Lamas, namely swidden agriculture, planting according to the phases of the moon, polyculture, and so on, they are much less likely to make offerings to the spirits of the *chacra*. In any case, the Kichwa-Lamas keep their ritual practices to themselves, careful to protect them from the contemptuous gaze of the members of the dominant society. Although the colonial laws of "extirpation of idolatry" are no longer enforced, the memory of the death-dealing ferocity with which they were enforced is still alive among the indigenous people.[9] In addition, evangelical movements have made deep inroads in the Peruvian High Amazon and those Kichwas belonging to Evangelical churches have ceased making such offerings, which are considered by Evangelicals to be the work of the devil.

It seems to me that such practices could well account for the broken ceramics found in the much more densely populated pre-Colombian patches of black soil all over the Amazon basin. Furthermore, it is well known that at least in the highland Wari pre-Colombian culture, elaborate ritual ceramics were dashed to pieces after an offering. I have admired such reconstituted vessels in the archaeological museum in Ayacucho as well as the one in Pueblo Libre in Lima. According to Harvard professor Thomas Cummins, a renowned specialist in Peruvian pre-Columbian ceramics, this practice of breaking the ceramics used in offerings could have been widespread, extending as far as the low Amazon.[10]

Since ceramics in the low Amazon antedate any other ceramics in the rest of the Americas it might even be possible that the practice originated there. The fact that the Peruvian archaeologist Alfredo Narváez has found Amazonian Dark Earth in the Chachapoyas culture area, full of ceramics, and that he claims that these are the remnants of offerings to the deities/ spirits is the strongest evidence so far for a continuous practice among the indigenous population of making such offerings in their food fields.[11]

Offerings to the Spirits and Cosmocentric Reciprocity

Although most of the literature on ADE does not speak of its spiritual aspect and is overwhelmingly quantitative and scientific, Gerry Gillespie, in his 2009 essay "City to Soil, Returning Organics to Agriculture: A Circle of Sustainability" comes close to it.[12] After pointing out that successful communities the world over have always returned organic matter to the soil and that these actions are the very basis of those communities' sustainability, he points out that such acts were "an intentional and conscious attempt to maintain a link between the individual and their food producer. As much as any other action, it was an act of respect."[13]

This is as close as the literature on ADE comes to something that could be called spiritual. In fact, such respect for the soil, as well as respect for all the other beings/spirits involved in growing food, is typical in peasant and indigenous societies the world over, including in pre-modern European agriculture. As I have argued, with the advent of the enclosure movement, the Reformation and the scientific revolution, the reciprocity between humans and those non-humans involved in growing food (such as the soil, the water, the sun, and the moon among others), began to be seen as magical acts devoid of efficacy.

Offerings made to the soil, locally embodied in its spirit Mama Allpa, emphatically enact a conscious and intentional bond of respect between humans and the soil, which simultaneously recognizes the agency of the earth. These offerings represent an awareness that without a return gift to the soil/earth, the success of agriculture is in danger. The earth/soil gives of its produce, enabling humans to live, and humans show their gratitude for those gifts by offering something in return to the soil. These reciprocal exchanges of gifts enact a *regenerative cycle* constituting the opposite of the extractive actions of a capitalist economy, where the soil is considered a "natural resource" rather than a sacred mother.

Agriculture is a series of concerted actions carried out by various actors: humans, who prepare the fields, choose the seeds, prepare and tend the soil, and harvest the produce; and non-human actors such as the earth, air, water, sun and moon, without whose aid agriculture would not be possible.[14] As I documented in my 2011 book, the agency of the non-human world is a feature that has become accepted in the field of critical science studies and among certain quantum physicists.[15] The Cartesian/Boylian/Newtonian paradigm of a mechanical, agency-less insentient world is being challenged, although this paradigm shift has barely begun to percolate in modern culture, even at the most sophisticated universities.

As the discoveries concerning Amazonian Dark Earth and other anthropogenic phenomena in Amazonia have revealed, the Amazonian rain forest is anything but a virgin forest. It is the result of millennia of concerted actions carried out by pre-Colombian humans and all the non-humans in that locality.[16] For example, the soil becomes Mama Allpa, a being to whom prayers and offerings are made, who is endowed with understanding, agency and sentience and responds to the actions of humans. In modernity the soil has become a "natural resource" bereft of agency, sentience and understanding—simply there for humans to exploit, without feeling that by doing so we are showing a lack of respect. A natural resource does not require us to reciprocate for what we take since it has no agency or sentience, rendering the idea of reciprocity meaningless. The logic of modernity calculates the value of the land and its products in terms of money. Even in today's so-called Green Economics, the agency and/or sentience of nature and the cosmos is not recognized. Modern humans need to take another look at what anthropologists have called "the gift economy," which is another term for what I have been pointing to as the reciprocal regenerative cycle existing between humans, the Earth, and the cosmos.

Re-casting the Gift Economy

The term 'gift economy' was coined by the French anthropologist Marcel Mauss in 1925, in what became a classic book in the field of anthropology, entitled "The Gift" (*Essai sur Le Don*).[17] Mauss studied the elaborate rituals of exchange in non-modern small-scale societies, entered into in what he called "the spirit of the gift"; his primary focus was the indigenous Maori people of New Zealand. Mauss analyzed the gift exchanges of the Maori in terms of how they created bonds between people, and his disregard for the role of the spirits in the ritual has dominated the anthropological literature on this topic ever since. However, traditional human gift exchanges always include gifts to invisible beings, namely the deities or spirits or ancestors. It is only then that these so-called gift exchanges become truly regenerative. Viewing gift exchanges as simply between human beings is in keeping with the strong tendency in anthropology to reject the importance and agency of spirits, deities, and the like. In general, anthropologists have not allowed agency to those aspects of the natural world responsible for human sustenance and have not recognized the need for humans to reciprocate with regenerative gifts in the form of constant ritualized offerings between people and the spirits.[18]

If the gift, according to Mauss and others, strengthens the bonds between humans, it also increases spirituality if we understand by this term a continuous flow beyond oneself and beyond one's human community toward the non-human world and its various spiritual embodiments. I consider such reciprocal exchanges as *cosmocentric reciprocity,* in which the regeneration of the sources of sustenance is not taken as an automatic natural or biological process but is recognized as dependent on the proper ritual action from humans. Regeneration emerges from the interactions between humans, non-humans, and the spirits. It is a radically non-anthropocentric type of reciprocity, in other words a reciprocity profoundly different from that imagined and performed by the anthropocentric extractivist capitalist economy.

For the Kichwa-Lamas, the spirits of the *chacra* are not projections of the human mind onto the non-human world or metaphors used by humans to *represent* the non-human world.

Rather, they literally embody that which enables the humans living in a particular place to draw from the natural world without depleting it. The spirits of the earth and cosmos are considered as real beings, spirits with independent agency; this prevents the exploitation of the natural world since any exploitative behavior would open one (and one's group) to the reprisal of the spirits. Such reprisals can also be recognized in the degradation of the soil, the forest, the water sources and so forth. Ritual offerings to the sources of sustenance ensure the regeneration of those sources and embody an implicit recognition that such regeneration depends on proper human actions; it is not automatic.

The difference between a natural resource and the spirit of the forest or of the soil/earth spells the difference between exploitation and regeneration.The spirits or deities make possible certain types of action and make other types of action difficult, reprehensible, or sinful, with consequences that are at once material, discursive and spiritual.[19] These rituals *enact* or *perform* continuous bio-cultural regeneration through a variety of actions and utterances which embody the entanglement of humans, non-humans, and the spirits—entanglements that I call "cosmocentric reciprocity." Cosmocentric reciprocity is a regenerative, non-exploitative system in which re-distribution among humans, non-humans and the spirit realm ensures the equitable regeneration of the sources of livelihood and sustenance for humans.

This stands in contrast to the Christian insistence on the total separation between humans, non-humans, Earth, and God. Ever since the Reformers' separation between matter and spirit, rituals of regeneration could only be understood as humans *representing* symbolically or metaphorically the non-humans, who became passive and silent. Just as the Puritans in New England felt righteous about expelling the Indians from the land, the conquistadors and the authorities in colonial Peru felt legitimate in preventing the indigenous people performing their regenerative rituals. For the Spaniards, the spirits were *diablos,* devils—which does recognize their existence, but demonizes them.[20] We are today still in the grip of the Reformation and its effect not only on the Church, but on all disciplines of study, including secularized anthropology.[21]

The Ecological Situation Today in the Peruvian High Amazon

When I first discovered the existence of *terra preta* in 2005, it immediately seemed worthy of further study and possible application in the region.[22] I had been coming to Lamas for some fifteen years by then and was aware of the urgency of the situation regarding the local practice of slash and burn agriculture by poor mestizo and indigenous farmers. Every year I return to Lamas there is less forest; indeed, San Martín has the dubious distinction of having the highest rate of deforestation in all of Peru.[23] The deforestation is the result of several factors. In the 1980s and 1990s the region saw an enormous increase in the production of coca for the illegal cocaine trade, which necessitated an enormous amount of deforestation to make way for coca fields.[24] In addition, ever since the region was opened with the construction of a road in the 1960's, there has been a dizzying amount of immigration on the part of land-hungry peasants from the highlands and/or the coastal areas of the country. Along with the government's official stimulus for industrial monoculture agriculture and the migrants' ignorance of the special nature of Amazonian clay soils, large tracts of forest have been clear-cut to make way for either cattle ranching or growing coca, rice, corn, sugar cane or cotton as cash crops.

Large-scale slash-and-burn agriculture was introduced when the Spaniards brought steel tools in the 16th century. Experts calculate that for this method of agriculture to be sustainable, a family must own a minimum of 50 hectares of land.[25] Since most small-scale farmers in Lamas own between 3 and 10 hectares,[26] there are shorter fallow periods between clearings, with the result that the secondary forest that regenerates in abandoned food fields or *chacras* is progressively less vigorous and eventually ceases altogether, leaving the land totally degraded: crops can no longer be grown, and the forest no longer regenerates.

The leadership of the Kichwa-Lamas is aware of the problem. The former president of the largest of the four Kichwa-Lamas organizations, the Ethnic Council of the Kichwa People of Amazonia (CEPKA is the Spanish acronym), Misael Salas Amasifuen, described the situation to my American undergraduate students in 2011:

> Our custom is to open chacras in the forest, cutting the trees, not uprooting them, and then burning the branches. After three to four years, we let the forest regenerate during some eight, ten, to fifteen years and then we cut the trees again. We are three brothers and our widowed mother. Together we own 18 hectares, and we are no longer able to open big food gardens. We can only make small chacras. We can no longer cut down the forest, and more and more land are being degraded. How are we going to survive if we cut down the little forest that remains for us? We will have to migrate, and we do not want to do that. We hope that your center can help us to learn another manner of growing food that does not require cutting down the forest.[27]

Most of the Kichwa-Lamas depend on their *chacras* for survival. Due to communal labor, called *maki-maki* or *choba-choba* in Quechua, where kin, neighbors and friends form work parties to work on each other's fields or projects, the need for cash has historically been minimal. Currently, however, the federal government requires all children to attend school, which means that uniforms and other supplies must be purchased by the parents, increasing the need for cash. Kichwas typically sell the surplus produce they raise in their chacras in the local markets and sell their labor at times of peak demands—during the coffee harvest, for example—to acquire cash. However, their ability to grow their own food is not only an economic necessity but also guarantees their autonomy, which in turn enables them to maintain their distinct identity. Thus, food sovereignty for the Kichwa-Lamas not only spells their physical survival but their political and cultural sustainability as well.

Given that slash and burn is their form of agriculture and that it requires forests, the Kichwa-Lamas are very actively engaged in negotiations with the regional government for stewardship of the local conservation reserve forest situated in the nearby mountain range of the Cordillera Escalera which is part of their ancestral territory. Unexpectedly for me, the Kichwa-Lamas leadership is not envisaging carrying out their form of agriculture in those forest reserves.

What surprised me in this attitude of the Kichwa-Lamas is that it seems to accept the logic of the separation between utilitarian activities on the one hand and conservation or preservation on the other. Even though they envision activities of hunting and gathering in the forest and others as well, they reject the making of chacra in it and thus food sovereignty through their traditional form of swidden agriculture. The area of forest conservation created by the Peruvian government and managed by the regional government of the State of San Martin is heir to the first historical such conservation areas. These were created in the United States in the second half of the 19th century as Nature Parks. As William Cronon's history of such parks has made us all aware these "wilderness preserves" were re-cast as God's Temple.[28] As Cronon shows, the enclosure of the Indians on reservations at the end of the Indian Wars in the second half of the 19th century as well as the disappearance of the frontier were key ingredients in the invention of such preserves. A nature park or preserve was constituted as a non-utilitarian space of sacred national wilderness. Cronon points out that: "to this day the Blackfeet continue to be accused of 'poaching' on the lands of the Glacier National Park that originally belonged to them and that were ceded by treaty only with the proviso that they be permitted to hunt there."[29] As is well known the idea of Nature Parks and later of Biodiversity Preserves was exported world-wide with the attendant require-ment of excluding the indigenous peoples who live in and from these lands. However, more recently several governments have changed course and allowed the people who used to live in such preserves the right to continue remaining in them.[30] Clearly for the Kichwa-Lamas, as for indigenous peoples everywhere, the sacred and the utilitarian are not separate.[31]

The explanation articulated by the Kichwa-Lamas leader-ship explains why they have agreed not to practice agriculture in the Area of Conservation Forest. They state that there is so little forest left that were they to continue practicing slash and burn in the conservation area it would lead to the same situ-ation now existing in the native communities. The leadership emphasized the urgency of preserving forests for the very iden-tity of future generations.[32] In his talk to my students in July 2011, Misael Salas Amasifuen emphasized the need of projects under the direction of experts to introduce new forms of per-manent agriculture in the native communities. As he confirmed to me at the end of his talk, he had in mind our own Chacra-Huerto project at Sachamama Center. It is precisely these kinds of conversations that led me to create a permanent agriculture project in collaboration with the Kichwa-Lamas beginning in the spring of 2010. We have called this project the *chacra-huerto* project to immediately communicate that the food chacra need not be in the forest, away from the settlements, but can be created near them, like the house gardens or *huertos*. Such huertos contain fruit trees, herbs, medicinal plants as well as the local tomato and chili, cultivars originating from the High Amazon region. They are tended mostly by the women of the house and are permanent.

To recap the foregoing, I have tried to suggest that the manner of growing food and other activities on the part of the Kichwa-Lamas, especially the reciprocal exchanges between the humans and the spirits of the cosmos, give rise to a self that is in daily and intimate connection with the non-human world and with the spirits, the invisible beings. In other words, the Kichwa-Lamas self has not been fully enclosed and thus alienated from nature and the spirit world.

Randy's Situatedness

The foregoing has drawn the broader cultural and natural context in which Randy lives. But Randy is not Kichwa-Lamas himself. His mother came from a poor mestizo farmer family that shared a great deal with their indigenous neighbors but in general not their spiritual practices. She and her husband are high school teachers with a secular worldview, rejecting the path of *curanderismo*, the shamanic path. So, although Randy grew up in some ways surrounded by the indigenous practices and beliefs that I have discussed in this chapter, he was not directly immersed in this context. His rather profound difference from indigenous practices made Randy try to refuse what his initiators were offering him. He did not want to become a shaman, but he was incapable of refusing what was being offered. When he lifted his arm to take hold of the sword presented to him, which sealed his acceptance of the shamanic path at the end of his first initiatory ayahuasca ceremony, this happened of its own accord, as he explained to me. The will of his discarnate initiators completely overwhelmed his own will and desire. Randy did not experience a long apprenticeship with living shamans, in which he would have learned their worldview and made it his own. The spirits suddenly sprang on him, unannounced and, at least to begin with, rather unwelcome.

In this region the normal way of becoming a shaman is through apprenticeship with a living shaman. Jacques Mabit, who was crucial in mentoring Randy at the beginning, had sought out living shaman teachers, with whom he apprenticed for many years. This is also the case for Davi Kopenawa, the Yanomami shaman who was taught by his father-in-law. Spontaneous initiation by spirits is extremely rare in this region and I had never heard of it in more than 25 years of regular attendance at aya-huasca ceremonies.[33] Although Randy had a hard time accepting the path of *curanderismo*, there was never any doubt for him that what he was experiencing, seeing and hearing was as real as what he experiences in this earthly dimension—so much so that he was often not sure which dimension he was in.

Randy is neither an acculturated modern with a thoroughly enclosed self, nor a Kichwa-Lamas with almost no enclosed self. He was a very reluctant initiate. There was no doubt in my mind that foreigners could become powerful shamans, because of my long acquaintance with Jacques Mabit, with whom I had done hundreds of ayahuasca ceremonies. I also know and participated in ayahuasca sessions with several mestizos who became shamans after apprenticing with indigenous shamans. But in these cases, the initiate participated in the apprentice-ship wholeheartedly; it was aligned with their own will and desire. Apprenticing with a living shaman is a slow process of familiarizing oneself with a new field or skill, knowledge, and expertise. Randy is closer to the indigenous world than Jacques Mabit or other foreign shamans, but he did not recognize that world as his own cultural inheritance. He showed no interest in participating in indigenous rituals with me and my students. He had no interest in belonging to the local indigenous culture.

In Randy's case, his own cultural identity, will and desire were completely overwhelmed by the will and desire of other beings, some of them 'nature beings,' some of them discarnate beings invisible to others besides Randy. Recall that when his indigenous master first appeared to him, his then-partner Kemy lay sleeping next to him in their bedroom. Randy woke her up and asked if she saw anything, and annoyed, she responded that she saw nothing and went back to sleep. The apparition was so real to Randy that he simply assumed Kemy would also see it. At that time, he was not under the influence of the aya-huasca potion and thus not expecting any visions.

I have known Randy since he was 15 years old, and he worked closely with me at my center for over two decades, where he was a reliable, stable, intelligent, extremely able and gifted painter, architect and builder. He has always been totally honest, not prone to dissimulation or lying. I am as certain as one can be of the complete honesty of what he has told me. It is impossible to understand Randy's experiences as imaginative fabrications, or lies, or as projections of his unconscious since he had no knowledge of the beings that appeared and spoke to him. Thus, I take it as a given that his experiences are completely real and the beings that speak to him and act on him are as real as their effect on him. Of course, I realize that my own lengthy experience with ayahuasca influences me in this acceptance, as well as my longstanding experience of Randy. However, none of my experiences with ayahuasca have been as vivid, concrete, and specific as Randy's and none of them involved receiving powers from any discarnate beings. That said, many of my experiences were profound mystical ones where the experience of the ultimate was so deep, so real, as to make experiences in this earthly dimension pale in comparison. They have remained an intense memory and have changed me.

5. IMPLICATIONS FOR SOCIETY AND THE NON-HUMAN WORLD

The enclosure of the self is something that resulted from the combined forces of three historical processes: 1) the extermination of Anima Mundi/shamanism; 2) the enclosure of the commons; and 3) the transformation of labor into a commodity. In the world of Anima Mundi, the person was connected to everything else in the cosmos, be it plants, stone, water, air, stars, animals, the angels, fairies, spirits, God, and of course other humans—*everything*. With the enclosure of the commons and the enclosure of the self, the integrality of the world and the cosmos, eventually vanished. This transformation was captured by Chaucer in his "Wife of Bath," in such verses as the following:

> All this wide land was land of faery
> The elf-queen, with her jolly company,
> Danced oftentimes on many a green mead;
> But now no man can see the elves, you know...
> For where was wont to walk full many an elf,
> Right there walks now the limiter himself... (lines 863-867)[1]

What Chaucer calls 'the limiter' refers to the encloser. The actions of the limiter disenchanted the land both by enclosing it and by transforming its former human inhabitants—the sowers and reapers, the herbalists and healers, the shamanesses and shamans—into paid laborers. Paid laborers need to own their labor force individually and exclusively, a necessary requirement to their being able to sell it. The land became an investment for a single man, who paid the laborers for their work and did not allow them to sow and reap on that land or to gather herbs, fish, or hunt on it or to reciprocate with the spirits.

It is only when we combine these forces with yet another that we can begin to grasp the deep meaning of what Karl Polanyi called *the Great Transformation*. This fourth force was the transformation of nature into an insentient mechanism, which was the onto-epistemological foundation for the mechanistic revolution.[2] As argued above, this was the solution for getting out of the interminable religious conflicts that were decimating Europe at the time. The natural philosophers who created the mechanistic revolution were not secularists themselves, as secularism did not take hold until the 18th century. In this period, God, the angels and all the supernaturals were understood as being above and thus outside of God's creation as the term "super-natural" says. This cleared the air for making creation or the cosmos the neutral domain that the natural philosophers required as the basis for the new knowledge. They could interrogate and investigate this machine-nature by remaining carefully and completely outside of it, neutral regarding the issues that so bloodily divided Protestants and Catholics.

When the Thirty Years War ended with the Treaty of Westphalia in 1648, the Nation State came into being. By the end of the 1700s, the new knowledge, which became known as science, became central to the functioning of the Nation State. James Scott details how the practice of scientific agriculture—agronomy—begun in Germany in the 1700s, led to scientific forestry, also invented in Germany, both of which became indispensable to running the Nation State.[3] The need for revenue on the part of the State required a drastic simplification of the landscape—the forests, the fields, in fact pretty much everything. This new political institution, the Nation State, needed revenue from commerce and industry. The commodification of the land and the establishment of fixed boundaries were facilitated by maps and surveys showing the extent, value, and ownership of land for taxation purposes. Metrics and mathematics were indispensable tools. For the State, a forest was potential revenue and all that was important was the volume of lumber and the revenue it would bring. The forest was subjected to a radical process of abstraction, what Scott calls 'simplification,' in which the trees, soil, and the actual life of the forest was reduced to calculations of board feet. The life of the land was irrelevant as productivity, revenue and profit became the motivation for the development of both scientific agriculture and scientific forestry. As we know, this scientific agriculture and forestry have drastically impoverished the biodiversity of trees and of cultivars. With industrial agriculture and its heavy reliance on chemical additives of all sorts, as well as the reliance on only a few cultivars, the soils and the waters are being poisoned and deadened. And at the same time, this transformation meant that those living with and from the land and waters no longer carried out their activities in intimate, constant and reciprocal conversation. They became hired laborers with enclosed selves subject to the demands of their bosses.

These processes amount to a thingification of the earth, transforming it from an erstwhile living integral cosmos to an insentient, mechanical thing devoid of agency and psyche. This insentient mechanical object could be manipulated to serve the ends of the new Nation State. Quantification, measurement, and simplification became the order of the day. By the end of the seventeenth century and the publication in 1687 of Newton's magnum opus *Principia Mathematica* the earlier worldview of Anima Mundi had been successfully eradicated and its practitioners, the shamanesses and shamans and their literate allies, the occult philosophers, successfully exterminated.[4] Their worldview came to be viewed as superstitious and irrational, even satanical in establishment circles. Soon the practices of those healers, herbalists, sowers, and reapers were consigned to the backward realms of the "primitive," "superstitious" and "pre-scientific." By the 18th century, the beginnings of the industrial revolution were under way.[5] By the 19th century it was going on at breakneck speed. By that time, the shift to a condemnation of the practices of those who lived in the world of Anima Mundi had become complete and such practices stood for a heretical form of religious understanding, as well as a totally irrational pre-scientific understanding. But incrementally heresy was replaced by a condemnation of such ways of thought and life in terms of their being wrong, erroneous, not based on scientific facts but rather on superstition. This became the dominant view especially with colonization in the 19th century and remains in force to this day.[6]

One of the most far-reaching entailments of Descartes' and Boyle's separation of mind from the cosmos was the disembedding or disengaging of humans, more specifically of their minds and psyches, from the cosmos. This was obviously necessitated by the new worldview of a mechanical, insentient cosmos introduced by the natural philosophers during the mechanistic revolution. The central and relevant characteristic of the human mind was rationality. Thus, this new knowledge differed radically from the classical Greek thinkers where knowledge was a matter of attunement with the cosmos.[7] The philosopher Charles Taylor writes:

> For Descartes, in contrast, there is no such order of Ideas to turn to and understanding physical reality in terms of such is precisely a paradigm example of the confusion between the soul and the material we must free ourselves from. Coming to the full realization of one's being as immaterial involves perceiving distinctly the ontological cleft between the two, and this involves grasping the material world as mere extension. The material world here includes the body and coming to see the real distinction requires that we disengage from our usual embodied perspective...We have to objectify the world, including our own bodies, and that means to come to see them mechanistically and functionally, in the same way that an uninvolved external observer would.

The ontological cleft between reason and body and cosmos means that the body and cosmos are no longer meaningful orders but rather that they are expressively dead. Understanding the body and the cosmos was no longer a matter of attunement with them as for the Classical Greek thinkers, even the non-Eleusinian initiated ones. The world as Max Weber put it, became 'disenchanted' bereft of the multitude of invisible beings that existed in medieval Europe and exist in non- or less modernized societies the world over. The cosmos became a despiritualized mechanism bereft of psyche, of soul, to be grasped by concepts and representations constructed by reason. This grasping for Descartes and after him for the functioning of the State, was construed as an instrumental control and mastery of nature. [8] What Boyle referred to as the "domination of the inferior creatures of God" as mentioned earlier.

This ontological cleft not only left the cosmos disenchanted, bereft of meaning and a multitude of invisibles, but imprisoned mind, rationality, psyche, in the subjectivity of the human being. Subjectivity was and still is considered to reside in the brain. Mind, and with it meaning and discarnate beings, became imprisoned in the human brain and separated from the cosmos. As we learned from Jill Taylor, this mind in fact was only the dominant left brain obscuring the view from the right brain. And this is the case still today in the 21st century. The neo-Jungian psychologist James Hillman states this unambiguously, pointing out the totally anthropocentric nature of the field of psychology. All schools of pyschology, Hillman says, agree that reality is of two kinds:

First, the word [reality] means the totality of existing material objects or the sum of conditions of the external world. Reality is public, objective, social, and usually physical. Second, there is a psychic reality, not extended in space, the realm of private experience that is interior, wishful, imaginational.[9]

Thus, the external world has no psyche or soul; soul has migrated and shrunk to the interiority of human beings. Psychology being a modern Western discipline, it could hardly be otherwise. It was born when the Anima Mundi, the Soul of the World, was replaced by a mechanical cosmos. Hillman notes that during the last hundred years, psychology has become increasingly individuated and intra-subjective. When mental pathology made its appearance, the focus of psychology consisted in readjusting inner psychodynamics. As Hillman puts it: "Complexes, functions, structures, memories, emotions—the interior person needed realigning, releasing, developing."[10] In the more recent field of family and group therapy, the problem was inter-subjective, located in the patient's close social relationships, so that therapy consists of improving inter-personal psychodynamics. Here too, the world remains "external reality," an objective backdrop to human action and subjectivity, without its own subjectivity, its own psyche.

Although the individual psyche is influenced by the small social group around the subject, it is not recognized as being part of, or in communication with, the outside world. The outside world, whether human-made or natural, has no psyche itself. It does not suffer; it does not communicate with the individual human psyche. That said, Hillman notes that the built environment, such as cities, buildings, and agriculture, are recognized in varieties of social psychiatry as possible objective causes of psychopathology:

> This was especially the American dream, an immigrant's dream: change the world and you change the subject. However, these societal determinants remain external conditions, economic, cultural, or social; *they are not themselves psychic or subjective.* The external may cause suffering but it does not itself suffer. For all its concern with the outer world, social psychiatry too works within the idea of the external world passed to us by Aquinas, Descartes, Locke, and Kant.[11]

Social psychiatry recognizes the built environment as a possible cause of psychopathology but like the "natural" environment, neither of them possess subjectivity. In other words, *res extensa*—whether built or natural, whether bodies or buildings—has no subjectivity, no psyche, no soul. This soulless *res extensa* therefore cannot be diagnosed with any sort of psychopathology of its own.

Because of the pivotal role given to a rationality separated from psyche, emotions, and the heart, from beauty, ethics, and any sort of numinosity, the laws of nature this new European science 'discovered' do not recognize any of these dimensions. As Albert Einstein has phrased it: "The concepts which [the scientific way of thinking] uses to build up its coherent systems do not express emotions. For the scientist, there is only 'being,' but no wishing, no valuing, no good, no evil—in short, no goal." [12] The separation demanded between the pursuit of truth and ethical concerns about the good is explicitly claimed to be necessary in the various methodologies devised to arrive at verifiable and therefore certain knowledge. [13]

As European powers colonized the rest of the world, the colonizers perceived non-European societies to need modernizing through scientific education. One of the most (in)famous statement of such a view comes from Thomas Macaulay, who served on the Supreme Council of India between 1834 and 1838. In his 1835 Minutes on Education in India, Macaulay argued that instruction in British Indian schools should be in English rather than Sanskrit and Persian. Those languages were not merely "a dead loss to the cause of truth" but also like "bounty money paid to raise up champions of error....We are to teach it because it is fruitful of monstrous superstitions." He adds that teaching the sacred literatures of India would mean that "we are to teach false history, false astronomy, false medicine." [14] Since then, education in India has been delivered in English, and has remained so for post-secondary school education and most elite private education. Macaulay's attitude can still be seen today in developmentalist literature that considers 'traditional' practices as a drain on productive resources, preaching that they should be replaced by productive scientifically based practices.

It is important to make visible the entanglement between the process of the commodification of land and the invention of 'natural resources' on the one hand and the commodification of labor on the other hand. Let us take a concrete example. Vandana Shiva shows how the transformation of certain tree species into commodities—valuable timber—transforms other tree species into weeds obscuring the role that these 'weed trees' play in protecting the soil from erosion, retaining ground moisture, increasing biodiversity, providing green fodder for local agro-pastoralists and timber for building.[15] The local communities who rely on the 'weed' trees are rendered irrelevant and invisible to business, government, and development experts.

Similarly, the work of those who use such 'weed' trees is typically not remunerated work but performed by members of agro-pastoralist communities for their own sustenance and continuity. This type of work has suffered a fate resembling that of 'weed' species. It has been generally labelled 'subsistence' work and not considered to be generative of wealth. The tending to the continuity of the life of human and non-human communities is generally seen as unimportant and backward in developmentalist literature, which focuses on increasing productivity and wealth by harvesting forests and replacing them with commercial monocultures, ignoring the profound damage done to biodiversity, the health of the soil, the atmosphere, the water sources, and the psyche of the agro-pastoralist communities and of the non-human world, not to mention the spirit world.

In agro-pastoralist or indigenous communities, the labor force of persons does not belong exclusively to them but is embedded in the community, both human and non-human, claimed by kin as well as by the spirits and other invisible beings. Many community celebrations, festivals, and life-cycle ceremonies mobilize the work of community members. With the extraction of work from its social and sacral context, these events become

relegated to a private domain that must take a secondary position vis-à-vis the official domain of the State and the economy
where wage labor reigns. Such community events are viewed by
the dominant society as the equivalent of weeds, a drain on the
creation of revenue for the State or profit for the corporation.

With the commodification of labor, the boss pays only for
the time worked, with the labor of maintaining the community
of humans, non-humans and the spirits completely disregarded. The time and space for reciprocity vanishes,[16] along
with the joyful communal labor of ritual, song, music, dance,
and food.[17] In time what is lost is the possibility of thriving
ecological and spiritual communities. In so-called 'advanced'
industrialized societies, the world has become thoroughly
anthropocentric and mechanical, with everything revolving
around the humans: their communities, their needs, their
psyches, their health. The sad irony is that this radical anthropocentrism has not led to thriving humans or thriving human
communities—quite the opposite, as human society is increasingly plagued by epidemics of mental disorders, drug addiction,
inequality and violence.

Is it possible to totally separate the world of humans from that of the non-humans?

The ontological cleft between the worlds of humans and the
world of non-humans has been radically questioned and troubled by quantum physics, though for quantum physics as with
just about all academic disciplines, the world of the spirits
exists only in humans' imagination. The quantum physicist and
feminist philosopher Karen Barad, in her 2007 book *Meeting the
Universe Halfway,* develops a theory she calls "agential realism"
that incorporates Niels Bohr's fundamental insight about physical reality being a function of the agencies of observation
rather than preexisting the measurements or perceptions of
the observer.[18] Barad shows how matter and human discursive

practices are always entangled, thereby putting into question the reality of an objective nature "out there."

Bohr challenged the Cartesian-Boylian-Newtonian framework by resolving one of the most well-known quantum quandaries, that of the wave/particle paradox. Early 20th century scientific observers sometimes perceived matter and light in wave form, and at other times as particles.[19] Paradoxically, under certain experimental conditions, light or matter displayed particle-like properties, while under different experimental conditions, incompatible with the former, they displayed wave-like properties. According to classical pre-quantum physics, this is a paradox since ontologically matter or light must be either a wave or a particle, they cannot be both. Barad shows how Bohr resolves this paradox by means of his "complementary principle," whereby both manifestations—wave and particle—are equally real or true but they can never manifest concurrently.

Bohr argues that theoretical concepts are defined by the circumstances required for their measurements. Therefore, there is no unambiguous way to differentiate between the "object" and the "agencies of observation" such as the observer, experimental apparatus, and of course the apparatus' builders. They form a whole. This lack of separation between objects and agencies of observation is what Bohr calls "quantum wholeness."

Central to Bohr's framework is his intertwining of the conceptual and physical dimensions of the measurement process. In Barad's reading of Bohr, measured properties refer to the *phenomenon* of material-conceptual "intra-actions" whose unambiguous account requires a description of all the relevant features of the experimental apparatus. Barad coins the neologism "intra-action" to signify the inseparability of objects and agencies of observation in the phenomena. She eschews the use of 'interaction' which presupposes an already existing separation between two entities. However, with the performance of an experiment, a cut is enacted that separates the "object" from the "agencies of observation." She calls this cut an "agential cut" and the principle it embodies "agential separability." But objects and agencies of observation emerge only within the phenomena, they are always contextual. They do not preexist separately, ontologically, before the enactment of an experiment or measurement or observation. The ontology has shifted from that of a pre-given universal nature, independent of acts of measurement, observation, or representation, to what she calls an agential reality.

In this framework or paradigm, the referent can no longer be an observation-independent reality but, to use Bohr's term, a *phenomenon* in which these two—observer and observed—form a whole. The implications of this new paradigm are profound: experimental apparatuses are no longer passive, transparent observing instruments as in the Cartesian-Boylian-Newtonian paradigm but are rather productive of and part of the phenomena. For Bohr, this inseparability "entails...the necessity of a renunciation of the classical [Cartesian-Boylian-Newtonian] ideal of causality and a radical revision of our attitude towards the problem of physical reality."[20] According to Barad, Bohr's complementarity principle was consciously offered as an alternative to the classical physics paradigm.

Using Michel Foucault's notion of 'discourses' as practices embodied in apparatuses,[21] Barad expands the theoretical reach of Bohr's insights to show how, with the abandonment of an ontology of pre-given, universal objects and with Barad's notions of intra-action and agential reality, the non-human world participates actively in the formation of reality. Humans are no longer the only actors, the pre-given 'subjects' observing, measuring, and representing the pre-given 'objects.' In this way the dualism between the human mind and a mindless natural, material world vanishes.

Barad does not explore the issue of the reality of spirits and other discarnate beings. Although her work in de-mechanizing the cosmos has been influential in the social sciences, including anthropology (an influence referred to as "the ontological turn"), this movement has not yet been ready to tackle the ontology of discarnate beings. This is something I cannot avoid since it is at the very heart of the arc of Randy's transformation.

6. SPIRITS AND OTHER DISCARNATE BEINGS

With the overcoming of the classical ontological cleft, the non-human world has acquired agency—observer and observed form a whole. Nature and the cosmos have lost their mechanical and inert nature and have become entangled with the observers and their apparatuses. Even using the term 'material object' now seems inappropriate, since it is entangled with the mind of the observer. Just as we humans are both body and mind, so it seems is the world, the cosmos. And there is no separation between human and cosmos, between mind and body.

Evidence from Near Death studies

It may be objected that the mind, usually thought to be in the brain, could not possibly also be in the cosmos since the latter does not have a brain. But neuroscientists have begun to contest the assumption that the mind is an emergent property of the brain. Reports of near-death experiences (NDE) back up the idea that mind is more than just brain. The scientific literature on NDE has grown enormously since the founding in 1978 of the International Association for Near Death Studies (IANDS).[1] A fair number of NDErs have mystical experiences of traversing a tunnel toward a light and being received at the other end by angelic guides or dead relatives who welcome them joyfully as they emerge into a sensation of pure unconditional love, which they often refer to as God. As the neuroscientist Mario Beauregard puts it:

> The effects of NDEs are intense, overwhelming, and real. A number of studies conducted in the United States, Western

European countries, and Australia have shown that most NDErs are profoundly and positively transformed by the experience. One woman says, "I was completely altered after the accident. I was another person, according to those who lived with me. I was happy, laughing, appreciated little things, joked, smiled a lot, became friends with everyone... so completely different than I was before."[2]

Such experiences are out-of-body (OBE), since their bodies are lying on a hospital operating table with no heartbeat and no brain activity, in other words dead. Such NDErs typically see their dead body from a point above it. Skeptics argue that such experiences rely only on the reports of the NDErs. They cannot be corroborated. But in the past few decades, the reports of a few NDErs have been independently corroborated by witnesses. One of the most well-known such cases is that of Maria, a migrant worker. She had a severe heart attack while visiting friends, was rushed to the hospital and a few days later had a cardiac arrest and was resuscitated. When her social worker, Kimberly Clark, visited her, Maria reported the following to her:

[D]uring her cardiac arrest she was able to look down from the ceiling and watch the medical team at work on her body. At one point in this experience, said Maria, she found herself outside the hospital and spotted a tennis shoe on the ledge of the north side of the third floor of the building. She was able to provide several details regarding its appearance, including the observation that one of its laces was stuck underneath the heel, and the little toe area was worn. Maria wanted to know for sure whether she had "really" seen that shoe and begged Clark to try to locate it.[3]

Clark found the shoe and was able to confirm all of Maria's descriptions of it. Clark remarked that the only way that Maria could have observed this shoe was from having floated near it since from where her body was lying while the doctors worked on it, she could not have seen it. This near-death experience, like so many others reported by Beauregard, Eben Alexander and many others, points to the mind or psyche being able to exist independently of the brain.[4]

The mystical experiences of NDErs are similar to experiences humans have with psychedelics. It is noteworthy that people in the region of Lamas routinely speak of ayahuasca experiences as going *al otro mundo*, literally going "to the other world," meaning the world after death. The experiences of NDErs and of those taking psychedelics are hauntingly similar. Roland Griffith, a neuroscientist from John Hopkins University who has been studying the effects of psychedelics for decades, said at a recent talk at the Center for the Study of World Religions at Harvard[5] that most participants in psychedelic studies have reported having profound mystical experiences that they considered to be the most important of their lives. Such experiences can also arise spontaneously without psychedelics or NDEs. I had an extremely powerful out-of-body mystical experience at the age of 12 or 13, which totally overwhelmed and frightened me but has remained so fresh in my memory that it feels as if it inscribed its lessons indelibly in my soul. I believe that this experience has been the foundation for my later drift toward spiritual experiences of various kinds. Nothing in my parents' worldview and lifestyle made such an event remotely likely.

As an anthropologist who by profession has read a great many ethnographies about cultures very different from the modern one, as well as having lived for many years in less modern cultures such as Morocco where I was raised, a pilgrimage center in Eastern India, and the Peruvian Upper Amazon, I am struck by the fact that I have yet to encounter any group or society for whom the reality of an "other world" does not exist. Such an 'other-world' is peopled with normally invisible beings of various kinds, often an amalgam of human and animal, and not infrequently including ancestors, and is taken completely for granted. Western European modernity is the exception, mostly due to the murder of the Anima Mundi, a murder foundational to the creation of a new knowledge system during the mechanistic revolution, a knowledge that required a neutral, inert mechanical basis for its investigation, one outside of religion and metaphysics.

The Experiences of Carl Jung

Forty-eight years after his death, Jung's private papers and paintings were finally published in 2009 in what is known as the Red Book. His paintings are stunningly beautiful, many of them mandala-like. There he writes about spontaneous experiences that happened to him between 1913 and 1919, when he was at the height of his professional success: "At that time, in the fortieth year of my life, I had achieved everything that I had wished for myself. I had achieved honor, power, wealth, knowledge, and every human happiness."[6]

The experiences Jung recounts in the Red Book are strikingly similar to Randy's experiences with or without ayahuasca, though Randy comes from a totally different class and world than Jung. In the Red Book, Jung recounts how he was transported to other places to meet with named figures, with whom he has lengthy conversations. He writes:

The years...when I pursued the inner images were the most important time of my life. Everything else is to be derived from this. It began at that time, and the latter details hardly matter anymore. My entire life consisted in elaborating what had burst forth from the unconscious and flooded me like an enigmatic stream and threatened to break me. That was the stuff and material for more than only one life. Everything later was merely the outer classification, the scientific elaboration, and the integration into life. But the numinous beginning, which contained everything, was then.

It is significant that he identifies the origin of these experiences as "the unconscious" rather than "my unconscious." This is in keeping with the theory he developed later of the collective unconscious and the archetypes.

While Randy's experiences were initiated during an ayahuasca ceremony and Jung to my knowledge never partook of any psychedelic, Randy also had several key experiences without ayahuasca, most notably the appearance of his indigenous Master who gave him powers from his own mouth to Randy's mouth, as well as the green-faced bird woman who gave him power from her eyes and mouth to his eyes and mouth. The beings that conversed with Jung were all named, whereas Randy's beings were unnamed and did not converse with him, certainly not at length; rather they only occasionally gave him brief verbal indications. Jung did not receive concrete, embodied powers from those figures as Randy has, and the conversations Jung had with them are lengthy and philosophical.

For example, when Jung encounters Philemon the Magician, he asks Philemon to share his knowledge of magic. "If magic were still taught today at university," Jung says to Philemon, "I would have studied it there. But the last college of magic was closed long ago. Today no professor knows anything anymore about magic."

Philemon replies: "It would be better if everything were buried with me. It can always be rediscovered later. It will never be lost to humanity since magic is reborn with each and everyone of us." Jung comments that he had often wondered how it is that "all peoples in all times and in all places have already thought along similar lines." Philemon says that ultimately "nothing at all about magic can be understood" because "Magic happens to be precisely everything that eludes comprehension."[7]

This is where the experiences of Randy and Jung differ most drastically. Randy lives in a place and time where magic and the black arts are very much alive and part of most of the people's everyday awareness whereas magic had been exterminated in Jung's European world more than three hundred years previously.

Jungian analyst Anne Baring gives us some crucial historical information in her book *The Dream of the Cosmos, a Quest
for the Soul,* clarifying that Jung's "near-overwhelming irrup-
tion of visions, dreams, and fantasies... took place just before
and during the First World War, whose catastrophic effects he
had foreseen in a series of dreams and visions he had during
the autumn of 1913 and the spring of 1914. The idea of war did
not occur to him at all, and so he drew the conclusion that he
must be threatened by a psychosis. But as events culminated in
the outbreak of war in August 1914, he began to understand the
meaning of these visions and dreams and to take the unconscious seriously as an unrecognized dimension of reality in
which all humanity participates."[8]

Unlike others who saw Jung as psychotic, Baring under-
stands his visions as "a shamanic initiation into the direct
experience of a deeper level of reality."[9] When I first read the
Red Book, I had the same reaction, recognizing the shamanic
quality of Jung's visions. Baring observes how Jung, "as a psychiatrist...had to interpret this raw material and embody it in
a form that people could understand, that could become the
basis of a contemporary understanding of the need for a relationship between the two separated aspects of the psyche—the
conscious mind and the deeper dimension of the soul that he
called the unconscious." In the Red Book, Baring says, Jung recognizes that the soul is *an independent living entity or dimension
of reality, something whose immense range we cannot grasp, whose
voice is "the Spirit of the Depths."*[10]

Like Randy, Jung had visions that persuaded him of the
reality of another world, the metaphysical world. But he was
guarded in sharing his insights, as he had to be, given the
European bias against any non-Church-authorized visionary
experiences. In the corridors of epistemological power, this
view still dominates. In Europe and America, magic and shamanism have been dismissed as superstition. Matter, space,
and time are all defined purely in mathematical terms, and any
thinking person must reject the notion of immaterial souls and

animating spirits. These are officially not real, or at most culturally bound and not universal.[11]

Jung's lost dimension of the soul, what he called the 'collective unconscious,' was deliberately murdered in Europe in the name of reestablishing certainty on the unshakable foundation of universal premises. By separating the mind/soul—the psyche—from matter, Science was able to claim universality for its findings since they all pertained to the same, universal, material world as perceived by all humanity endowed with the same perceptual apparatus. This created a system of knowledge with universal validity, totally separated from either the individual psyche/mind of the scientist or the collective mind of the culture or religion of the scientist. The mechanistic science born in Western Europe could travel anywhere under its self-invented guise of a religiously and culturally neutral knowledge system. Hence the ease of its global spread under the mantle of universality, totally free from any specific cultural, religious, or political moorings. Nevertheless, this mantle of universality is an illusion since it renders invisible the very Western European foundations upon which it is built.

Jung's notion of the "collective unconscious" was not only based on what he learned through his own visionary experiences but also through the dreams and experiences of his patients. Jung reported dreams of his patients which neither they nor he could decipher. He researched the world's mythology and rituals and often found astonishing confirmation of such dreams in very remote and exotic cultures that the patient could not possibly know. He traveled to Africa and other areas and researched the libraries on such topics as alchemy, kabbalah, Tantric texts, the I Ching, and the world's mythologies and rituals[12] in pursuit of the possible origins of the dreams and visions of his patients as well as his own. What he found was that the esoteric traditions of medieval and Renaissance Europe share with the esoteric traditions of the East and with shamanic traditions of indigenous peoples everywhere, is precisely the lack of separation between this world—or nature—and another dimension that one might label 'numinous' or 'spiritual,' since in those the two dimensions are alive with spirits.

Jung called into question the universality of mechanistic science by arguing that rationality, the conscious mind, "rests like a lily-pad on this greater substratum of our psychic life."[13] Together with one of the early physicists of the quantum revolution, Wolfgang Pauli (1900–1958), Jung formulated the concept of 'synchronicity,' which challenged the separation between matter and mind and brought together Jung's notion of the collective unconscious with the quantum revelation of the inseparability of the observer and the observed.

Quantum physicist David Peat, in his 1987 book *Synchronicity: The Bridge Between Matter and Mind*, relates one of the classic examples of synchronicity, which was observed by Jung during a therapeutic session:

> Jung's patient was a woman whose highly rational approach to life made any form of treatment particularly difficult. On one occasion the woman related a dream in which a golden scarab appeared. Jung knew that such a beetle was of great significance to the ancient Egyptians for it was taken as a symbol of rebirth. As the woman was talking, the psychiatrist in his darkened office heard a tapping at the window behind him. He drew the curtain, opened the window, and in flew a gold-green scarab—called a rosechafer, or Cetonia Aureate. Jung showed the woman "her" scarab and from that moment the patient's excessive rationality was pierced and their sessions together became more profitable.[14]

The usual reaction to synchronicities is to dismiss them as pure coincidence, just chance events. They differ from the way the observer in a quantum experiment intervenes to collapse a wave function. It is true that such interventions make a radical break between the standard separation of the observer

from the observed in classical Newtonian science. In the physicist John Wheeler's words, cited in Peat: "the old word *observer*
simply must be crossed off the books, and we must put in the
new word *participator*."[15] However, such a participator remains
a far cry from the synchronicities recorded by Jung and Pauli
and later by many others. The difference is that in synchronicities the issue of meaning to the person experiencing them is
at the core of the event in a way that is absent from the participator in a quantum experiment. No golden scarabs or their
equivalent appear during such experiments. This is how David
Peat puts it:

> For while random events may always throw out patterns by
> pure chance, the essence of a synchronicity is that the par-
> ticular pattern has a meaning or value for the individual
> who experiences it. While the conventional laws of physics
> do not heed human desires or the need for meaning—apples
> fall whether we will them to or not—synchronicities act as
> mirrors to the inner processes of the mind and take the
> form of outer manifestations of interior transformations.[16]

Another difference is the profusion of symbols that Jung
has been able to identify as belonging to far-flung spiritual traditions from all over the world. Even a brief perusal of Jung's
extraordinary paintings in the original Red Book makes clear
the central importance of the Eastern mandala pattern in them,
a pattern shared by most of the Indic traditions and present
in Christian mysticism as well, for example in the great rose-
shaped stained glass in cathedrals like Notre Dame or Chartres.
Jung's own experience and those of his patients tapped into an
extremely rich world-wide store of mystical and spiritual themes
and designs. What stands out for me is that the mystical, esoteric
streams of most of these traditions share a lack of separation
between nature and the divine or sacred. This world shimmers
with numinosity; all sacrality is not relegated to a "supernatural"
domain above nature as it is in the mainstream of monotheistic

Abrahamic religions. The same is true for mystical strains within Eastern traditions such as Taoism, Tantra, the I Ching, Vajrayana Buddhism, the Shakta tradition, and so on.

According to Anne Baring, Jung understood the word 'unconscious' to mean an infinitely greater consciousness of cosmic proportion, the invisible psychic aspect of the cosmic matrix out of which the conscious human mind has evolved. This understanding of the collective unconscious makes clear the intimate kinship between Jung's and Randy's shamanic experiences and approach. In Baring's words:

> This great consciousness or greater dimension of the soul has a focus or center of consciousness within it, functioning there as an autonomous intelligence—a dynamic, structuring, ordering, and integrating principle that Jung called the Self. In his view, this deeper intelligence (even when unrecognized) initiates and oversees the alchemy of the transformation of consciousness—whether in the individual or in our species as a whole—whereby the center of gravity gradually shifts from the personal to the transpersonal or, to put it another way, where the conscious personality or ego grows and expands through aligning itself with the unseen ground of life. The creation of this relationship over the span of a life is the quintessence of the process of individuation.[17]

In other words, the collective unconscious is the unrecognized ground of life, the cosmic dimension of the psyche/ soul/mind. Jung names the unconscious 'collective' because it underlies all of humanity and sentience and exists in a planetary and cosmic dimension.[18] Neuroscientist Eben Alexander comes to an almost identical understanding in his analysis of his week-long NDE experience:

> Our little individual theater of consciousness appears at first glance to be ours alone, but the evidence emerging

from quantum physics and from the deepest study of the nature of consciousness and the mind-body problem indicates that we are all truly part of one Collective Mind. We are all in this together and are slowly awakening to a common goal—the evolution of conscious awareness.[19]

Like Jung, Alexander and his partner and co-author Karen Newell perceive that much of humanity, particularly in the West, is currently unaware of the true nature of consciousness/mind/psyche. A greater awareness is present in the Indic family of traditions—Hinduism, Buddhism, Jainism, Shaktism, South Asian Sufism—as well as in Taoism, in indigenous traditions and in the esoteric or mystical traditions of the Abrahamic faiths. Throughout the Red Book it becomes clear that Jung's use of the Self comes from his familiarity with many of the Indic traditions, in which the individual small self, the 'atman,' and the cosmic Self, 'Brahman,' correspond to his usage. The scent of the European occult traditions—alchemy, hermeticism, Kabbalah/Cabala—also pervades the Red Book. The awareness of the unity of consciousness/mind/psyche/cosmos was suppressed by the Church in the 15th century, along with the folk peasant healing traditions and shamanism, which were all eradicated along with the Anima Mundi, the Soul of the World, to establish certainty upon the neutral ground of a soul-less, inert, and insentient matter. Religion kept the domain of the 'supernatural,' and science remained on a purely material, secular plane. These foundational events in European history are at the root of the continued Western resistance to fully recognizing the philosophical and metaphysical implications of the quantum revolution as well as the evidence about the nature of reality that has come from depth psychology, psychedelic research, NDE experiences and shamanism.

There is also the matter of the power dynamics inherent in the strict separation between observer/observed and mind/matter. Matter that is inert, insentient and without agency cannot resist the manipulations of the conscious observer. As the late Australian philosopher Val Plumwood observed,[20] this reduction of matter to a mindless object extends not only to nature but also to women and most non-European men. This consensus view of philosophical materialism carries immense weight and influence in contemporary human civilization, as is evident in the dominant skepticism of anything supernatural that reigns in academia and many other areas of modern society.

What Jung and Pauli named synchronicities are natural events that speak directly to a particular human's experience and have deep meaning for that person. These events collapse the alleged separation between matter and psyche. The Western worldview sees synchronicities as fortuitous because of the effects of the Age of Reason and the Burning Times, which led to the conflation of shamans and occult philosophers with "witches." In most other cultures, signs from the natural world that speak to an individual were considered omens, to be observed, recorded, and heeded. But in Western modernity all such occurrences are dismissed as superstitious, belonging to an archaic, superseded, primitive world.

Signs from the natural world are not the only ones that irrupt in the dreams, visions, or experiences of humans. I make a distinction between the categories of 'other-than-human' and 'non-human,' the latter referring to natural entities and the former to entities that do not occur in nature but do occur in human dreams or visions. Other-than-human entities in Randy's visions include: the phoenix bird; dragons; the winged horse that preceded the apparition of his indigenous master; the green bird-woman that gave him powers from her eyes and mouth; the virgin of Guadalupe; his indigenous master; the human-like entities that came out of Grimaldo's body; and the spirits of various plants appearing as humans with flowers growing out of their heads. Such 'other-than-human entities' do not occur in nature—when they appear in human dreams and visions they are recognized as being different from any existing animal, plant, or landscape but rather peculiar to the human imagination. In the West, to call such entities products of human imagination immediately calls into question their reality. However, most people in the world would agree with Henry Corbin that the '*mundus imaginalis*' is quite real.[21]

Randy's experience supports the reality of other-than-human entities. Before his initiation, Randy had absolutely no ability to cure anyone of anything. This changed radically after his initiation, increasing as he was given powers by such entities as his indigenous master, the green bird-woman, the Virgin of Guadalupe, and the Eagle embodiment of the mountain Waman Wasi. He did not seek out those entities or ask for any powers; initially he refused to accept what his indigenous master offered him. The Virgin of Guadalupe specifically told him she was giving him powers so he could heal suffering people—and heal people he did. The efficacy of his healing ability can be illustrated by the story of one of his early patients, a woman who was suffering from what looked like second or third-degree burns all over her body. Her skin was peeling, raw and very painful, though she had not been burned. She had gone to the hospital and been seen by various doctors; they could not find any natural cause for her condition. Randy conducted an ayahuasca session for her. The next morning, she called him and asked him to come to her house. He was astounded to find her completely cured, displaying normal skin. Randy is always careful to ask people coming to him for a physical ailment whether they have been to a doctor or hospital and ascertained that the condition is not due to natural causes. If he is not sure, he sends them to be seen by a doctor before he will do a ceremony for them. Randy's reputation has grown rapidly in the small town of Lamas and beyond, where he has cured not only physical complaints but also disorders of the psyche such as addictions to gambling, drugs and alcohol.

The fact that other-than-humans appear in dreams and visions but not in our daily experience of space-time leads the modern Western mind to assert that they are products of the human psyche. However, in the view of Jung, Corbin and many others, the human mind is part of a larger cosmic matrix. Once we break the wall between matter and psyche, recognizing that we are all part of One Collective Mind or Psyche, in Eben Alexander's words, the modern bafflement at such beings begins to wane. That the One Collective Mind/Psyche—or in Jung's term, the collective unconscious—is perfectly able to produce a myriad of other-than-human beings as well as the wildly diverse natural beings on this planet and in the cosmos, is evidence of the infinite creativity of the Cosmic Mind.

7. COLLECTIVE MEMORY IN THE COSMOS

It is often the case that people conceive of the mind/soul/psyche in a human-centered way. We tend to have an anthropocentric bias, for example assuming that only humans are truly sentient. At times I too tend to assume that mind/soul/psyche is human or human-like, even when I am speaking of the cosmic mind or Self or Brahman. In contrast, Rupert Sheldrake's theory of the collective memory,[1] with its emphasis on a vibratory pattern of activity he names "morphic fields," is radically non-anthropocentric, non-materialistic, non-dualist, and holistic. These vibratory morphic fields interact with the electromagnetic and quantum field of any self-organizing system, from non-human to human ones, including atoms, molecules, cells, tissues, organs, organisms, and societies. At each level, the whole is more than the sum of the parts, which are themselves wholes made up of parts. These morphic fields are patterns of probability, like quantum fields, and work by imposing patterns on otherwise random events in systems under their influence.[2] Through the process Sheldrake calls 'morphic resonance,' an existing pattern of activity in a vibratory morphic field resonates across time and space in ever-evolving patterns that Sheldrake hypothesizes could be called habits. "A growing crystal of copper sulfate, for example, is in resonance with countless previous crystals of copper sulfate, and follows the same habits of crystal organization, the same lattice structure," Sheldrake says.

A growing oak seedling follows the habits of growth and development of previous oaks. When an orb-web spider starts spinning its web, it follows the habits of countless ancestors, resonating with them directly across space and time. The more people who learn a new skill, such as snowboarding, the easier will it be for others to learn it because of morphic resonance from previous snowboarders.[3]

Sheldrake's language and arguments carefully build up a holistic, non-anthropocentric, non-materialist theory that shows how patterns in morphic fields, repeated through morphic resonance, are habits that are not restricted to human or human-like entities but belong to all earthly and cosmic entities. Sheldrake concludes that memories reside outside the brain, with the brain acting more like a radio receiver. Following the work of neuroscientist Karl Pribram, Sheldrake views the brain as a 'wave-form analyzer,' comparing it to a radio receiver picking up wave forms from what quantum physicist David Bohm called the 'implicate order,' and rendering them explicate.[4] Sheldrake argues that rather than being carried around in the head of humans, memories are transferred through resonance with similar patterns in the past.

Sheldrake widens this theory beyond the human sphere by hypothesizing that all self-organizing systems—from atoms to human societies—have morphic fields that are patterns of vibratory activity that, through morphic resonance across space and time, create habits and memories. This leads to the crucial recognition that "individual memory and collective memory are different aspects of the same phenomenon; they differ in degree, not in kind." As evidence for this hypothesis, Sheldrake points to experiments conducted with rats: "If rats learn a new trick in one place, then rats all over the world should be able to learn the same trick quicker." And indeed, he says, in time "All similar rats learned quicker, just as the hypothesis of morphic resonance would predict." This was also borne out in studies concerning the IQ of humans, which have shown that average IQ test scores have been rising for decades by 30% or more.[5]

A crucial implication of Sheldrake's theory is that since neither individual nor collective memory are stored in the brain, the death of the brain or the person or animal or plant, or society does not imply the erasure of memory. As the data from Near Death Experiences shows, memory, and perception are retained after the heart and the brain are dead. NDE experiences, which are growing in numbers since hospitals' ability to revive patients is increasing, also seem to show that memories, perception and thought are not emergent properties of neuronal activity in the brain. Sheldrake proposes an alternative to both the radical materialist position (which asserts that consciousness/mind/psyche/soul do not exist) as well as the dualist position (which sees mind/soul/psyche/consciousness, as immaterial, outside of time and space, and therefore 'supernatural'). Instead, Sheldrake sees the human mind as a self-organizing system with morphic fields that extend beyond brains both in time and space, linked to the past by morphic resonance and to virtual futures through hopes and wishes.

Sheldrake's third way between materialism and dualism opens the possibility of building bridges between shamanism and science since shamanism sees nature and the cosmos as not only alive but more importantly as having soul/mind/consciousness. When indigenous people in the region of Lamas in the Peruvian Upper Amazon speak of the 'spirit of the rain forest' (Sachamama), the 'spirit of the moon' (Mama Killa) or the 'spirit of the sun' (Taita Inti), they are referring to sentient entities that possess mind, soul, and consciousness. Sheldrake directly muses about shamanism, asking:

What if shamans really do have ways of learning about plants and animals that are completely unknown to scientists? What if they have explored the natural world for many generations, discovering ways of communicating with the world around them that depend on subjective rather than objective methods? [6]

Sheldrake provides a way of making sense of shamanism in general, and Randy's experience in particular. In Randy's case, the authority of the invisible entities he encountered both in and outside of ayahuasca sessions overwhelmed his own worldview, his own preferences and desire. He found it initially difficult to accept this alternative reality, but eventually he was profoundly transformed, a transformation that severed his relationship with his partner and his parents, and dramatically changed his abilities. From never having been able to heal anybody, he became an effective healer; from never having sung or played an instrument he became an adept musician and singer while leading ayahuasca sessions. What happened to Randy cannot be explained, as many traditional anthropologists would, by his belonging to a particular regional cultural group. Nor can it be subsumed under the category of conversion.[7] In my view, anthropological explanations, however distinct they might be among themselves, all refer to the collective patterns of thought, belief, disposition of a particular human group. In other words, they are all based on cultural phenomena that are about human beings and not about nature or the cosmos per se. Sheldrake's theory offers us a truly non-anthropocentric manner of understanding shamanism, one not rooted in cultural phenomena, but rather rooted in what might best be called natural-cultural phenomena.

An example of synchronicity and evidence of an integrated, sentient cosmos can be seen in an incident which happened to Randy some three months after his initiation in 2016. Randy had recently created his very first altar in a room of his apartment, which he used for quiet periods of meditation and learning ikaros. One day, as he was leaving that room, he came face to face with a green snake. He stopped cold and the snake raised itself up so that they were able to stare into each other's eyes. The snake then entered Randy's room and coiled itself under the small low altar table, right underneath the image of the Virgin of Guadalupe that Randy had recently installed there. Randy's first vision of the Virgin of Guadalupe had happened shortly before this incident, in Jacques' office; Randy saw an image of a young woman with copper skin like his own, a mantle and a sweet smile. When he described his vision to Jacques, Jacques showed Randy an image of the Virgin of Guadalupe, asking him if that was the woman he saw. It was, and soon after this incident Randy created his altar and installed on it a small statue of this Virgin, about whom, at that time, he was totally ignorant.[8]

A year and a half later, the Virgin of Guadalupe appeared to Randy during an ayahuasca session with Grimaldo on the 12th of December, the special date when this Virgin is worshipped in Latin America—a "coincidence" Randy did not know about at the time. During this vision, the Virgin gave him special healing powers by covering him from head to toe with serpents, which slowly sank into his body while he experienced an almost unbearable force entering him. Later, during the same session, the Virgin asked Randy to make her image and showed him exactly where to build her chapel, which he did.

This synchronicity expresses the profound transformation taking place in Randy's psyche. The rudimentary altar under which the snake coiled itself, right underneath the small statue of Maria Guadalupe, was Randy's very first expression of a sense of the sacred. His pre-initiation life was singularly secular. He was preoccupied with visiting friends, having affairs with a variety of women, drinking with his buddies, painting, and designing and building bungalows, and constructing and maintaining my center.[9] His buddies were all mestizos and although he may have been unusual in not going to church or celebrating the Catholic festivals such as Easter and Christmas, he shared in the local mestizo youths' typical secular activities. But during his initiation he had the following experience:

I am seated, destroyed, bent over and I raise my eyes and I see three lights in the shape of lozenges. In that moment I understood that these three lights were the whole: the only God. The creator of the whole universe. The light was so strong that I could not withstand it. I raised my head twice. And all the while there were some grandmothers playing the shacapa; they were ancient shamanesses.

This epiphany profoundly transformed Randy and initiated him to the sacred dimension. I believe that the presence of the ancient elder shamanesses during this vision indicates that his discovery of the sacred was under their auspices. The shacapa is the symbol of shamanism in this region, and in shamanism the world is both alive and sacred, as Anne Baring writes in a section entitled "The Essence of the Shamanic Experience":

Because the clear distinction we now make between an inner and outer world did not then exist, and because they felt they lived *within* a Sacred Order, the psyche of that time lived within that Order, in communion with it. The words spoken, the music heard, the dreams and visions seen came not from 'inside' them, but from the soul of the Cosmos, from daemonic beings, goddesses and gods and the spirits of animals, trees, mountains, and rivers as well as from the ancestors who were never thought of as dead but who formed a continuous line in connection with the living.[10]

Baring writes about the Lunar Era as a shamanic, pre-patriarchal time when the Earth was considered our mother, and humans had a participatory consciousness as being part of a wide kinship net with the whole cosmos. This consciousness remains alive in many contemporary indigenous societies but almost everywhere else has been overwhelmed by the more dominant patriarchal formations. Baring's Lunar Era persists in several places in the world today, but even in the Indian state of Odisha, where I studied the tradition of temple dancers, priestesses embodying the goddess Kali, this tradition has now ended as a public ritual in a great temple and remains mostly in its esoteric, secret Tantric form.

In their 2001 book in three voices, *Chaos, Creativity and Cosmic Consciousness,* Rupert Sheldrake, the mathematician Ralph Abraham, and the psychedelic expert Terence McKenna discuss the repression of Chaos, a mythologically female figure, by the male gods of law and order, some 2000 years ago. The potential of Chaos as a stimulant for the imagination was also repressed.[11] McKenna situates this repression in the context of psychedelics and shamanism, pointing to the ego-dissolving power of psychedelics and arguing that women's bodies give them a more immediate experience of boundary dissolution than male bodies, principally through birthing and being penetrated in intercourse. McKenna writes:

> We have lost touch with chaos because it is feared by the dominant archetype of our world, the ego. The ego's existence is defined in terms of control...The beginning of wisdom, I believe, is our ability to accept an inherent messiness in our explanation of what's going on...The imagination is chaos. New forms are fetched out of it. The creative act is to let down the net of human imagination into the ocean of chaos in which we are suspended and then to attempt to bring out of it ideas...The key is surrender and dissolution of boundaries, dissolution of the ego, and trust on the love of the Goddess that transcends rational understanding [12]

It may be that we are witnessing a resurgence of the Goddess happening in tandem with a global increase in interest in shamanism. Though there is a risk of commodification of shamanism, especially in Amazonia, Randy's story shows that we cannot discard the notion that this revived interest may have in part been initiated in the hidden realm of a collective memory. Randy was such an unlikely candidate for becoming a shaman that his story makes a strong case for the intervention of beings from a cosmic realm that we can perhaps name the 'collective memory,' following Sheldrake. The fact that the

Virgin of Guadalupe was seen by both Grimaldo and Randy in that crucial session where she gave Randy two kinds of powers, is prima facie evidence that she was not a fiction of either of their imaginations, and neither of them were previously 'believers' in her. It is relevant here to note that Grimaldo, founder of the Peruvian NGO PRATEC, with whom I have collaborated for ten years, has chosen to identify with his indigenous legacy and has left Catholicism behind. So, as Randy confirmed to me, Grimaldo was initially not expecting or even thrilled to come into the presence of this Catholic virgin.

Sheldrake, Abraham, and McKenna discuss discarnate entities, which dominant reductionist theory considers to be part of our human psyche, usually repressed to our unconscious. Sheldrake wonders whether all such entities emerge from our imagination or from our unconscious, or whether, alternatively, they may come from an autonomous, totally separate realm of entities, perhaps fitting into Jung's collective unconscious.[13] Abraham responds that "On the soul level, everything is connected up and all is one, as in the oversoul of Emerson and Thoreau. This great pancake in the sky participates in the material world by ripping off a piece of itself to incarnate in matter." He continues:

> In this view, which is the essence of the Hermetic tradition, everything has soul and souls are permanent. Their occupation as animals or rock or trees is temporary. In this Hermetic view, we may have the best chance to understand ourselves and our history. History on the scale of the world soul is a process of morphogenesis. Incarnation is the materialization of the morphic form, the entity, in the body. It is the morphic resonance of soul and body. Spirit is the abode of the entities, which are particular aspects of morphic forms. The interaction between these different planes has been described as a resonant wave phenomenon.[14]

Later in the same conversation Sheldrake points out that the view of the spirit world being a projection of the human mind has created an anthropocentric universe which is known as humanism. He invokes the Faustian myth retold by Goethe, in which "the paradigmatic scientist sells his soul to the devil in return for unlimited knowledge and power." Sheldrake adds that "The guiding spirit of modern science, according to the Faustian myth, is a satanic demon, a fallen angel called Mephistopheles."[15] To my mind, Sheldrake, Abraham, and McKenna do a great service by translating shamanistic ideas and images into ideas and theories familiar to the modern Western rational mind, thus building a bridge between shamanic experience and Western modernity. Sheldrake's theory of morphogenesis and morphic resonance existing in all cosmic systems offers a powerful instrument to help us free ourselves from the grip anthropocentrism has on our modernized minds.

8. ACADEMIA AND ITS DISCONTENTS

It is not easy to build a bridge between shamanism and the modern knowledge system as taught and developed in academia. Sheldrake, Abraham, and McKenna have been considered in academic circles as controversial at best and sometimes as downright heretical. During my 26 years of teaching at Smith College,[1] the idea of linking shamanism with a scientific understanding of the cosmos would have been immediately tarred and feathered with the label of New Age, a sure death knell for anyone's academic reputation. Nevertheless, this bridge continues to be constructed, mostly in the fields of psychology, psychiatry, and neuroscience, which have begun to explore "non-ordinary reality" once again in what is being called "the psychedelic renaissance." I will have more to say about psychedelics in the next chapter; here I will sketch my understanding of why the social and natural sciences have avoided shamanism and psychedelics. When—as in the case of anthropology—they have studied it, it has been generally in the third-person mode, as an object of study and not as a personal experience.

I began thinking seriously about such issues many years ago in the context of my academic discipline, in which the anthropologist ponders other peoples' lives while keeping their own life apart from such pondering. Some anthropologists have turned to what is often referred to as 'post-modern poetics' to address this quandary. However, as the anthropologist John Watanabe points out:

post-modern poetics fares no better than artless positivism in resolving the inherent political asymmetries in ethnography's problematic—indeed, inescapable—appropriation of its subjects' lives for purposes beyond the living of those lives....[W]hatever its textual form, ethnography always diverges from the 'native's' point of view, if only because anthropologists ponder worlds that other people live.[2]

In general, anthropologists and other professional researchers live their work lives within the parameters and paradigms of their academic professions or disciplines. These boundaries can sometimes be changed but, as Kuhn taught us long ago, this is typically done by pushing at the margins rather than by more radical reformulations.[3] The reason for this, to my mind, lies principally in the social organization of academic disciplines. To earn a PhD and secure a job, and then to keep the job and acquire legitimacy—to say nothing of prestige—one must attend to the discipline's theories, concepts and methodologies, attention that must take place in strict separation from one's personal life. Passion and value belong to the latter whereas sobriety—what Boyle called 'modesty'—and attention to facts belong to the former. In the case of my discipline, anthropology, there is an irony to that situation. In most societies typically studied by anthropologists, namely small-scale non-Western ones, life is not as strictly separated between a public domain of work and a private domestic domain.[4] In Europe and America this division became much greater with industrialization; as E.P. Thompson put it, industrial capitalism brought about "the separation of work and life."[5]

Another aspect of industrialization that has profoundly impacted the organization of knowledge in the autonomous university is the factory mode of production, which economist Stephen Marglin has described as 'the fragmentation of the task at the point of production.'[6] In industrialization, the making of an object was broken down into many separate activities, performed by different sets of workers, with the goal of higher efficiency. Marglin argues compellingly that there are in fact no efficiency gains in this method of production; its true function, he demonstrates, is a political one—control of the workers. I have built on that work and argued that in the industrial age workers' skills were disembodied and transferred to the heads of the experts—today's academics—hired by the business owners.[7] This gave rise to a corresponding fragmented, disembodied, and dispassionate form of knowledge held in the experts' minds, paralleling the fragmentation of the tasks in the factory.

Immanuel Kant, in his famous 1798 treatise *The Conflict of the Faculties,* explicitly makes this association between the factory and the university. This treatise is recognized as laying down the foundation for the modern university, which first saw light in Germany in the 19th century, was emulated in the United States and has since spread globally.[8] At the beginning of this treatise, Kant invokes the factory (the word he uses is *fabrikenmässig*) with its division of labor as the model for the university and the organization of knowledge "so that for every branch of the sciences there would be a public teacher or *professor* appointed as its trustee, and all of these together would form a kind of learned community called a *university."*[9] Kant's work also contains the germ of the idea of knowledge for knowledge's sake, embedded in the notion of the unhindered pursuit of truth separated from state and other controls. The notion of knowledge for knowledge's sake, that is the pursuit of 'pure' science with no practical application, became an established norm by mid-19th century. Kant's separation of theoretical and practical reason, and his vision of the university as modelled on the factory, provided the intellectual legitimacy for the insulation of science from politics, morality, religion, and emotion—in general, from lived life. The ideology of knowledge for knowledge's sake divorces knowledge from the constraints and requirements arising from community and earthly life. It also is completely anthropocentric since only knowledge held in the mind of humans has value. The continuity of life for communities of non-humans upon which human life depends and in which it is embedded simply disappears, and with it the continuity of life for both humans and non-humans, that is the health of the world or nature, disappears as a worthy telos for knowledge. For natural and social scientists, the telos of science was knowledge for knowledge's sake.

In the polity though, it would be more accurate to say that the telos of the non-human world was its utility for humans. Nature became known as "natural resources," the study of which focused on the production system which, by definition, is for humans. In this modern paradigm the life of non-humans becomes relevant only as an input in the production system of goods for humans. The study of an objectified and mechanized nature was the basis for the new knowledge whose applications outside academia served economic and political ends, rendering the continuity of the natural world invisible.[10]

In the university, the production of knowledge, like the production of goods, has become an end in itself, unmoored from humans' lived life. Lived life is always entangled in the lives of other humans, non-humans, and other-than-humans, that is the spirits, ancestors, deities, demons or angels and other such discarnate beings that the new mechanistic knowledge has simply banished from its purview. These were cavalierly pronounced pure products of the human imagination and generally ceased being considered real active participants in living communities.

What I have been at pains to make visible here is the tight embrace between the modern form of knowledge as institutionalized in the modern university and the pursuit of a type of knowledge removed from concerns with the continuity of the life of both humans and non-human communities.[11] Of course medicine and related scientific disciplines focus on saving human lives and have been remarkably successful in that endeavor, but saving individuals' lives does not necessarily address those humans' communities and their continuity. In cases where university-trained experts are called upon to help undo or prevent damage to a particular species or landscape, such political requests have often arisen in response to the demands of indigenous people, for whom that species or that landscape has a spiritual meaning. This was the case in the removal of four dams on the Klamath river in Oregon and California, that had prevented the free life cycle of the salmon, sacred to native peoples along that river.[12]

The case of the Yavapai indigenous peoples of Arizona reveals something that is central to my argument. In the case reported by Wendy Espeland in her 1998 book *The Struggle for Water: Politics, Rationality, and Identity in the American Southwest*, the US Bureau of Reclamation had sent a team of experts to conduct a cost-benefit analysis concerning the economic and environmental advantages and disadvantages of building such a dam. As part of this study, members of the Yavapai community were interviewed on their views concerning the building of such a dam. The Yavapais did not want the dam. The experts, after their cost-benefit analysis was accomplished, decided that the dam should not be built, basing that decision on the results of their cost-benefit analysis. To their surprise, the Yavapai were not happy about the decision. This is what one of the Yavapai elders told them:

> God gave Indians the land...for use. They don't really own the land. The Anglo with title says "it's mine, no one else's." Land is part of nature. Humans are here temporarily. They live from the land where all life comes from. They are one. Without the Indian land can't be land, because it needs to be taken care of in order to survive life.[13]

The Yavapai people felt betrayed by the experts' analysis because it only took into account the economic and environmental costs and benefits of building or not building the dam, ignoring the moral and spiritual reasons for the Yavapais' refusal of the dam. Such a manner of reaching a decision, with a complete elision of moral and/or spiritual considerations, was experienced as an insult to the land and the people. The continuity of the land, with its human and non-human life, simply disappeared from the rational calculation of the experts, who deliberately ignored the Yavapais' understanding of both people and land as integral to each other, where humans and non-humans form a unified whole.

It could hardly be otherwise for those university-trained experts since the factory- inspired fragmentation of knowledge in universities constitutes the very structure of their expertise. Though this fragmentation has yielded some remarkable breakthroughs in medicine and other technologies, these have come at the expense of an awareness of the constraints and requirements of the continuity of the life of the whole. Although this strategy may be necessary for achieving certain goals, it has resulted in terrible destruction and impoverishment of the natural world, including the climate crisis and the Sixth Great Extinction of species, as well as the growing epidemics of addiction and mental illness among humans, especially in highly industrialized regions.[14]

In my view, anthropology has not helped. The Yavapais' view on the oneness of the life of humans and land (like many similar views from the indigenous or peasant groups typically studied by anthropologists) is too quickly explained by the beliefs existing in this type of culture. I am not saying that these beliefs are not taken seriously by anthropologists—they are. Such beliefs are recognized as profoundly affecting and in many cases also regulating the social, political, economic, spiritual, or other aspects of life for such peoples. I am also not saying that understanding how such beliefs affect other aspects of life in those societies does not amount to enlightening and important knowledge. It typically does. What I am saying is that bracketing the anthropologist's own life and the context in which that life is embedded, especially the academic life that has led this anthropologist to study an indigenous society, results in the bracketing of any possibility of a genuine dialogue between different worldviews. The construction of a bridge between profoundly different worldviews is all too often aborted, sacrificed on the altar of knowledge for knowledge's sake.

For the Yavapai, the oneness of humans and the land is more than a simple fact, and more than a belief held in the mind—it is something viscerally experienced, imbued with spirituality or numinosity. For the cost-benefit experts, spirituality or religion is, by definition, excluded from their rational intellectual process. The modern university, ever since Kant's "Conflict of the Faculties" treatise, conceives of itself as a value-free institution, a position that was inextricably intertwined with academic freedom. Kant argued for the autonomy of the philosophy and sciences faculties—what later became the liberal arts faculty—because he saw its role as that of a watchdog, critic, and guardian of the truth vis-à-vis the three higher faculties of theology, law, and medicine. Those latter three were properly the purview of the state and under its control. According to Kant, the argument used to convince the state to relinquish its control over what is today the liberal arts faculty was for the latter to be impartial and non-partisan, devoted solely to the pursuit of truth, separate from utility or any other telos. In today's world, where corporations and other powerful institutions are wielding more and more power in the universities, this is clearly a worthy goal.

By the mid-19th century, the pursuit of 'pure science' by salaried professionals in the autonomous university was established in Germany, and later taken up in the United States.[15] The ideology of knowledge for knowledge's sake divorces knowledge from the constraints arising from community life embedded in its non-human environment and its purpose of regeneration and continuity. The well-being and continuity of communities ceases to be tied to the production of knowledge. Knowledge becomes an end in itself.

Kant chose the word 'university' from the medieval Latin *universitatem*, also related to the word 'universe.' The Anglo-French *université* also meant what we today mean by 'universal.'[16] The separation of the pursuit of knowledge from

231

INITIATED BY THE SPIRITS

moral, political, and religious constraints was a result of the mechanistic revolution with its invention of a nature completely devoid of anything remotely sacred, religious, or metaphysical, at least where the natural sciences were concerned. But with Kant's university and the neo-Kantians in Germany, this separation was extended to all the disciplines in the liberal arts faculty. Knowledge thus separated from moral, political, or spiritual considerations is not only non-local, but becomes universal. The sacrifice of a dialogical bridge between different lived realities amounts to a sacrifice in the name of a universal type of secular knowledge. Thus, the non-locality of the knowledge of the anthropologist is due to the universality of his or her knowledge. The knowledge of the experts in the Yavapais' dam example is a universal knowledge that can be used in any context whatsoever. It is rational whereas the Yavapais' notion of the oneness of the land and the people is only a local belief, bereft of rationality. However, the devaluation of local knowledges rests entirely on the fundamental assumption of a mechanistic, inert, insentient, and agency-less nature deemed universal by its inventors but in fact deeply rooted in European culture and history.

The fundamental assumption underlying rational, secular knowledge today, giving it legitimacy to supersede any other mode of knowing, must be recognized for what it is: an invention by a select group of male upper-class European thinkers, rooted in the 16th and 17th religion conflicts of Western Europe, characterized by the non-positioned investigator, what the feminist anthropologist Donna Haraway has ironically named "the God's eye view"—ironic since it is so entangled with the rejection of any traces of religion or numinosity but exact since in the Western non-mystical religious traditions God has overwhelmingly been seen as outside and above His Creation.

A requirement for the non-positioned investigator is for her own voice to disappear totally. This requirement was instituted in Robert Boyle's public laboratory in mid-17th century England and soon became *de rigueur* everywhere. The passive voice and what came to be known as the 'objective' style of writing is still the norm in the natural sciences and most of the social sciences and humanities. The disappearance of the first-person perspective has had an especially lethal effect on those experiences that reveal the numinosity of the world. Such experiences, whether occurring spontaneously or induced by psychedelics or in other ways, are by nature profoundly personal. But because they cannot be submitted to replication and verification, a protocol invented by Boyle to clearly break from his alchemical past, they are generally simply discarded in academic knowledge production.

In the West and in modernity today, a person's personal experience has little currency, especially in academia, where it has been relegated to the creative arts. This has meant that the investigation of psychedelic exploration has been off-limits in the modern university. However, the renewal of scientific investigation of the effects of psychedelics on people has begun again, mostly carried out by neuroscientists interested in observing and measuring the neurological and/or psychological effects of such substances. An early scientist in this field is William Richards at John Hopkins University, who began his research before psychedelics became illegal and then was able to re-start it later. In his 2016 book *Sacred Knowledge: Psychedelics and Religious Experience* Richards writes:

> The mind may undergo one or more intense experiences of death and rebirth and awareness of the ego (that is, that part of your mind that function with your name in everyday life) may ebb and flow. Similarly, awareness of the body lying on the couch may come and go as one might expect to experience in a state of deep trance... This threshold between the personal (that is, the everyday self) and the transpersonal (that is, more fundamental or universal dimensions of consciousness) is conceptualized by different people in different ways. Most commonly, the term 'death' is employed as the ego (everyday self) feels that it

is quite literally dying. Though one may have read that other have reported subsequent immersion in the eternal and experiences of being reborn and returning to everyday existence afterward, in the moment imminence of death may feel acutely—and for some terrifyingly—real.[17]

I can personally attest to the veracity of the intense experience of death in many of my ayahuasca experiences. The way the ego dissolves and disappears is experienced as a death and at the beginning it was terrifying for me. With repeated ayahuasca ceremonies, I came to understand this ego death as necessary for accessing a fundamentally other, transcendent, or transpersonal level of reality, typically imbued with numinosity or sacrality.

Michael Pollan also speaks of the death of the ego in relating his own experience with psilocybin.

'I' now turned into a sheaf of little papers, no bigger than Postits, and they were being scattered to the wind. But the 'I' taking in this seeming catastrophe had no desire to chase after the slips and pile my old self back together... And then I looked and saw myself out there again, but this time spread over the landscape like paint, or butter, thinly coating a wide expanse of the world with a substance I recognized as me...the 'personal' had been obliterated...I was present to reality but as something other than my self.[18]

The experience of the annihilation of the self/ego comes with a shift in worldview, as Pollan describes:

One of the gifts of psychedelics is the way they reanimate the world, as if they were distributing the blessings of consciousness more widely and evenly over the landscape, in the process breaking the human monopoly on subjectivity that we moderns take as a given...Psychedelic consciousness overturns that view, by granting us a wider, more generous lens through which we can glimpse the subject-hood—the spirit!—of everything, animal, vegetal, even mineral, all of it somehow returning our gaze. Spirits it seems are everywhere. New rays of relation appear between us and all the world's Others.[19]

With the death of the self/ego, we gain the ability to experience our lack of separation from the cosmos, and to glimpse the subjecthood of everything in nature, as well as non-natural spirits, deities, angels, and demons. This kind of spiritual awakening can also be caused by near-death experiences (NDE). The scientific method enshrined in the academy requires observers to be in perfect control of their rationality. The experience of dying, whether provoked by the dying of the ego in a psychedelic event or in a near-death experience means that those undergoing such an experience have lost their ability to think rationally. This is how the Yanomami shaman Davi Kopenawa puts it: "White people are surprised to look at us become spirits with the *yãkoana*. They think that we are losing our minds..."[20] *Yãkoana* is a psychedelic that contains DMT, like ayahuasca. Kopenawa often refers to taking this psychedelic as "dying," which is perceived by the whites as losing their minds. The dying of the ego opens one to a realization of consciousness as a cosmic reality, a shift that Jeffrey Kripal, in his 2019 book *The Flip: Epiphanies of Mind and the Future of Knowledge,* calls an "epiphany of mind" that deeply transforms and "flips" those who have experienced it.[21]

Both near-death and psychedelic experiences lead to a form of first-person knowing where rationality essentially disappears. In both cases the experience is often mystical, giving access to a level of reality that seems truer and more real than space-time reality. Kripal expresses this as follows: "One can think of this [direct knowledge] as knowing something directly without or outside the "filter" of the brain and its various cognitive and sensory mediations."[22] However, in the light of the work of Jill Taylor and Iain McGilchrist, the experience may in fact be due to the brain function as well.

This is the kind of knowing reported by mystics in all traditions as well as by shamans everywhere and by many who have partaken of the shamans' psychedelics. These, ever since the mechanistic revolution, have been either violently eradicated or dismissed as either unreliable or irrelevant. Many of the flipped scientists that Kripal interviewed, and Kripal himself—a scholar of philosophy and religion—are now looking forward to a new form of knowledge where first-person experience is taken seriously and where the sacrality of the experience is not swept under the rug but rather is brought into dialogue with the rational third-person manner of knowing dominant in academia and the culture of modernity at large.

The resistance and obstacle to achieving such a dialogue has much to do with the fact that religious conflicts were at the root of the invention of the third person mode of knowing. By radically separating the new mechanistic knowledge from religiosity, and with it the sacred and the metaphysical, and inventing nature as purely material, mechanistic, and devoid of sacrality, the Western academy indeed made this new knowledge universal in respect to the great diversity of knowledges and sacred traditions of humanity. Most likely this played an important role in the globalization or universalization of the modern form of third person knowledge. However, since the invention of an inert, mechanistic, and desacralized nature arose in western Europe it also paradoxically makes of the modern knowledge system a specifically western European one and belies its purported universality.[23]

One scholar who has to my mind addressed this paradox profoundly and persuasively is Iain McGilchrist in his 2010 book *The Master and His Emissary: The Divided Brain and the Making of the Western World*. McGilchrist first trained as a psychiatrist specializing in neuroimaging and later acquired a doctorate in literature at Oxford where he currently teaches. This book has quickly become a classic and with trepidation

I will try to briefly summarize its thesis expounded at great length and with enormous scholarship. McGilchrist first gives neuroscientific and other evidence debunking the popular view of the right hemisphere as the intuitive, feminine brain and the left as the dominant, rational, thinking brain. With evidence ranging from neuroscience to physical anthropology, to ethnology and more, he shows that the right hemisphere is in fact the dominant part of the brain where language first emerged most likely from music, gesturing and dancing. The right hemisphere gives us the picture of the whole and imparts meaning, whereas the left hemisphere is the one that allows us to focus with extreme clarity on any specific part of the environment. One of his examples are hunters who, to catch their prey, must focus with razor sharpness on their target, bracketing it from anything else in the environment. In order to focus so exclusively on their target, hunters need to ignore their own feelings, thoughts or perceptions, which could distract them from their prey. In other words, hunting involves a third person type of knowledge, the bracketing of the whole along with the bracketing of the hunter's own inner environment.

In non-modern hunting societies, these requirements for a successful hunt have not, however, led to a system of knowledge and practice that has enshrined this mode as the preferred, desired mode of cognition and perception across the board. In fact, as the ethnology of hunting societies has clearly shown, hunters typically do two things: they carefully divide the prey to distribute it among the hunters' group and they perform a ritual of gratitude to the animal for sacrificing its life so that humans can live. In other words, as McGilchrist shows us, the mode of knowing required during the hunting of a prey is immediately bracketed after the success of the hunt and placed in the wider natural, personal, and social context of the hunter. Typically, the person who has shot the prey does not boast of the fact and comes back to camp either in silence or demeaning the catch.[24] McGilchrist maps these two forms of cognition and perception onto the left and the right hemispheres of the brain and shows that the left-brain mode—which in the hunters' example corresponds to the third-person mode of knowing—is vital for human survival as mammals here on this planet. He also shows that in hunting societies—and I would add in other non-modern societies—this third-person mode of knowing has always been subsumed by the whole which corresponds to the right hemisphere. The second part of his book is a sweeping survey of the history of the modern western world where he tracks the inbalance that the dominance of the left hemisphere over the right has wrought, hence the title of his book. The right brain for McGilchrist is really the master and the left brain should be its emissary, a situation reversed in western modernity both in its artistic as well as in its scientific tradition. I will quote from the last lines in his conclusion titled "The Master Betrayed":

> What all these [great European philosophers] point to is the fundamentally divided nature of mental experience. When one puts that together with the fact that the brain is divided into two relatively independent chunks which just happen to broadly mirror the very dichotomies that are being pointed to—alienation versus engagement, abstraction versus incarnation, the categorical versus the unique, the general versus the particular, the part versus the whole, and so on—it seems like a metaphor that might have some literal truth. But if it turns out to be 'just' a metaphor, I will be content. I have a high regard for metaphor. It is how we come to understand the world.[25]

However, thanks to neuroscientist Jill Bolte Taylor's observations of left and right brain functioning, we now know that what McGilchrist writes in his conclusion is *not* a metaphor. It is the literal truth. So perhaps the paradox between the universality of the modern form of knowledge as it is understood seemingly the world over and what the history of its creation reveals, namely its specificity rooted in the soil of 16 and 17th century western European religious conflicts, resolves itself

under McGilchrist's gaze into an imbalance between two complementary but unequal parts of our brain. In his view the
left brain, with its disengaged third person rational mode of
knowing, should be the servant and emissary of the right brain,
with its first-person mode of knowing and perceiving. Both
modes are vital, but the right brain, which brings us engage-
ment and wholeness, should be the dominant hemisphere.
When that relationship is inversed, as it has been for much of
modern civilization, the results can be extremely problematic.

The danger of the dominance of the left-brain type of
knowing with its third person epistemology is nowhere better
illustrated than in Zygmunt Bauman's 2000 book *Modernity and
the Holocaust*. Bauman, a sociologist, is a concentration camp sur-
vivor. He begins by highlighting the role of rational bureaucratic
organization, which for him includes the scientific management
of the bureaucratic organization of the death camps:

> It [the Holocaust] arrived (...) in a factory-produced vehicle,
> wielding weapons only the most advanced science could
> supply, and following an itinerary designed by scientifi-
> cally managed organization. Modern civilization was not
> the Holocaust's *sufficient* condition; it was, however, most
> certainly its *necessary* condition. Without it the Holocaust
> would be unthinkable. It was the rational world of modern
> civilization that made the Holocaust thinkable.[26]

The "final solution" was justified not only through the
language of biology but also its conceptual framework and
certainly its third person mode of knowing. The Jewish people
(and other groups such as homosexuals and gypsies) were
defined as an infection that had invaded the national body.
This malignant virus was sickening and would eventually kill
the collective body and thus needed to be exterminated, just as
viruses and other dangerous foreign entities invading an individual's body need to be killed. Bauman argues that the typical
removal of the observer from the thing observed, in science in

general and biology especially, was what enabled the inventors and executors of this death-dealing 'final solution' to bracket any broader view of the shared humanity between all involved. Bauman also stressed that such horror could happen again given the right circumstances. For me, this danger was brought close to home by the sight of a parade of neo-Nazi men marching with tiki torches in Charlottesville, Virginia, shouting "Jews will not replace us!"—and former US president Trump affirming that there were "good people on both sides." This is another example of how urgent it is that the right brain, first-person mode of knowing become dominant in modern civilization.

For many years in academia, feminist scholars have urged the use of the first-person voice in scholarly writing. When I have required this practice from my students at Smith College, an elite women's college, I frequently heard from students that they had no idea how to write in the first person since they had always been taught the third-person mode of thinking and writing. I had to coach them and explain there was no need to hang their rational left brain in the vestibule before speaking, feeling, and thinking in the first-person in their papers. In general, after initial coaching, they felt released and energized by this shift.

The invisibility of one's own participation in the world has reached such an extreme degree as to become pathological. A small personal incident is revealing in this regard. I had just been introduced to my son-in-law's grandfather, a Nobel prize physicist, who waxed eloquent about a mutual acquaintance, another well-known nuclear physicist, Victor Weisskopf (my ex-father-in-law). He commented on Victor Weisskopf's generous and warm personality, adding: "Weisskopf was very unusual in our profession. I am a bastard! Most physicists are bastards, unlike Weisskopf, who was an exception. Weisskopf was generous and considerate." What was communicated to me by his tone and manner was a kind of pride in the ferocious competitiveness and nastiness in his field, a pride that could only arise from an entrenched habit of third-person thinking and writing in academic science. The total separation of a scientist's psychological or ethical inclinations from his professional work seems to imply an inverse relationship: the more brilliant the thinking, the less important the personality and feelings of the scientist.

Victor Weisskopf, a Jew who had fled Austria two years before the Nazis invaded, was part of the team of scientists who gathered in Los Alamos in New Mexico from 1943 to 1945 to make the atomic bomb. What pushed the team to successfully produce this bomb was their collective belief that Hitler was also engaged in the same pursuit. It was therefore necessary to work as fast as possible and defeat the evil of Nazism. The bomb was tested in a deserted area not far from Los Alamos on July 16, 1945. However, the project team had learned three months earlier, in April 1945, that Hitler was defeated, thus annulling the reason for continuing the work on the bomb. Weisskopf writes about this in his memoir:

> With Hitler defeated there was no danger that the Nazis would develop their own bomb, but this did not rise to the surface of our consciousness. By then we were too involved in the work, too deeply interested in its progress, and too dedicated to overcoming its many difficulties. We were committed to the project not only for pragmatic reasons but also because of the purely scientific search for answers. No matter what happened in Europe, we knew our work had to be completed.[27]

I knew Victor Weisskopf to be a profoundly ethical person and a very warm and generous man. Given his life-long dedication to nuclear arms control and peace after the end of World War II, this quote is even more remarkable. What it shows is that when a project is driven by the third-person mode of knowing, the larger whole and purpose in which it is embedded recedes to the point of becoming invisible, or unconscious as Weisskopf puts it. This mode of pursuing knowledge has resulted in the deep ecological and climate crisis we find ourselves in today as well as in the epidemics of addiction and mental illness that plague us. If even such a man as Victor Weisskopf, deeply dedicated to arms control and peace, could have acted in this way, it only shows that the third-person mode of knowing dominant in science and in much of academia still today and certainly in the 1940's, needs to be critically addressed and transcended.

In my own experience in academia, I started out totally unaware of most of the issues I have raised in this and other chapters. I believed in the pursuit of knowledge for knowledge's sake and took for granted the whole structure of knowledge in the university.[28] My transformation was so slow as to be for a long time imperceptible. It began with the effect that both my dance and ethnographic work in India had on me. I realized that I was being transformed from a secular person into someone whose spiritual third eye had been awakened. However, unlike for Randy, for me this transformation was so subtle and slow that it took many years before it manifested as a crisis that changed both my ethical and my spiritual sensibilities. Finally, by 1993—some 18 years after having started ethnographic fieldwork in India—I simply found that my body refused to take notes and perform all the other necessary actions required of an ethnographer. While in "the field" in Puri, Odisha, all I wanted to do was participate in the rituals and other practices of the people there. I had lost the ability to behave like a proper ethnographer. Ethically, I came to feel that my decision to do fieldwork based on an agenda I had chosen myself, without a serious consideration for my ability to reciprocate the knowledge I had received, was simply unacceptable.[29] Spiritually, I had been deeply transformed by all I had experienced in India. I became aware that even if my book were translated into Oriya, it would not be relevant to the people who had transformed me. This caused me great anguish. I felt I had taken advantage of my informants' generosity for my own purposes of pursuing research and earning a doctorate. These transformations led me to start a ritual practice at home based on the rituals that were significant and made sense to my friends in Puri, unlike the intellectual cogitations in my first book. I also started a daily meditation practice. These practices somewhat assuaged my feeling of betraying the people who had transformed me.

It soon became evident, however, that it was impossible to show this new self in my department, or in any academic environments whatsoever. Having to hide my spiritual self troubled me greatly and I finally reached out to a quantum physicist who was also spiritually inclined; together we created a Five College Faculty Seminar we named Epistemology and Contemplation. I wanted to recruit interested faculty by sending a mass email, but he immediately dissuaded me, saying that any potentially interested faculty would not want their interest in spiritual issues made public. By word of mouth, within a couple of years we were able to gather some eighty faculty from the Five College consortium in our region. We met monthly and these meetings enabled me to heal my split academic self enough to stay in academia until my daughter graduated from college in 2006.

Another major decision I took in 1993 was that I would only go for research to a place that had been colonized by Europeans (people like me) if I were invited because I had something to reciprocate with that was of interest to them. This happened when I met Grimaldo Rengifo of PRATEC at a conference in Canada in 1992, which eventually resulted in PRATEC inviting me to collaborate with them in Peru in 1994. A year after my daughter Jessica graduated from college I retired and pursued my collaboration in Peru more intensely. Such a collaboration blurred the distinction between research and activism, a distinction very much emphasized in my discipline and department. Activism was clearly quite low on the prestige scale, whereas I felt that theory without reciprocity was ethically deeply problematic as well as intellectually problematic. Of course, my experiences with ayahuasca had to remain private while I was still in academia.

9. PSYCHEDELICS AND THE HEALING OF MODERNITY'S ILLS

In his excellent 2018 book[1] on what is generally referred to as 'the renaissance of the scientific study of psychedelics,' Michael Pollan gives many examples of the efficacy of psychedelics for treating addiction, depression, fear of death, and other mental illnesses, which have reached epidemic proportions in the United States and Europe, particularly during the Covid pandemic.[2] I call these "ills of modernity" not because such problems do not occur in less modernized places, but because they are most acute and widespread in the modernized sectors of the world,[3] reaching epidemic proportions. Scientists are once again beginning to study psychedelics, which were declared illegal drugs in 1970 in the United States, thus interrupting for some thirty years research on them begun in the 1950s. While the psychedelics used in scientific research, mostly psylocibin and LSD, are still illegal, government agencies in the US, Canada and Europe have resumed funding this research because of the pressing need to find effective therapies.[4] Current central nervous system drugs are losing their efficacy, so that pharmaceutical companies are no longer investing in them. Anti-depressant drugs are less and less effective, although depression affects a tenth of Americans and world-wide is the leading cause of disability.[5]

Pollan cites the findings of Rosalind Watts, a clinical psychologist working for the National Health Service whose interviews with volunteers in research on psychedelics uncovered two master themes. The first "is a state of disconnection, whether from other people, their earlier selves, their senses

and feelings, their core beliefs and spiritual values, or nature."
The second "referred to living in 'a mental prison,' others to
being 'stuck' in endless circles of rumination they likened to
mental 'gridlock.'"[6] These themes are characteristic of much
mental illness and can also be a factor in drug addiction.

I would say that these volunteers were suffering from
being disembedded from their social and/or natural environments as well as having strongly enclosed selves. These states
are the result of the emergence of capitalism through the commodification of land, labor, and capital. As argued earlier, such
a disembedding and enclosure of the self were less common
in pre-modern Europe, and mostly absent among the contemporary Kichwa-Lamas. The cosmologist Brian Swimme has
identified mental illness and addiction as endemic to modern
capitalist society:

> I now think alcohol and drugs are an intrinsic feature
> of the consumerism lifestyle. To state my conviction as
> bluntly as possible, I think that hoping for a consumer
> society without drug abuse is as pointless as hoping for a
> car without axle grease. Drugs of one form or another are
> necessary for consumerism to continue.... Consumerism
> is based on the assumption that the universe is a collec-
> tion of dead objects. It is for this reason that depression is
> a regular feature in every consumer society.[7]

The drug addictions and mental illnesses of consumer
societies are most acute in the global north simply because
more of it has been thoroughly modernized. However, it has
appeared in those parts of the global south where modernity
has penetrated more intensely. In fact, the use of traditional
shamanic indigenous or mestizo cures in Latin American cities
to treat drug addiction as well as other mental health issues has
risen markedly.[8] By 'modernity's ills' I do not want to convey
that such ills do not exist in non- or less-modern societies, only
that modernity has greatly exacerbated them.

Brian Swimme emphasizes the effect of living in a dead world of insentient objects, as contrasted with the many spirits enlivening and peopling the cosmos in indigenous cultures. We in modernity are bereft of our cosmic and earthly relations, with whom we no longer reciprocate and converse as do the Kichwa-Lamas, and many other indigenous people. We modern denizens of a dead cosmos unconsciously suffer from a state of permanent mourning. Such a loss is difficult to acknowledge in modernity since the beings peopling the cosmos are not considered real.

Michael Pollan is willing to discuss his spiritual experiences with psychedelics, but he excludes the possibility of "supernaturals" from such experiences. "I have no problem using the word "spiritual" to describe elements of what I saw and felt as long as it is not taken in a supernatural sense," he says.[9] For Pollan, however, psychedelics do begin to open a crack in his secular positionality. "Even for atheists... *like me*...psychedelics can charge a world from which the gods long ago departed with the pulse of meaning."[10]

> Psychedelic consciousness overturns that view, by granting us a wider, more generous lens through which we can glimpse the subject-hood—the spirit!—of everything, animal, vegetal, even mineral, all of it somehow returning our gaze. Spirits it seems are everywhere. New rays of relation appear between us and all the world's Others.[11]

All the world's Others except, it seems, supernatural beings. I wonder how he might have reacted had he encountered the Virgin of Guadalupe or any other religious figure during his psychedelic experiences. Would he have rejected them as unwanted and unacceptable supernaturals?

Pollan's rejection of religious figures in psychedelic experience is not shared by William Richards or Roland Griffiths, two of the most prominent scientific psychedelic researchers. In his 2016 book *Sacred Knowledge: Psychedelics and Religious*

Experience, Richards uses the words 'God' and 'transcendence' repeatedly and calls for increased dialogue between different religious traditions:

> Instead of arrogantly viewing shamans as primitive "witch doctors" who have been deprived of the brilliant knowledge of Western allopathic medicine, it is becoming increasingly apparent that some shamans indeed possess valuable knowledge to share with us, not only concerning exotic herbs and concoctions, but also about techniques of navigating within consciousness and the spiritual interconnectedness of us all. The sharing of knowledge and worldviews in the respectful interaction of professional healers, whether in Brazil, Tibet, Gabon, the United States, or elsewhere, is likely to prove to be a win-win situation for all.[12]

Among some religiously inclined denizens of modernity, the supernaturals continue to exist and exert their influence on humans. However, the nature spirits have mostly departed, with the natural world and the cosmos understood as an insentient, mechanical order.

What is becoming clearer is the therapeutic value of mystical experiences through psychedelics. A 2017 scientific study of mystical experiences with psychedelics concludes as follows:

> RSMEs [religious, spiritual, or mystical experiences] occasioned by the use of psychedelic substances are dismissed by many as illegitimate—that is, the bugaboo of morbid origin continues to scandalize. The results of the present study, however, suggest that psychedelic experiences can equal or even surpass the intensity and impact of experiences derived through nonpsychedelic means.[13]

It is relevant to note that in this study "There was an unusually high number of atheists in this sample (25%), compared with the general population (1.6%; Pew Research Center, 2008)." In other words, mystical experience occasioned by psychedelics affect atheists equally or more strongly than religiously inclined persons—which was the case with Randy.

In Pollan's section on dying, he reports on a volunteer in NYU's psilocybin cancer trial named Patrick Mettes, diagnosed with terminal cancer. Pollan chats with the two psychiatrists present in the NYU treatment room administering psilocybin to Mettes. Pollan was struck by those psychiatrists' "excitement, verging on giddiness, at the results they were observing in their cancer patients—after a single guided psilocybin session."[14] Pollan records Patrick Mettes' own words, reflecting on the effect of the psilocybin:

> I could feel my physical body trying to vibrate in unity with the cosmos...The sheer joy...the bliss...the nirvana... was indescribable... I've had no earthly pleasure that's ever come close to this feeling...no sensation, no image of beauty, nothing during my time on earth has felt as pure and joyful and glorious as the height of this journey...Never had an orgasm of the soul before...I was learning a song... it was one note...C...it was the vibration of the universe...a collection of everything that ever existed...all together equaling God.[15]

When his wife came to pick him up at the hospital, he told her that he "had touched the face of God." He and his wife were both certified atheists. Before this experience he had been extremely anxious, overwhelmed by a fear of death. Two months after his psilocybin journey, slowly dying of cancer, he told his psychiatrist "I am the luckiest man on earth."

Pollan also relates the story of another secular volunteer at NYU, Dinah Bazer, also diagnosed with terminal cancer. Although a "solid atheist," she said: "the phrase that I used—which I hate to use but it's the only way to describe it—is that I felt 'bathed in God's love.'"[16] Randy said something very similar during his initiation: "I raised my eyes and saw three lights of diminishing size in the form of lozenges. In that moment I understood that those three lights were everything, the only God, the creator of the whole universe." Randy, like Patrick Mettes and Dinah Bazer, was then a 'solid atheist.' The difference, and it is a major one, is that Randy was given healing powers both by nature spirits and by supernaturals and as a result has become profoundly spiritual as well as an effective healer. The spirits and the supernaturals chose a secular young man to initiate into the path of healing and shamanism. His initiation, he told me later, erased his fear of death, which in his case was clearly weaker than in the case of the terminally ill volunteers.

As Pollan remarks, the findings of psychedelic therapy and research seem "to be operating on a frontier between spirituality and science that is as provocative as it is uncomfortable." [17] Given the history I sketched earlier of the extermination of shamanism in Europe, making way for the mechanistic revolution, I cannot but see a deep irony in shamanic plants and fungi coming to the rescue of modernity's intractable ills. Here we are, seventeen centuries after the closing in late 4th century CE of the psychedelic Eleusinian mysteries, on the verge of the collapse of our planetary ecology, with humanity engulfed in spiking epidemics of drug addiction and mental illness. How remarkable that the plants and fungi so persecuted throughout the past centuries are precisely the ones that can rescue us, through their ability to transform our view of the earth and the cosmos by converting them from dead objects into living sentient beings.

It is my belief that psychedelics should be made widely available for therapeutic purposes, to be administered by trained shaman-like psychotherapists who would ingest the psychedelic along with their patients, reversing Boyle's strict edict of the absolute separation between the observer and the observed. Such widespread use of psychedelics under the care of trained specialists would lead us away from violent extractivism and toward reciprocating with the other-than-humans and the non-humans.[18] Hopefully, as predicted by Pollan, these substances will soon be legalized not only for therapeutic purposes but also for spiritual and ecological ones.[19] If their use becomes widespread, they may have an enduring effect on slowing or even stopping the ecological destruction of our planetary home.

The decision by the United States to make all psychedelics illegal, without distinguishing between those that cause addiction and those that do not (the latter being all the shamanic ones)[20] is in keeping with the long history of the eradication of shamanism in the West. The psychedelics were used by European shamanic practitioners who were all lumped under the invective of 'witches' and thus irremediably associated with heresy and satanic practices as well as superstition, ignorance and even madness. That these substances were classified as illegal is not surprising. What is surprising is their recent emergence in scientific studies attesting to their therapeutic efficacity in healing intractable maladies of modernity. Could it be that the impotence of mainstream therapeutics is related to their lack of spiritual or sacred dimensions?

The twin modern ills of human mental illness and ecological destruction are both rooted in an intensification of the separation of the self/ego from the whole, namely from nature/cosmos, which has led to a steady diminution in spirituality and a concurrent intensification of secularism. By spirituality, I mean a continuous flow beyond oneself and one's human community toward the more than-human world and its varied and multifarious discarnate beings. Following William Richards, I would not restrict discarnate beings only to nature spirits, as Pollan does, but would include the supernaturals of all the spiritual and religious traditions of the world—which is the reality that Randy has experienced since his initiation by the spirits, one much closer to Jung's collective unconscious.

The enclosure movements that turned the earth into 'natural resources' and commodities for the exclusive use of humans also transformed the spirits and the supernaturals into imaginary figments of our minds. Our very consciousness has been enclosed, fenced off from the numinous powers of the earth and the cosmos. Psychedelics, by their ability to dissolve the ego, enable us to experience the numinous heart of the cosmos once again.[21] Modernity has made us blind and deaf, altogether insensible, to the Soul of the World, the Anima Mundi, but psychedelics miraculously restore our sense of the sacred, even for certified atheists.

Rupert Sheldrake's theory of morphic resonance returns to the cosmos the sentience and consciousness recognized by the 'religion without a name' since Paleolithic times and by shamanism and many other spiritual or religious traditions today. Sheldrake's theory of memory in the cosmos allows us to understand discarnate beings existing as resonance patterns in the cosmos, which are not lost with the demise of individuals, cultures, or civilizations. This means that discarnate beings from various traditions can and do appear during the muting of our left brain under psychedelics. These resonant patterned vibratory fields can be accessed even by those who have never heard of these beings. For example, Randy made a sketch of a goddess that I initially thought might be Yemaya. However, when I sent the sketch to friends, specialists, or devotees of this tradition, they were immediately able to identify her as Olokun—an Orisha of the sea with whom Randy was not familiar at all.[22]

For me, the fact that confirmed atheists and secularists have profound spiritual or mystical experiences with psychedelics and that such experiences have a powerful therapeutic effect means that sacrality or numinosity is inherent to the cosmos. Such numinosity is muted or made invisible by our intensely enclosed modern minds, with their dominant left brains. It also means that the *experience* of such sacrality or numinosity is healing, whereas the prolonged lack of such experience can lead to mental illness. A direct experience of the sacred hidden heart of the cosmos[23] is therapeutic and transformative and can of course be achieved without psychedelics through practices such as meditation, prayer amd sensory deprivation.

However, psychedelics, used by all shamanic cultures of the world, including indigenous Europeans, seem to act with surprising rapidity and efficacy.

Based on Randy's and my own memory of such mystical experiences under the influence of ayahuasca, along with the reports from volunteers in the scientific study of psychedelics, what characterizes the numinosity at the heart of the cosmos is non-specificity. Many name it 'God.' Patrick Mettes called it 'Love,' a cosmic vibration that Sheldrake names "morphic fields." I typically experience my body vibrating during ayahuasca ceremonies and Randy also mentions this experience. It is remarkable, however, that such a cosmic vibration has been experienced in a psychedelic scientific experiment. Although mechanistic modern science has enabled enormous advances in our understanding of the cosmos, it has not been able to reveal its numinous heart. This can only be experienced via a dissolution of the ego, an endeavor made illegal in the US in 1970 and one that remains taboo in academia and most other areas of modern society. The powerful therapeutic efficacy of this ego dissolution is due to psychedelics' ability to liberate us from the strictures of our severely enclosed self, allowing us to fully experience the sacrality of the heart of the world.

Psychedelic mystical experiences do not necessarily lead confirmed atheists or secular people to become 'religious' in the sense of adopting a particular religious tradition. They are content with being characterized as 'spiritual,' open to the idea of sacrality being a universal reality, like language is a universal human reality. As with languages, the manner of capturing such experiences of numinosity varies from language to language. I am reminded of the work of French anthropologist Jean Pouillon on the Dangaleat of sub-Saharan Africa. The Dangaleat experience and affirm the reality of their spirits and name them. When Pouillon pointed out to them that their neighbors, another ethnic group, do not believe in those same spirits, they were completely non-perturbed by this revelation. They calmly answered that of course their neighbors did not since they live in a different place with different spirits. Pouillon's reflections on this report focus on the absoluteness of the otherworldly realm, which he identifies as being a Christian belief. He points out that for the Dangaleat the encounter with otherness "confirms [their] experience of the world, which is relative from the beginning and so cannot be disturbed by diversity."[24]

Christianity views the non-physical realm as populated by specifically Christian beings who are considered universal, or absolute. The absoluteness of the otherworldly Christian realm has been transposed by the fathers of the mechanistic revolution to the material cosmos, preserving its absoluteness in a different key, that of the knowledge of an insentient mechanical nature. Universality could be recognized both in the religious Christian sphere as well as in the non-overlapping sphere of the new knowledge of a mechanical nature. The onto-epistemological European terrain was divided into two mutually exclusive domains, one exclusively material and the other exclusively religious, what naturalist Steven Jay Gould has famously called Non-Overlapping Magisteria or NOMA. Today the material terrain is considered universal, the same everywhere in the world, whereas the religious part is recognized to be diverse world-wide. To my mind, Sheldrake's theory of morphic fields and morphic resonance, encompassing both the 'natural' and the 'cultural' domains, transcends the duality of NOMA and that of culture and nature, psyche and *phusis*. If indeed we humans have emerged from a whole, and that whole is a vibratory field, it would follow that to experience ourselves as radically other than "the material world" and separate from it would constitute a fundamental alienation. This existential situation is what generates epidemics of drug addiction and mental illness.

Under the new forms of scientific knowledge, another form of separation also emerged: the separation between the life and emotions of the scientist and his object of study. The expulsion of women during the formative years of the mechanistic revolution had everything to do with their purported inability to separate their rationality from their emotions. This separation was made operative in the rule forbidding *ad hominem* criticism in Boyle's public laboratory. The feelings of the scientist were to be kept strictly separate from his witnessing of the experiment being carried out in the public laboratory—a separation that led to the subject/object dualism of modern knowledge. That dualism has been transcended by the quantum revolution in physics, which identified the way the perceptions and ideas of the scientist are inevitably entangled with the results of the experiments.

Traditional scientific 'objectivity' is related to the forced use of the third person mode of knowing and writing, which is the dominant mode taught in schools and academia, as well as in journalism. Under this system, one's own participation in the world becomes invisible to oneself; the alienation from nature/cosmos also becoming an alienation from one's own emotions, from one's embodied life. This is a primary symptom of what I have called the 'ills of modernity.' These ills cannot be resolved by technological solutions alone. It is necessary to address the climate crisis by lowering carbon emissions, instituting regenerative agricultural practices and so on. However, if we do not simultaneously address the siloed nature of our modern knowledge system and its denial of the existence of a mind and heart of the cosmos—if we ignore and dismiss the diversity of spiritual experiences in the world—we will not succeed in healing modernity's ills. Mental illness and drug addiction, along with ecological destruction and other such diseases of the soul, will most likely continue, to our common detriment.

CONCLUSIONS

M odernity, born during the Age of Reason and the Burning Times in the 16th and 17th centuries in Western Europe, brought about what I have called the enclosure of the self, namely a separation of the human individual from the whole reality in which it is embedded and from which it receives its sustenance and meaning. This severance of the person from their life-giving source creates alienation, which is at the heart of the rampant ecological devastation and mental illness (including drug addiction) that plagues human society today, especially in the global north.

The refusal of modern science to admit its Western European foundation has unmoored science and the modern worldview from its actual politico-cultural foundations, clothing it in the garb of universality as it has spread worldwide its dogma of an insentient mechanical nature/cosmos as the only reality. This colonizing impulse has transformed all other knowledge systems into archaic local knowledge, casting the numinosity of the planet and the cosmos as the pre-scientific beliefs of "less advanced" peoples. This development has opened the whole planet to extractivism and exploitation as well as spread the virus of alienation.

I am not saying that Western science is a wrong-headed knowledge system—rather, it is one among many other knowledge systems, with its own strengths and weaknesses, as is the case for all espistemologies. It is, however, unique in divesting itself from ethical, aesthetic, and spiritual constraints through its invention of a mechanical, insentient nature/cosmos and the third person mode of knowing. This position has unleashed a gigantic expansion of technological inventions, but at tremendous cost. We are truly seeing the Faustian myth being played out in real time.

The scholar of Chinese science, Jatinder Bajaj, has pointed out that China was much more advanced technologically than Europe in the 16th century but did not create a science based on an insentient mechanical world. In 16th century China, Bajaj says:

> Nature was self-governed, unfolding itself according to its own internal harmonies. The object of science for the Chinese therefore was not to decipher the law in order to put nature to human uses, but to find out the way of nature, the Tao of Heaven, in order to be able to go along with it, to live according to the Tao.[1]

For the Chinese of that time, nature was sentient and alive, and the aim of life and knowledge for them was to attune themselves to its ways, rhythms, and harmonies. They developed a knowledge system based on values and ethics as well as aesthetics. One consequence of this difference was that China did not develop the kind of devastating weaponry developed by the Europeans. In the 16th century, the Chinese created a powder capable of explosion, but it was used for fireworks, not for weaponry. For the Chinese, knowledge pursuits required for survival were always subsumed under the wider umbrella of the whole, the Tao.[2] This is something that has been declared outside of the domain of 'science' ever since the mechanistic revolution in Western Europe. To bring in considerations of the whole in the pursuit of the mechanistic knowledge system is considered a serious category mistake. As Einstein said, science must be silent as to the good, the just and the beautiful. In the Western European tradition, a consideration of 'the whole' was displaced onto religion, metaphysics, and art. The religious domain pertains to 'beliefs' while science pertains to rationality and empirical evidence, also referred to as 'facts' and 'reality.' However, by dissolving our ego, our very enclosed modern selves, shamanic psychedelics allow the emergence to consciousness of something that is simultaneously true and numinous, as well as therapeutic. Nevertheless, since this is a personal experience of those ingesting a psychedelic, mainstream science declares it to be anecdotal evidence and thus not valid. The renaissance of the scientific study of psychedelics since 2000 constitutes a serious challenge to this view. Psychedelics ingested (or injected) under careful and skilled monitoring, ideally by a shaman, allow us to mute our left brain safely and temporarily, thus enabling our right brain to reveal the numinosity of the world.

Benny Shanon titled his sociological study of ayahuasca partakers "The Antipodes of the Mind."[3] It may have been more exact to have titled his book 'the antipodes of the modern mind.' The shamanic ayahuasca experience is indeed the antipodes of the modern mind. The unmuting of our right hemisphere reveals the numinosity of the cosmos as well as the presence of a myriad of discarnate sacred beings in the world. Such an experience makes purely instrumental relationships to the world much more difficult as we begin once again to see ourselves as relatives of all the other beings in the cosmos rather than unique, exceptional, and superior. It is also an experience that heals us of secularism, the inability to experience the numinosity of the world.

The fact that the experience of the numinous heart of the cosmos has seemingly never manifested itself as a specific being with a specific name and specific attributes corresponding to any tradition is, I believe, extremely significant. Discarnate sacred supernatural beings have appeared to Randy, such as the popular and well-known Virgin of Guadalupe. However, as his retelling of his visions and the illustrations in this book make clear, sacred supernatural beings from various traditions have also appeared to him, such as the Hindu god Ganesh and the Yoruba orisha Olokun, mistress of the deep sea. Randy's abandonment of secularism did not propel him into a particular religious tradition. The diversity of his visions attests to that.

Here I would like to insert an anecdote. Jacques Mabit organized an encounter for several Catholic priests and nuns on the theme of ayahuasca. They came and visited the shrine to the Virgin of Guadalupe that Randy has built near our center, and we were able to chat with some of them. One of them was a Catholic priest belonging to an Amazonian indigenous group in Bolivia, who had a parish in an indigenous village. He told Randy and me that because most of his parishioners took ayahuasca, he also was partaking of it, in order to confirm its therapeutic efficacy. In one of his ayahuasca visions the dark blue Hindu god Krishna appeared and spoke to him. Krishna held a beautiful flower in his hand and explained that this flower was sacred and that sacrality was not the exclusive property of any one spiritual tradition. Rather, sacrality and numinosity pervaded the world if you had eyes to see it. The priest told us that this visionary encounter profoundly touched him; he found the message of the Hindu divinity to be a deep revelation. Given the violent history between both branches of Christianity and shamanism in Europe, this priest's embrace of what a Hindu god had revealed to him is remarkable. As we saw in earlier chapters, Church violence was also visited on other traditions deemed heretical, such as the Cathars, Jews and Muslims. I would bet that if there had been Hindus in medieval and Renaissance Europe, they would also have been declared heretics.

With the development of science came the introduction of a new practice, that of the scientific study of sacred texts. Religions historian Karen Armstrong notes that:

Mythical language could not satisfactorily be translated into rational language without losing its raison d'être. Like poetry, it contained meanings that were too elusive to be expressed in any other way. Once theology tried to turn itself into science, it could only produce a caricature of rational discourse, because these truths are not amenable to scientific demonstration.[4]

Armstrong describes how this endeavor led to religious fundamentalism, the idea one's own religious tradition is the only true one.[5]

However, the spirits and sacred supernatural beings who initiated and gave shamanic powers to Randy either did not declare their spiritual affiliations or belong to a diversity of spiritual traditions. This, combined with the fact that the ultimate, sacred heart of the cosmos, what many call God, has no attributes or visible form in psychedelic-induced mystical experiences, means that the mind and heart of the cosmos is beyond any human language. Spiritual traditions are inherently diverse, paralleling the dizzying biodiversity on the planet as well as the great diversity of languages, a diversity which under the onslaught of modernity is sadly but steadily diminishing. It is remarkable that a Catholic priest and philosopher of religion, Raimundo Panikkar, calls himself a Catholic, a Hindu, and a Buddhist.[6] Rabbi Zalman Schachter-Salomi, the founder of Jewish Renewal, has also embraced diversity in his re-imagining and revival of the ancient Jewish mystical tradition. He personally learned from the practices of many other mystical traditions such as Sufism, Buddhism, Hinduism, mystical Christianity, and Shamanism from the Americas and enfolded many of them in this new Jewish tradition. Reb Zalman partook of ayahuasca and participated in other indigenous practices.

The moment human beings try to capture the ineffable experience of the sacred heart of the cosmos, it becomes clothed in the fashion of the linguistic, cultural, and historical tradition of those humans. The diversity of this fashioning of the ineffable is inevitable given the diversity of languages and cultures. I believe it should be appreciated and preserved. It is to be celebrated and treasured as we have come to treasure biodiversity as well as the linguistic diversity of the planet. Modernity has sadly generated a reverse trend of intensifying fundamentalisms, each warring with its others. The cure, however, is not secularism, itself centrally implicated in the emergence of fundamentalism. As I have argued, secularism is closely implicated in the pursuit of certainty and absolutism, which in turn has generated what Karen Armstrong has called "the God-shaped hole in the consciousness of wholly rational human beings."[7] This hole has much to do with the epidemics of alienation and mental disorders.

One often hears calls to overcome the divorce between science and religion. A bridge between these two domains requires a transformation of both, as well as the recognition that rationality needs to be subsumed into the whole. Many religious traditions have begun to recognize that the sacred heart of the cosmos is ineffable and cannot belong to only one human tradition. When that ineffable heart is clothed in one of the many linguistic traditions of the world it becomes easier to forget that it is of the whole nature/cosmos and belongs to all its beings, including the humans. When humans speak of it, this ineffable heart of the cosmos inevitably clothes itself in a glorious variety of forms mirroring the great diversity of human languages. Such a diversity of religious forms and practices is to be celebrated and treasured, reminding us, the humans, that it also emerges from all the non- and other-than-human beings in the cosmos.

Mechanistic science itself is also changing. One only needs to invoke quantum physics, chaos theory or morphic fields and their resonances to quickly become aware of how radically different such scientific theories are from the classical scientific paradigm. There is no doubt that in the 21st century the bridge between science and religion is already being built.

I would like to end with a note addressing the perceived difference between specifically religious discarnate beings— what are commonly referred to as 'supernaturals'—and nature spirits. Both kinds appeared to Randy and gave him shamanic healing powers as well as protection. I think it is difficult to give these two classes of discarnate beings a different ontological status. The supernaturals tend to belong to a given religious tradition and emerge from the vibratory fields and resonance emerging from those human collective systems. The nature spirits exist for indigenous peoples but today, at least among upper Amazonian curanderos, the two kinds are considered equally sacred, effective, and real. As I have argued, the eradication of shamanism in the West and its categorization as a satanic heretical pursuit is completely entangled with the birth of Western modernity during the mechanistic revolution. The result is that for secular denizens of modernity both types of discarnate beings are considered hallucinations or inventions, possessing no reality at all. For religiously inclined people, too often the only real discarnate beings are those certified by their own tradition. Randy's experience, as well as my own, forces us to recognize that discarnate beings can effect real changes, even in people who initially did not believe in their existence or were unable to recognize their specific cultural identities. For me Sheldrake's theory makes these phenomena both understandable and possible.

With the psychedelic renaissance we now have more evidence coming from secular people who have been profoundly transformed by ingesting a shamanic psychedelic substance. Although Randy's shamanic initiation was vastly broader and more complex, he also, as a secular person, was led to deeply question the assumption in modernity of the illusory nature of such discarnate entities. These entities show an extraordinary compassion and generosity toward skeptic denizens of modernity, heirs to the bloody extermination of shamanism. Such compassion emerges from the heart of the cosmos, which bathes us all in unconditional love, even though many of us are oblivious due to our intensely enclosed selves and muted right brains.

Given that Randy has also encountered negative discarnate entities, such as the Amazonian sorcerer who tried to make him blind, there is no doubt that evil exists in the dimension from whence such discarnate beings originate, a fact that is well attested to in the ethnographic literature on shamanism. Sorcery really exists and really harms, sometimes lethally. The decision of the Catholic and the Protestant churches to consider *all* shamanic practices evil may have to do with the fact that evil is considered by them as being wholly separate from the divine sphere. The healing efficacy of shamanism could simply not be conceptualized as existing simultaneously, or side by side as it were, with the harming or evil aspects. Since harm did exist in those practices, the early European churches simply decided that shamanism in its entirety was heretical. As for the natural philosophers—the inventors of the mechanistic revolution—their need to effectively distance themselves from occult philosophy forced them to the same attitude, one that even made metaphysics out of bound. We are heir to this lengthy and rather brutal history.

It is truly extraordinary that shamanic plants and fungi can cure some of the most intractable ills of modernity. It is my profound hope that once they are made legal, not only for therapeutic purposes but also for ecological and spiritual ones,[8] they will deeply transform our relationship with nature and the cosmos from an insentient object to be commodified into a numinous being with whom we are graced to interact in a reciprocal exchange.

BIBLIOGRAPHY

Abram, David. *The Spell of the Sensuous: Perception and Language in a More-Than Human World*. New York: Pantheon Books, 1996.

Adas, Michael. *Machines as the Measure of Men: Science, Technology, and Ideology of Western Dominance*. Ithaca, NY: Cornell University Press, 1989.

Alexander, Eben and Karen Newell. *Living in a Mindful Universe: A Neurosurgeon's Journey into the Heart of Consciousness*. Emmaus, PA: Rodale Wellness, 2017.

Alvarado Bremer, Jaime. "Las Fases de la Luna y su Influencia en los Cultivos Agrícola." CD, Universidad Nacional de San Martin, 2005.

Apffel-Marglin, Frédérique. "Rationality, the Body, and the World: From Production to Regeneration." In *Decolonizing Knowledge: From Development to Dialogue*, edited by F. Apffel-Marglin and S.A. Marglin, 142-181. Oxford: Clarendon Press, 1996.

—. *Rhythms of Life: Enacting the World with the Goddesses of Orissa*. Delhi: Oxford University Press, 2008.

—. *Subversive Spiritualities: How Rituals Enact the World*. New York: Oxford University Press, 2011.

—. "Under the Guns." *Cultural Survival* 33, no. 4, (Winter 2009): 20-27.

—. *Wives of the God-King: The Rituals of the Devadasis of Puri*. Delhi: Oxford University Press, 1985.

Apffel-Marglin, F. and Pramod Parajuli. ""Sacred Grove" and Ecology: Ritual and Science." In *Hinduism and Ecology: The*

Intersection of Earth, Sky, and Water, edited by Christopher Chapple and Mary Evelyn Tucker, 291-316. Cambridge, MA: Harvard University Press, 2000.

Appleby, Joyce Oldham. *Economic Thought and Ideology in Seventeenth-Century England.* Princeton: Princeton University Press, 1978.

Armstrong, Karen. *The Battle for God.* New York: Alfred Knopf, 2000.

Bache, Christopher. *LSD and the Mind of the Universe: Diamonds from Heaven.* Rochester, Vermont: Park Street Press, 2019.

Baez, Fernando. *El Saqueo Cultural de América Latina: De la Conquista a la Globalización.* Mexico City: Random House, 2008.

Bajaj, Jatinder. "Francis Bacon, the First Philosopher of Modern Science: A Non-Western View." In *Science, Hegemony, and Violence: A Requiem for Modernity,* edited by Ashis Nandy, 57-58. Delhi: Oxford University Press, 1988.

Balée, William. *Cultural Forests of the Amazon: A Historical Ecology of People and Their Landscapes.* Tuscaloosa, AL: Alabama University Press, 2013.

—-. *Footprints of the Forest: Ka'apor Ethnobotany: The Historical Ecology of Plant Utilization by an Amazonian People.* New York: Columbia University Press, 1994.

Barad, Karen. *Meeting the Universe Halfway: Quantum Physics and the Entanglement of Matter and Meaning.* Durham, NC: Duke University Press, 2007.

—-. "Reconceiving Scientific Literacy as Agential Literacy, Or Learning How to Intra Act Responsibly Within the World." In *Doing Science + Culture,* edited by Roddey Reid and Sharon Traweek, 232. New York: Routledge, 2000.

Barbira-Freeman, Françoise. "'Vegetalismo' and the Perception of Biodiversity: Shamanic Values in the Peruvian Upper Amazon." In *Cultural and Spiritual Values of Biodiversity,* edited by Darrell Posey, 277-278. London: United Nations Environment Program, 1999.

Baring, Anne. *The Dream of the Cosmos and the Quest for the Soul.* Shaftsbury, UK: Archive Publishing, 2019.

Batnitzky, Leora. *How Judaism Became a Religion: An Introduction to Modern Jewish Thought.* Princeton: Princeton University Press, 2011.

Bauman, Zygmunt. *Modernity and the Holocaust.* Ithaca, NY: Cornell University Press, 2000.

Bayou, François. *Ils portaient l'écharpe blanche: l'aventure des premiers réformés, des guerres de religion à l'édit de Nantes, de la Révocation à la Révolution.* Paris: Bernard Grasset, 1998.

Beauregard, Mario. *Brain Wars: The Scientific Battle Over the Existence of the Mind and the Proof That Will Change the Way We Live Our Lives.* New York: HarperOne, 2013.

Belmont, Nicole. "Superstition and Popular Religion in Western Societies." In *Between Belief and Transgression: Structuralist Essays in Religion, History, and Myth,* edited by Michel Izard and Pierre Smith, translated by John Levitt, 9-23. Chicago: Chicago University Press, 1983.

Bigwood, Carol. *Earth Muse: Feminism, Nature, and Art.* Philadelphia: Temple University Press, 1993.

Bohm, David and David Peat. *Science, Order, and Creativity: A Dramatic New Look at the Creative Roots of Science and Life.* New York: Bantam Books, 1987.

Bohr, Niels. *Essays 1958-1962 on Atomic Physics and Human Knowledge. The Philosophical Writings of Niels Bohr,* v. 3, 59-60. New York: Interscience Publishers, 1963.

Boyle, Robert. *A Free Inquiry into the Vulgarly Received Notion of Nature,* edited by Edward B. Davis. Cambridge: Cambridge University Press, 2012 [1685].

Bruckmann, Monica. *Le Monde Diplomatique.* September 2009.

Buckley, Thomas, and Selma Gottlieb. *Blood Magic: The Anthropology of Menstruation*. Berkeley, CA: University of California Press, 1988.

Butler, Judith. *Gender Trouble: Feminism and the Subversion of Identity*. New York: Routledge, 1990.

Carroll, James. *Constantine's Sword: The Church and the Jews*. Boston: Houghton Mifflin Company, 2001.

Clottes, Jean and David Lewis-Williams. *Les Chamanes de la Préhistoire*. Paris: Réalisations Cursives, 2007.

Connolly, John. "The Academy's Freedom—The Academy's Burden." Lecture on the inauguration of Smith College President Ruth Simmons, Northampton, MA, September 1995. Copy of the written but unpublished lecture given to F. Apffel-Marglin by John Connolly.

Corbin, Henry. *Alone with the Alone: Creative Imagination in the Sufism of Ibn 'Arabi*. Princeton, NJ: Princeton University Press, 1998.

—-. *Spiritual Body and Celestial Earth: From Mazdean Iran to Shi'ite Iran*. Princeton, NJ: Princeton University Press, 1977.

Craffert, Pieter F., John R. Baker, and Michael Winkelman, editors. *The Supernatural After the Neuro-Turn*. Routledge, 2021.

Cronon, William. "The Trouble with Wilderness or Getting Back to the Wrong Nature." In *Uncommon Ground: Rethinking the Human Place in Nature*. New York: W.W. Norton, 1996.

Descartes, René. [1641] 1998, *Pr. Phil.*, Pt. 4, § 187

Diamond, Jared. *Guns, Germs, and Steel: The Fate of Human Societies*. New York: W.W. Norton and Co., 1997.

—-. *How Societies Choose to Fail or Succeed*. New York: Viking, 2005.

Duerr, Hans Peter. *Dreamtime: Concerning the Boundary between Wilderness and Civilization*. New York: Basil Blackwell, 1985.

Eliade, Mircéa. *Shamanism: Archaic Techniques of Ecstasy*. Princeton, NJ: Princeton University Press, 1972.

Espeland, Wendy. *The Struggle for Water: Politics, Rationality, and Identity in the American Southwest.* Chicago, IL: Chicago University Press, 1998.

Federici, Silvia. *Caliban and the Witch: Women, the Body, and Primitive Accumulation.* Brooklyn, NY: Basic Books, 2004.

Foucault, Michel. *Discipline and Punish: The Birth of the Prison.* Translated by Allan Sheridan. New York: Vintage Books, 1979.

Ghosh, Amitav. *The Nutmeg's Curse: Parables for a Planet in Crisis.* Chicago: The University of Chicago Press, 2021.

Gill, Penny. *The Radiant Heart of the Cosmos: Compassion Teachings for our Time.* Housatonic, MA: Green Fire Press, 2022.

Gillespie, Gerry. "City to Soil: Returning Organics to Agriculture: A Circle of Sustainability." In *Amazonian Dark Earths: Wim Sombroek's Vision,* edited by William Woods, 465-472. Berlin: Springer, 2009.

Ginzburg, Carlo. *The Cheese and the Worm: The Cosmos of a Sixteenth-century Miller.* Baltimore: John Hopkins University Press, 1980.

—-. *Ecstasies: Deciphering the Witches' Sabbath.* New York: Pantheon Books, 1991.

——. *Night Battles: Witchcraft & Agrarian Cults on the Sixteenth and Seventeenth Centuries.* New York: Penguin Books, 1985.

Glass-Coffin, Bonnie. *The Gift of Life: Female Spirituality and Healing in Northern Peru.* Albuquerque, NM: University of New Mexico Press, 1998.

Gould, Stephen Jay. *Rocks of Ages: Science and Religion in the Fullness of Life.* New York: Ballantine Books, 1999.

Grahn, Judy. *Blood, Bread, and Roses: How Menstruation Created the World.* Boston: Beacon Press, 1993.

Green, Arthur. "Jewish Mysticism in Medieval Spain." In *Essential Papers on Kabbalah,* edited by Lawrence Fine, 27-66. New York: New York University Press, 1995.

Halifax, Joan. *Shaman: The Wounded Healer*. London: Thames and Hudson, 1991.

Hancock, Graham. *Supernatural: Meetings with the Ancient Teachers of Mankind*. Revised edition. San Francisco, CA: Disinformation Books, 2007.

Haraway, Donna. Modest Witness Second Millennium: FemaleMan Meets OncoMouse: *Feminism and Technoscience*. New York: Routledge, 1997.

—-. "Teddy Bear Patriarchy." In *Primate Visions: Gender, Race, and Nature in the World of Modern Science*, 26-58. New York: Routledge, 1989.

Hecht, Susanna, Morrison, Kathleen and Christine Padoch. *The Social Lives of Forests: Past, Present, and Future of Woodland Resurgence*. Chicago: Chicago University Press, 2014.

Hillman, James. *The Thought of the Heart and the Soul of the World*. Dallas, Texas: Spring Publications, Inc., 1992.

Hyde, Lewis. *The Gift: Imagination and the Erotic Life of Property*. New York: Random House, 1983.

Jacobs, Margaret. *The Cultural Meaning of the Scientific Revolution*. Philadelphia, PA: Temple University Press, 1988.

James, William. *The Varieties of Religious Experience*. New York: Penguin Classic, 1985.

Jung, Carl G. *The Red Book: Liber Novus, A Reader's Edition*. Edited by Sonu Shamdasani. Translated by Mark Kyburz, John Peck, and Sonu Shamdasani. New York: W.W. Norton, 2009.

Kant, Immanuel. *The Conflict of the Faculties*. Translation and introduction by Mary J. Gregor. New York, NY: Abaris Books, 1979.

Kimmerer, Robin W. *Braiding Sweetgrass: Indigenous Wisdom, Scientific Knowledge, and the Teachings of Plants*. Minneapolis, Minnesota: Milkweed Editions, 2013.

Knight, Chris. *Blood Relations: Menstruation and the Origins of*

Culture. New Haven, CT: Yale University Press, 1991.

Kopenawa, Davi and Bruce Albert. *The Falling Sky: Words of a Yanomami Shaman*. Translated by Nicholas Elliott and Alison Dundy. Cambridge, MA: The Belknap Press of Harvard University Press, 2013.

Kripal, Jeffrey J. *The Flip: Epiphanies of Mind and the Future of Knowledge*. New York: Bellevue Library Press, 2019.

Kuhn, Thomas S. *The Structure of Scientific Revolutions*. 2nd edition. Chicago: University of Chicago Press, 1970.

Lamp, Frederick. "Heavenly Bodies: Menses, Moon, and Rituals of License among the Temne of Sierra Leone." In *Blood Magic: The Anthropology of Menstruation,* edited Buckley, Thomas and Selma Gottlieb, 210-231. Berkeley, CA: University of California Press, 1988.

Latour, Bruno. *We Have Never Been Modern*. Translated from French by Catherine Porter. Cambridge, MA: Harvard University Press, 1993.

Lee, Richard. *The Dobe !Kung*. New York: Rinehart & Winston, 1984.

Lehmann, Johannes, editor. *Amazonian Dark Earth: Origin, Properties, Management*. Boston: Kluwer Academic Publishers, 2003.

Lewis-Williams, David. *A Cosmos in Stone: Interpreting Religion and Society through Rock Art*. Walnut Creek, CA: AltaMira Press, 2002.

Lincoln, Bruce. *Emerging from the Chrysalis: Rituals of Women's Initiation*. New York: Oxford University Press, 1991.

Luna, Luis Eduardo, and Pablo Amaringo. *Ayahuasca Visions: The Religious Iconography of a Peruvian Shaman*. Berkeley, CA: North Atlantic Books, 1999.

Mabit, Jacques. "Ayahuasca and the Treatment of Addictions." In *Psychedelic Medicine: New Evidence for Hallucinogenic Substances as Treatments,* Vol 2, edited by Michael Winkelman and Thomas B. Roberts, 87-105. Westport, CT: Praeger Publishers, 2007.

—-. "The Sorcerer, the Madman, and Grace: Are Archetypes Desacralized Spirits? Thoughts on Shamanism in the Amazon." In *Contemporary Voices from Anima Mundi: A Reappraisal,* edited by F. Apffel-Marglin and Stefano Varese, 113-154. New York: Peter Lang, 2020.

Macaulay, Thomas. "Minute on Education (1835)." In *Selection from Educational Records, Part I. 1781-1839,* edited by H. Sharp. Calcutta: Superintendent Government Printing, 1920.

Malinowsky, Bronislaw. *Coral Gardens and Their Magic.* Volume I and II. New York: American Book Co., 1935.

Mann, Charles. *1491: New Revelations of the Americas Before Columbus.* New York: Knopf, 2005.

—-. *1493: Uncovering the New World Columbus Created.* New York: Vintage Books, a division of Random House, Inc., 2012.

Marglin, Stephen A. *The Dismal Science: How Thinking Like an Economist Undermines Community.* Cambridge, MA: Harvard University Press, 2008.

—-. "Farmers, Seedsmen, and Scientists: Systems of Agriculture and Systems of Knowledge." In *Decolonizing Knowledge: From Development to Dialogue,* edited by F. Apffel-Marglin and S.A. Marglin, 185-248. Oxford: Clarendon Press, 1996.

—-. "Losing Touch: The cultural Conditions of Worker Accommodation and Resistance." In *Dominating Knowledge: Development, Culture, and Resistance,* edited by F. Apffel-Marglin and S.A. Marglin, 217-282. Oxford: Clarendon Press, 1990.

—-. "What Do Bosses Do? The Origins and Functions of Hierarchy in Capitalist Production, Part I." *Review of Radical Political Economy,* 6 (1974): 60-112.

Mauss, Marcel. *The Gift: Forms and Functions of Exchange in Archaic Societies.* Translated by Ian Cunnison. New York: Norton, 1967.

Originally published in French as *Essai sur le Don* in 1925.

Maxwell, Nicholas. *From Knowledge to Wisdom: A Revolution in the Aims and Method of Science.* Oxford: Basil Blackwell, 1984.

McGilchrist, Iain. *The Master and His Emissary: The Divided Brain and the Making of the Western World.* New Haven, CT: Yale University Press, 2019.

McKenna, Dennis. "The Healing Vine: Ayahuasca as Medicine in the 21st century." In *Psychedelic Medicine: New Evidence for Hallucinogenic Substances as Treatments*, edited by Thomas Roberts andMichael Winkelman, 21-44. Westport, CT: Praeger Publishers, 2007.

Merchant, Carolyn. *The Death of Nature: Women, Ecology, and the Scientific Revolution.* San Francisco, CA: Harper and Row, 1980.

Morgan, Davis. *Chachapoyas, The Cloud People: An Anthropological Survey.* Unpublished folio deposited in Harvard University Tozzer Anthropological Library, 1985.

Morin, Edgar. *La Voie: Pour l'avenir de l'humanité.* Paris: Fayard, 2011.

Muraresku, Brian. *The Immortality Key: The Secret History of the Religion with No Name.* New York: St. Martin's Press, 2020.

Narby, Jeremy. *The Cosmic Serpent: DNA and the Origins of Knowledge.* New York: Putnam, 1999.

Noble, David. *A World without Women: The Clerical Culture of Western Science.* New York: Knopf, 1992.

Pacheco, Luis Calderón. "Relaciones entre Kechwa-Mestizo en Lamas en el contexto de la globalización." In *Comunidades Locales y Transnacionales, Cinco Estudios de Caso en el Perú*, edited by Ivan Digreori, 1-100. Lima: Instituto de Estudios Peruanos, 2003.

Panduro, Rider and Grimaldo Rengifo. *Montes y Montaraces*: la visión del bosque en los quechua-lamas : una aproximación. Lima: PRATEC Proyecto Andino de Tecnología, 2001.

Panikkar, Raimundo. *The Cosmotheandric Experience: Emerging Religious Consciousness.* Maryknoll, NY: Orbis Books, 1993.

Parpola, Asko. "From Ishtar to Durga." Unpublished manuscript, 1988.

Peat, David. *Synchronicity: The Bridge Between Matter and Mind.* Toronto: Bantam Books, 1987.

Plumwood, Val. *Feminism and the Mastery of Nature.* London: Routledge, 1993.

Polanyi, Karl. *The Great Transformation.* New York: Rinehart and Company, 1944.

Pollan, Michael. *The Botany of Desire: A Plant's-Eye View of the World.* New York: Random House, 2002.

—-. *How to Change Your Mind: What the New Science of Psychedelics Teaches Us About Consciousness, Dying, Addiction, Depression, and Transcendence.* London: Penguin, 2018.

Poole, Richard Stafford. *Our Lady of Guadalupe: The Origins and Sources of a Mexican National Symbol, 1531-1797.* Tucson, Arizona: University of Arizona Press, 1995.

Posey, Darrell, ed. *Cultural and Spiritual Values of Biodiversity.* Nairobi: UN Environment Program, 1999.

Potter, Elizabeth. *Gender and Boyle's Law of Gases.* Bloomington, IN: Indiana University Press, 2001.

Pouillon, Jean. "Remarks on the verb "To Believe."" In *Between Belief and Transgression: Structural Essays in Religion, History, and Myth,* edited by Michel Izard and Pierre Smith. Chicago: Chicago University Press, 1982.

Proctor, Robert N. *Value-Free Science? Purity and Power in Modern Knowledge.* 2nd edition. Cambridge, MA: Harvard University Press, 1991.

Ramanujan, A. K. "Is there an Indian Way of Thinking?" Paper presented at the first workshop of the ACLS-SSRC Joint Committee on South Asia, Chicago, September 1980; mimeo.

Published in *The Collected Essays of A.K. Ramanujan.* General editor Vinay Dharwadketr. New Delhi, New York: Oxford University Press, 1999.

Richards, William. *Sacred Knowledge: Psychedelics and Religious Experience.* New York: Columbia University Press, 2016.

Schultes, Richard Evan, Hoffman, Albert, and Christian Rätsch, eds. *Plants of the Gods: Their Sacred, Healing, and Hallucinogenic Powers.* Rochester, VT: Healing Arts Press, 2006.

Scott, James. *Seeing Like a State: How Certain Schemes to Improve the Human Condition have Failed.* New Haven, CT: Yale University Press, 1998.

Shanon, Benny. *The Antipodes of the Mind: Charting the Phenomenology of the Ayahuasca Experience.* Oxford: Oxford University Press, 2006.

Shapin, Steven, and Simon Schaffer. *Leviathan and the Air-Pump: Hobbes, Boyle, and the Experimental Life.* Princeton, NJ: Princeton University Press, 1985.

Sheldrake, Rupert. *The Science Delusion: Freeing the Spirit of Enquiry.* London: Coronet Press, 2013.

Sheldrake, Rupert, Terence McKenna, and Ralph Abraham. *Chaos, Creativity, and Cosmic Consciousness.* Rochester, VT: Park Street Press, 2001.

Shiva, Vandana. *Monocultures of the Mind: Perspectives on Biodiversity and Biotechnology.* London: Zed Books, 1993.

Silva, Fabiola Andrea. "Cultural Behaviors of Indigenous Populations and the Formation of the Archaeological Record in Amazonian Dark Earth: The Asurini Do Xingú Case Study." In *Amazonian Dark Earths: Origin, Properties, Management,* edited by Johannes Lehmann, 373-385. Dordrecht; Boston: Kluwer Academic Publishers, 2003.

Silverblatt, Irene. *Moon, Sun, and Witches.* Princeton, NJ: Princeton University Press, 1987.

Stengers, Isabelle. "Reclaiming Animism." *e-flux Journal* 36, no. 7 (2012).

Swimme, Brian. *The Hidden Heart of the Cosmos: Humanity and the New Story*. Maryknoll, NY: Orbis Books, 1996.

Swimme, Brian, and Thomas Berry. *The Universe Story*. San Francisco, CA: HarperCollins, 1992.

Takiwasi. *Medicinas Tradicionales, Interculturalidad y Salud Mental: Memorias del Congreso Internacional, Tarapoto 2009*. Centro Takiwasi, 2012.

Tambiah, Stanley Jeyaraja. *Culture, Thought, and Social Action: An Anthropological Perspective*. Cambridge, MA: Harvard University Press, 1985.

Taylor, Charles. *Sources of the Self: The Making of Modern Identity*. Cambridge: Cambridge University Press, 1989.

Taylor, Jill Bolte. *My Stroke of Insight: A Brain Scientist's Personal Journey*. New York: Viking, 2008.

—-. *Whole Brain Living: The Anatomy of Choice and the Four Characters that Drive Our Life*. Carlsbad, CA: Hay House, 2021.

Thomas, Keith. *Religion and the Decline of Magic*. New York: Scribner & Sons, 1971.

Thompson, E. P. "Time, Work-Discipline, and Industrial Capitalism." *Past & Present*, no. 38 (1967): 56–97.

Tindall, Robert, Frédérique Apffel-Marglin, and David Shearer. *Sacred Soil: Biochar and the Regeneration of the Earth*. Berkeley, CA: North Atlantic Books, 2017.

Todorov, Tzvetan. *The Conquest of America*. Translated from the French by Richard Howard. New York: Harper and Rowe, 1984.

Toulmin, Stephen. *Cosmopolis: The Hidden Agenda of Modernity*. New York: Free Press, 1990.

Tucker, Mary Evelyn, and Brian Swimme. *Journey of the Universe*. New Haven, CT: Yale University Press, 2011.

Urbano, Henrique. *La Extirpación de la Idolatría en el Pirú*

(1631). Cuzco, Perú: Centro de Estudios Regionales Andinos Bartolomé de las Casas, 1999.

Varela, Francisco, Evan Thompson, and Eleanor Rosch. *The Embodied Mind: Cognitive Science and Human Experience.* Cambridge, MA: MIT Press, 1993.

Varese, Stefano. *The Art of Memory: An Ethnographer's Journey.* Translated by Margaret Randall. Raleigh, North Carolina: Raleigh Press, 2020.

—-. "La etíca cosmocéntrica de los pueblos indígenas de la Amazonía: Elementos para una crítica de la civilización." In *Selva Vida: de la destrucción de la Amazonia al paradigma de la regeneración*, edited by S. Varese, F. Apffel-Marglin & Róger Rumrrill, 61-81. Copenhague, Dinamarca: Grupo Internacional de Trabajo sobre Asuntos Indígenas, IWGIA, 2013. 2013.

Vitebsky, Piers. *The Shaman: Voyages of the Soul: Trance, Ecstasy and Healing from Siberia to the Amazon.* New York: Barnes & Noble, 2008.

Vivanco, Luis. *Green Encounters: Shaping and Contesting Environmentalism in Rural Costa Rica.* New York: Berghahn Books, 2006.

Viveiros de Castro, E.B. "Exchanging Perspectives: The Transformation of Objects into Subjects in Amerindian Ontologies." *Common Knowledge* 10 (2004): 463-84.

Wasson, R. G., Hoffman, Albert, and Carl Ruck. *The Road to Eleusis: Unveiling the Secret of The Mysteries.* Berkeley, CA: North Atlantic Books, 2008.

Watanabe, John M. "Unimagining the Maya: Anthropologists, Others, and the Inescapable Hubris of Authorship." *Bulletin of Latin American Research* 14, no. 1 (1995): 25–45.

Weisskopf, Victor. *The Joy of Insight: Passions of a Physicist.* New York: Basic Books, 1991.

Wertheim, Margaret. *Pythagoras' Trousers: God, Physics, and the*

Gender Wars. New York: Times Books/Random House, 1995.

Whitehead, A.N. *Science and the Modern World.* New York: MacMillan, 1925.

Woods, William, ed. *Amazonian Dark Earths: Wim Sombroek's Vision.* Berlin: Springer, 2009.

Yaden, David B., et al. "Of Roots and Fruits: A Comparison of Psychedelic and Nonpsychedelic Mystical Experiences." *Journal of Humanistic Psychology* 57, no. 4 (July 2017): 338-53.

Yates, Frances. *Occult Philosophy in the Elizabethan Age.* London: Routledge & Kegan Paul, 1979.

ENDNOTES

Epigraphs

1 James, *The Varieties of Religious Experience*, 388.

2 Kimmerer, *Braiding Sweetgrass*, 49.

3 Morin, *La Voie*, 22. My translation.

4 Ghosh, *The Nutmeg's Curse*, 201.

PART I
Introduction by Frédérique Apffel-Marglin

Chapter 1. Introduction: Science and Shamanism in the Peruvian Rainforest

1 Although as we will see, initiation by the spirits is well attested to in the anthropological literature but almost unknown in this region: the Peruvian, Ecuadorian, and Brazilian Upper Amazon.

2 In Mexico the mushroom containing psylocibin has been used for millennia by indigenous shamans. See our project's Facebook page: Proyecto Teonanácatl.

3 Some of those can be seen on our website, asociacionsachamama.org, under Hospedaje Sangapilla.

4 Ayahuasca is a brew made from boiling together two plants: one is called ayahuasca, a vine, and the other is a bush called chakruna. Their scientific names respectively are: banisteriopsis caapi and the other is psychotria viridis. The vine or creeper grows on trees abundantly in the Amazonian rain forest as does the bush, which is from the same family of plants as coffee. The chakruna plant contains DMT (demethyltriptamine). DMT is also a natural constituent found in the human brain and the pineal gland and is a psychedelic. However, there exist some substances called monoamino oxidase (MAO) in the human liver and the gut that inhibit the DMT in the chakruna plant from producing visions. As it turns out the ayahuasca vine contains potent MAO inhibitors. Thus, by combining these two plants one can produce the well-known psychedelic effects of this brew. The anthropologist Jeremy Narby who was

cured of an intractable back problem in the Peruvian Amazon by a shaman using ayahuasca, wrote a book titled The Cosmic Serpent in which he makes a probability calculus about the possibility of such a precise combination of plants having come about through trial and error. He concludes that the number is so astronomical that the time required would be longer than the existence of our species. He is convinced that what his shaman told him, namely that the plants themselves communicate their properties to shamans, is true.

5   *The Antipodes of the Mind* is the title of Benny Shanon's sociological study of ayahuasca partakers, published by Oxford University Press in 2006.

6   As we will see in part III of the book, the Lutheran Swedish Church eradicated the Sami shamans in Scandinavia in the 18th and 19th century.

7   However, in Peru the psychedelic brew ayahuasca is legal.

8   My own long-standing association with the Takiwasi center in Tarapoto, Peru, close to my own center in Lamas, made me aware of the therapeutic efficacy of ayahuasca many years ago.

9   Taylor, *My Stroke of Insight*, 51.

10   Taylor, *Whole Brain Living*, 47, 48.

11   Taylor, *Whole Brain Living*.

12   Taylor, *Sources of the Self: The Making of Modern Identity*. Harvard UP, 1992.

13   I personally have only ingested the ayahuasca brew, as has Randy. In Part I 4 I give details concerning this.

14   Bache, *LSD and the Mind of the Universe*, 232–233.

15   The late Harvard anthropologist Stanley Tambiah critiqued Malinowsky on this point with his performative theory of ritual; see Tambiah, *Culture, Thought, and Social Action*. This is however only a partial correction since in this performative theory Tambiah only considers its effect on humans and not on the world. Tambiah rightly gets rid of the description of such actions as "false science" as well as of the distinction between magic and ritual, an enormous achievement. However, he maintained a matter/mind dualism. Tambiah also pointed out to me that Keith Thomas retains this same Malinowskian distinction in his very influential book *Religion and the Decline of Magic*.

Chapter 2. Shamanism in the Upper Amazon

1   The other two smaller indigenous groups are: the Awajun in the north and the Shawi in the southeast of the state of San Martin.

2   During my collaboration with PRATEC I had sent one of their Kichwa-Lamas collaborators from Lamas who did video filming in the place in Ecuador near Sarayaku that had been ecologically devastated by oil companies to do a report. This person was astounded to discover that they spoke the same language and used to be one people before the two nation states of Peru and

Ecuador were created by descendants of the conquistadors.

3   I am deeply grateful to my friend and colleague, Stefano Varese, who brought back from his visit to Sarayaku with UC Davis students in July of 2018 this document and gifted it to me and our center.

4   The Quechua word *yachakkuna* is made up of the substantive *yachak* meaning a person with *yachay*, namely knowledge/power. The suffix *-kuna* makes the substantive plural.

5   For a scientific explanation of the chemical substances making up this brew see the essay by Dennis McKenna "The Healing Vine: Ayahuasca as Medicine in the 21st century" in *Psychedelic Medicine: New Evidence for Hallucinogenic Substances as Treatments*, edited by Winkelman and Roberts, 21–44.

6   Davi Kopenawa was taught how to be a shaman by his father-in-law. He was not initiated directly by the spirits, as Randy was.

7   Kopenawa and Albert, *The Falling Sky: Words of a Yanomami Shaman*.

8   Dimethyltryptamine, a substance also found in the human brain that alters consciousness.

9   Kopenawa and Albert, *The Falling Sky*, 393, 382.

10   See Mann, *1491*, pages 3–30 on what scholars euphemistically call "the demographic collapse" of the indigenous people.

11   Kopenawa and Albert, *The Falling Sky*, 418.

Chapter 3. Relations Between Kichwa-Lamas and Mestizos

1   Pacheco, "Relaciones Entre Kechwa-Mestizo en Lamas en el Contexto de la Globalización" in *Comunidades Locales y Transnacionales, Cinco Estudios de Caso en el Perú*, edited by Digreori, 1–100.

2   This information is from the local amateur historians in Lamas. There is no scholarly published work on that Jesuit mission.

3   It is only after a few Kichwa-Lamas men acquired university degrees toward the end of the 20th century that overt racism towards them began to slowly change.

4   My friend and colleague, the Italo-Peruvian anthropologist Stefano Varese, was key in the naming and creating of this law since he worked for the organization created by Velazco to protect Indigenous peoples of the Amazon during his regime. With the countercoup that brought this government down (with the help of the CIA), Varese became persona non grata and sought refuge in Mexico where he was invited by colleagues at the university there. He later became professor in the Indigenous Studies department at the University of California in Davis. See Varese's recently published memoirs *The Art of Memory: An Ethnographer's Journey*.

5   As I learned later, many businesses and NGO's must show proof of a collaboration with an indigenous organization to secure foreign funding and

this Kichwa-Lamas farmer organization was quickly created to fulfill this requirement of a mestizo agricultural business and the only indigenous farmers who would join a mestizo business were evangelical ones.

6   My translation from Pablo José de Arriaga, de la compañía de Jesús con estudios preliminares y notas de Urbano, *La Extirpación de la Idolatría en el Pirú* (1631), XXIV–XXV.

7   Silverblatt, *Moon, Sun, and Witches*.

8   Glass-Coffin, *The Gift of Life: Female Spirituality and Healing in Northern Peru*.

9   Varese, "La Etíca Cosmocéntrica de los Pueblos Indígenas de la Amazonía: Elementos Para Una Crítica de la Civilización" in *Selva Vida*, 61–81. My translation.

10   I should add that recently several of the schools we work with have introduced students to recycling and composting and other basic ecological practices. But the Lamas municipality does not require households to recycle, and trash is of one kind only.

Chapter 4. Situating Ourselves in Our Social Contexts

1   This acronym stands for Proyecto Andino de Tecnología Campesina (Andean Project about Peasant Technology).

2   Much greater detail as well as references are given in our 2017 book *Sacred Soil: Biochar and the Regeneration of the Earth* with Robert Tindall and David Shearer writing their own chapters and four chapters of my own. In 2019, a Spanish translation was published by Apus Graph in Lima under the title *Yana Allpa: El Biocarbón, una Solución Ancestral Amazónica a la Crisis Climática*.

3   I have reproduced the diagram Randy made of his oven with the explanation of how it works, how it recycles and neutralizes the gasses emitted in carbonization in the barrel with the biomass. See my book with Tindall and Shearer, *Sacred Soil*, 164.

4   Because the earliest archaeological digs that found this black earth were in Brazil.

5   I have previously used the English version of the Spanish word *microorganismos*, namely 'microorganisms,' used by the Costa Rican farmers who taught me how to harvest them from the forest floor. But the scientific term is mycelium that symbiotically attach to plant roots as mycorrhyzal webs. Mycelium are microscopic fungi.

6   In our book *Sacred Soil* I bring together a series of correlating evidence to make this contemporary practice of the Kichwa-Lamas more than plausible as an explanation for the presence of broken ceramics wherever this pre-Columbian anthropogenic black soil has been found by archeologists; see pages 134–136.

7   In the documentary we made of this work at SCBR, "Re-Weaving the Web," Royner and Cindy can be seen making those offerings in the presence of my students. It can be found on our center's website:

www.asociacionsachamama.org.

8   I had the student read Jaques Mabit's essay "Ayahuasca and the Treatment of Addictions" in *Psychedelic Medicine: New Evidence for Hallucinogenic Substances as Treatments,* 87–105.

9   I should clarify that beginning in 2013 I began having other universities hold courses in my center, taught by colleagues and friends of mine. One couple was from the University of British Columbia and the other one from the University of Victoria, both in Canada. In those university courses I would be one of the co-teachers.

10   I had from the beginning decided against support known as soft money— reliance on temporary grants. This is how PRATEC functioned, and I witnessed what it involved, namely constant traveling and stress for purposes of raising money. I had learned with my first trials of holding study abroad courses in PRATEC's first center in Lamas, called Waman Wasi, that I could sustain a center through such courses and be self-sustaining and that is what I have been doing ever since.

11   My mother had recently passed away, and I inherited enough to build a swimming pool.

12   Some years later Randy learned about a machine that hydrolyzed water with sea salt that could completely purify and sanitize the water. We bought the machine since the aquatic plants began to exude a noxious odor and that machine has ever since sanitized the pool with that hydrolyzed sea salt water. The encircling shallower ring became a pool for small children.

13   See Eliade, *Shamanism,* 33–66.

14   Halifax, *Shaman: The Wounded Healer.*

15   Randy has since revised his part in the version in Spanish and made corrections where necessary.

16   The region of Alsace in the eastern part of France (as well as Lorraine) along the German border had been until the 17th century an independent duchy and was made part of the French kingdom then and given permission to keep its protestant as well as Jewish inhabitants who had been expulsed from the rest of the French kingdom. The upper class in Alsace tends to be Lutheran and the farming rural people tend to be Catholic. Alsace and Lorraine were conquered by the Germans in 1870 but lost again to France at the end of the First World War. At the fall of France to the Nazis in 1940, Alsace was de facto taken and administered by the Nazis, and finally liberated in 1945 became French again.

17   I had been initiated some four years previously to a Dzogchen practice which enriched my Hindu Shakta (focused on the Goddess) practice which I garnered from my years of fieldwork in Odisha.

PART II: INITIATED BY THE SPIRITS
RANDY'S VOICE AND ILLUSTRATIONS

Introductory remarks by Frederique Apffel-Marglin

1   I have since gifted my image of Tonantzin to Randy who always places it on his altar during ayahuasca sessions he leads.

Chapter 1. The Initial Session at Don Aquilino Chujandama's Center, June 2016

1   Text within backets [] are Frédérique's explanations or clarifications.

2   Randy and most of the staff at our center address me as "doctora." I tried hard to change this and was unsuccessful.

3   When Randy says "they showed me" he is referrig to the discarnate spirits that initiated him.

4   A tambo is a palmleaf indigenous structure.

Chapter 2. Randy Receives Shamanic Knowledge/Power from a Discarnate Master, June 2016

1   The cushma is the loose-fitting knee-high garment worn by low Amazonian indigenous men.

2   The talega is the cotton woven shoulder bag worn by indigenous men.

3   The chumbe is a narrow band made of cotton grown by indigenous people and woven by the women of the Kichwa-Lamas.

4   By the time Randy retold me this incident he knew that this originally unidentified man was a curandero, a master. Randy did a sketch of this man and I tentatively identified him as belonging to the low Amazonian indigenous group known as the Ashaninkas.

5   *Mariri* is the Quechua word for shamanic knowledge/power. A synonym is *"yachay."*

6   The *mapacho* is a ritual cigarette made with locally grown organic tobacco. Tobacco is considered the food of the spirits and the mapacho is an indispensable tool for a curandero with which he smudges his patients.

Chapter 3. Randy's First Visit and Ceremony at Takiwasi Drug-addiction Treatment Center, July 2016

1   The ikaros are the songs sung by the shaman during an ayahuasca ceremony.

2   Vomiting after ingesting the ayahuasca psychedelic brew typically happens and is a positive purging.

Chapter 5. Randy Receives Mentoring from Dr. Jacques and a Vision, July and August 2016

1   The Quechua word yachay is a synonym to mariri and means the same thing, namely the knowledge/power of a shaman.

Chapter 7. Second Session with Don Aquilino in Chazuta; Randy Acquires More Tools and Powers, September 2016

1   "Making someone blind" coming from a curandero means to destroy another person's ability to have visions.

2   Floripondio is a flower in the category of daturas, powerful psychedelics.

Chapter 8. Randy Receives Mentoring from Dr. Jacques Mabit, September to December 2016

1   This is something that Jacques Mabit also told me. Jacques eventually acceded to the spirits of the forest's request to heal drug addicts and opened Takiwasi center in 1992.

2   In the context of shamanism, the dieta refers to a retreat usually under the guidance of a shaman of various length of time and usually in the forest, during which one fasts, takes 'master' plants and isolates. This can be done by shamans to strengthen their powers or by anyone needing healing.

3   Don Simeon is a beloved elder in Wayku and a friend of ours, an expert in cane weaving among other gifts.

Chapter 9. Randy's First Dieta in Takiwasi in February 2017, Followed by Four Months of Depression

1   Purging before an ayahuasca ceremony is standard practice.

2   "To cut the dieta" means to stop eating only a little food without salt; usually this meal consists of a small salad with salt.

3   Colleagues and friends from the University of British Columbia who taught a course at our center.

Chapter 10. Randy Learns How to Prepare Ayahuasca, July 2017

1   Sauce is a small town on the shore of a mountain lake at some two and half hours from Lamas.

2   Mukura is a medicinal plant that both purifies and protects.

Chapter 11. Randy Leads His First Ayahuasca Session and His First Workshop, August 14–16, 2017

1   Erin was a Navajo from the United States.

Chapter 12. Randy Decides to Abandon the Path of Curandismo; Session with Grimaldo on December 8, 2017

1   Randy came to know about the Hindu elephant-headed deity Ganesh through me. I taught him a simple invocation for Ganesh which he adapted as a brief ikaro.

2   Suy suy is the name of a small blue bird and the name of an ikaro.

3   Cinnamon bark was given to Randy by Don Aquilino in one of his first two sessions there. It is often used by curanderos to calm a patient.

Chapter 13. Randy's Turning Point on December 12, 2017: The Virgin of Guadalupe Empowers Him

1   The shacapa is used by shamans to mark the rhythm; it is made from the dried leaves of the tree of that name and is the very symbol of curanderismo in this region. This shacapa is agitated by the curandero to mark the rhythm of the session.

2   Agua Florida is a cologne used by all curanderos to cleanse. The shaman typically sprays it on the patients by mouth.

Chapter 15. Prophetic Session with Karen and the Virgin, December 15, 2017

1   The *shacapa* long necklace is made from the seeds of the tree of that name and is used by indigenous dancers to mark the rhythm as they dance. It is very long and is held in both hands.

Chapter 16. Prelude to Receiving Powers from the Sacred Mountain, February 16, 2018

1   Urkumamanwasi—meaning the place of the sacred mountain—is a land in the forest on the outskirts of Lamas I purchased for Randy shortly after his June initiation. Randy has built a maloca—an indigenous structure to hold ceremonies—and individual huts for retreats. The land faces the mountain sacred to the Kichwa-Lamas, named Waman Wasi. It is shaped like a tilted pyramid.

2   Julio Valladolid in one of the three founders of PRATEC, with a long experience with Andean sacred mountains or Apus.

3   The name Waman Wasi means the house of the eagle.

Chapter 17. The Sacred Mountain Comes to Randy and Gives Him Powers, February 23, 2018

1   These pairs are masculine and feminine, a common practice in the Andean region that Grimaldo taught to Randy.

2   The *pinchudos* are pre-Colombian funeral effigies placed on cliffs in certain sites of the pre-Colombian cultural area of Chachapoyas to the north of Lamas.

Lamas itself is situated in the eastern border of the cultural area of Chachapoyas.

Chapter 18. Randy Learns to Exorcise a Possession, April–May 2018

1   Don Abilio is a mestizo shaman in Lamas.

Chapter 21. Randy is Blinded by a Jealous Curandero, March 2019; and Second Dieta in Takiwasi, April 2019

1   The shipibos are one of the Amazonian indigenous groups. They are well known for selling their intricately geometrically designed cloths everywhere in the region.

2   Randy was blinded shamanically, meaning he lost his ability to have visions.

Chapter 22. Randy Has a Beautiful Vision, Late Spring 2019

1   Karito is the diminutive of Karen, the name by which Randy calls his current partner.

2   White attire echoes both with weddings and with ayahuasca ceremonies where everyone usually wears white cotton clothing.

3   Although Karen had been shown to Randy shortly after his initiation in 2016, when he was told she would be his wife, he did not approach her until shortly before the celebration of the virgin of Guadalupe near our center on December 12, 2019. She had always been involved in those preparations. Randy went to her house for the purpose of discussing details of the celebration and that is when they kissed for the first time in this worldly realm.

Concluding Remarks on Part II by Frederique Apffel-Marglin

1   Randy has behaved extremely honorably and generously in giving Kemy, his former partner of twelve years, a large house in Lamas that he owns, which is rented to the provincial judiciary. Randy is now the owner of Sangapilla which I donated to him a few months before his initiation.

2   I go into much more detail on that issue in Part III.

PART III: REFLECTIONS ON THE ERADICATION OF SHAMANISM IN THE WEST

by Frédérique Apffel-Marglin

Chapter 1. The Oldest Destructions of Cosmocentric Worldviews in the West

1   See my book *Wives of the God-King: The Rituals of the Devadasis of Puri*.

2   The Vedic scholar Asko Parpola gave me in 1988 a typewritten version of his essay "From Ishtar to Durga," which was published much later as two separate essays. In it he shows with both linguistic as well as ethnographic and other kinds of evidence, the close similarity between the West Asian goddess Ishtar and the South Asian goddess Durga.

3   See Muraresku, *The Immortality Key*, 32.

4   Wasson, Hoffman and Ruck, *The Road to Eleusis: Unveiling the Secret of The Mysteries*.

5   On the influence of the Greek/Hebrew alphabet on Classical Greek and subsequent thinking see David Abram's *The Spell of the Sensuous*.

6   Muraresku, *The Immortality Key*, 21.

7   Eliade, Shamanism, 51; quoted in Hancock, *Supernatural*, 89.

8   Lewis-Williams, A Cosmos in Stone, 243; cited in Hancock *Supernatural*, 89.

9   Clottes and Lewis-Williams, *Les Chamanes de la Préhistoire,* 105. My translation; emphasis in the original.

10   Hancock, *Supernatural*, 406.

11   Muraresku *Immortality Key*: 289.

12   Muraresku *Immortality Key*: 289.

13   Muraresku *Immortality Key*: emphasis in the original.

14   Muraresku *Immortality Key*: 73.

15   Muraresku *Immortality Key*: 79–80.

16   Muraresku *Immortality Key*: 296.

17   See Buckley and Gottlieb, *Blood Magic*; Grahn, *Blood, Bread, and Roses*; Knight, *Blood Relations*; Lincoln, *Emerging from the Chrysalis*.

18   Lamp, "Heavenly Bodies," 210–231.

19   Buckley & Gotlieb, *Blood Magic*, 187–209.

20   Teaching at Smith I learned from my students that an English vernacular form of naming the menses is "the curse," which refers to the curse God put on Eve that brought mortality to humans. It is noteworthy that the Eleusinian Mysteries bring about the opposite, Immortal Life through Demeter, her daughter Persephone, and the child that is born to her, that is, the cycles of birth, death, and rebirth. Modernity's obsessive desire to obliterate any sign of menses in women is the sad inheritor of such a legacy.

21   I was stunned to learn this term from a mestizo shaman in Lamas since it is the very same term that is used in the Shakta esoteric rituals where menstrual blood is included; there it is called by its Sanskrit name Swayambhu Kusuma, meaning 'self-born flower.'

22   This is often mistaken for an either/or situation such as much feminist

literature on menstruation in India where the impurity of menstrual blood is seen by some as causing the classification of women as inherently inferior. However, this is a profoundly mistaken view. My second period of fieldwork in Odisha was focused on the rural festival of Raja Parba, celebrating the menstruation of the earth, the sea, and women everywhere in the rural areas. It is a grand festival observed by everyone that lasts four days. Menstrual blood is indeed impure and pollutes anyone who comes into contact with it, but it is simultaneously auspicious and life-giving. See Apffel-Marglin, *Rhythms of Life*, 159–275.

23   Merchant, *The Death of Nature*, 143 and passim.

24   Butler, *Gender Trouble*.

25   Bigwood, *Earth Muse*, 56–57.

26   Noble, *A World without Women*, 125 and passim.

27   This was made clear to me in twenty-six years of teaching in an elite women's institution, Smith College. See Bigwood, *Earth Muse*, 18.

Chapter 2. The Burning Times as a Foundation for the Scientific Revolution

1   'The religion without a name' is in Muraresku's subtitle for his 2020 book and refers to this psychedelic, shamanic extremely ancient tradition in the West and the Middle East.

2   Although we will see in the coda added at the end of this chapter that this happened later in Scandinavia.

3   All those three terms: hylozoism, Anima Mundi, and cosmocentrism, share the view that the cosmos is alive, sacred, and interrelated. Another closely related term is "Animism." I will be using sometimes one or the other of those terms, overlooking for my purposes the differences that may exist between them.

4   I place the term "scientific revolution" in quotation marks because it does not acknowledge that this knowledge system is profoundly rooted in a Western worldview and communicates that this science owes nothing to any one culture, western or otherwise. Later I will switch to referring to this event by another term: "the mechanistic revolution" which I consider much more precise and accurate. However, I will continue until necessary to refer to the 'scientific revolution,' a phrase that has become canonical and refers to a supposedly "universal" knowledge to make sure the reader knows what I am referring to.

5   It is, however, well established that the 'witches,' shamanesses and other female healers vastly outnumbered the male ones as the victims of the Inquisition's burnings. This is not true of the occult philosophers since most women were illiterate, having no access to education.

6   See Noble, *A World without Women*, 207. Noble does a thorough study of the role of women and heresy in the flight from popular healing on the part of the Church, the natural philosophers, and the Protestants.

7   For a thorough study of the Church and its position of supersessionism, namely

the view that Christianity had rendered both 'paganism' as well as Judaism superseded see Carroll, *Constantine's Sword*. On the relation between occult philosophers and the oral peasant healers, see especially Noble, *A World without Women*.

8   On scholarship about European witches see inter alia Ginzburg, *The Cheese and the Worm*. Also, by the same author *Ecstasies and Night Battles*, as well as Federici, *Caliban and the Witch*.

9   Descartes [1641] 1998, Pr. Phil., Pt. 4, § 187

10   Picco de la Mirandola, quoted in Potter *Gender and Boyle's Law of Gases*, 89.

11   Bayou, *Ils portaient l'écharpe blanche*.

12   For a fuller treatment of this topic, see Apffel-Marglin, *Subversive Spiritualities*, chapters 2–3.

13   The information on the civil wars in France in the 16th century as well as on the role of a Protestant inquisition comes from François Bayou's book *Ils portaient l'écharpe blanche*.

14   See Green, "Jewish Mysticism in Medieval Spain," 27–66. The Zohar was written in thirteenth-century Spain in Aramaic (a language no longer spoken at that time). In Spain in the thirteenth century, Ramon Lull wrote a Christianized version of the Kabbalah (called Cabala to distinguish it from the original Jewish version) in Arabic. Among other features he introduced in this version was the notion that the unpronounceable, four-letter name of God was a foreshadowing of Jesus's name.

15   Toulmin, *Cosmopolis*.

16   On Boyle's invention of the scientific experimental method, the two classic works are Steven Shapin and Simon Schaffer's *Leviathan and the Air-Pump: Hobbes, Boyle, and the Experimental Life* and Elizabeth Potter's *Gender and Boyle's Law of Gases*.

17   Boyle, *A Free Inquiry into the Vulgarly Received Notion of Nature*, 15.

18   Yates, *Occult Philosophy in the Elizabethan Age*, 174.

19   Shapin and Schaffer, *Leviathan and the Air Pump*, 45.

20   Also of interest is Potter, *Gender and Boyle's Law of Gases*.

21   See Gould, *Rocks of Ages*.

22   A key work on this topic is Donna Haraway's *Modest Witness Second Millenium: FemaleMan Meets OncoMouse: Feminism and Technoscience*.

Chapter 3. The Enclosure of Land in Europe Then and in South America Now

1   Monica Bruckmann in the French edition of the September 2009 *Le Monde Diplomatique* (p. 17) reports that the Peruvian territory has become a center of operation for the US military on the grounds of 'informational support' and 'training in anti-drug activities' while the Peruvian coast is a center of

operation for the IVth US Pacific Fleet.

2   Survival International (in its internet communiqué of August 26, 2009) has awarded its Stamp it Out Racism Award challenging racist description of indigenous peoples in the world's media, to the Peruvian national newspaper *Correo*. *Correo* called indigenous people 'savages,' 'Paleolithic,' and 'primitive' and said that their languages have no more than eighty words and declared that in the protests that have engulfed much of Peru's Amazon in the spring of 2009, they were manipulated by 'communist excrement.' *Correo* called for the napalm bombings of these savages.

3   I was directed at that time to a YouTube video filmed by a Peruvian concerned citizen precisely showing these actions on the part of the police. After viewing it, I unfortunately did not think of taking down the reference, being physically ill by what I had just viewed.

4   A shortened version of my piece was published in *Cultural Survival*, titled "Under the Guns," 20–27.

5   Alan Garcia was later condemned for corruption and fraud and as the police were about to take him, he committed suicide in 2019.

6   True, prior to enclosing provisioning was far from equal, with aristocrats and wealthier members receiving the lion's share, but nevertheless a safety net existed. See especially Appleby, *Economic Thought and Ideology in Seventeenth-Century England*.

7   I thank my friend, the writer Robert Tindall, for this reference.

8   Quoted in Federici *Caliban and the Witch*, 195.

9   Cited in Duerr *Dreamtime*, 123.

10   See the works of historians Carlo Ginsburg and Hans Peter Duerr cited earlier, as well as Michael Pollan in his chapter on cannabis in *The Botany of Desire* and Richard Evan Schultes, Albert Hoffman, and Christian Rätsch, editors of *Plants of the Gods*, among other works.

11   Stengers, "Reclaiming Animism."

12   Scholars Thomas Berry, Brian Swimme, and Mary Evelyn Tucker have argued for an integral approach to the world where humans and non-humans are one integrated whole, with no separation between nature and culture. Swimme and Berry, *The Universe Story*; Tucker and Swimme, *Journey of the Universe*.

13   Cited in Stengers, "Reclaiming Animism." [Robert Boyle 1685].

14   For an excellent and highly readable account of the impact of silver mining in a place like Potosi by the Spanish authorities on the global economy beginning in the 16th and 17th century see Mann, *1493: Uncovering the New World Columbus Created*.

Chapter 4. The Enclosure of the Self and Cosmocentric Reciprocity

1   Polanyi, *The Great Transformation.*

2   Randy really did not have stones in his kidneys, and he really was cured of the pain and the impossibility of urinating or eliminating, for example. He was still sufficiently under the spell of the mainstream worldview that he had an ultrasound done on his kidneys to acertain whether the pain came from malevolent beings or from physical causes. Though he failed to convince his doctor, he has been able to cure others suffering from recognized maladies. Most surprisingly for him—and for me—he was able to see malevolent entities coming out of the body of some of his patients, as in the case of his first session with Grimaldo. Unfortunately, he was also able to receive magical darts from such malevolent entities. He realized he needed to acquire effective protection, which took time. After the first excruciatingly painful virote Randy decided to quit the path of curanderismo. It is only later that he acquired sufficient protection that reassured him he could protect himself from such future attacks.

3   The two most important publications on this pre-Columbian soil are Lehman, *Amazonian Dark Earths: Origins, Properties, Management* and Woods, *Amazonian Dark Earths: Wim Sombroek's Vision.*

4   *Shaño* is the local Quechua word that refers to pieces of broken ceramics that the women who are the ceramicists also ground to a powder and add to the new clay to make new pots. Mama Allpa is the earth spirit, *allpa* also means 'soil.' *Chacra* is a Quechua word, which has entered the local Spanish language, for a swidden food garden.

5   *Ingenieros* refers literally to agronomists who overwhelmingly are mestizos (descendants of indigenous and European persons) and whose scientific education generates this kind of attitude. However, as Fernando Baez writes in his 2008 book *El Saqueo Cultural de America Latina,* the act of making the indigenous people ashamed started as soon as the Spaniards invaded Latin America.

6   There are two major agricultural campaigns in these tropical eastern foothills of the Peruvian Andes. In June and December indigenous farmers practice swidden agriculture using the slash and burn technique to open food fields in the forest that produce from one to four years until the soil is exhausted and another chacra is opened in the forest.

7   Silva, "Cultural Behaviors," 373–385.

8   Dr. Narvaez bases his identification of broken ceramics as being from offerings on his findings in a site in Tucume on the Northwest Peruvian coast where he found a great quantity of such fragments in a small altar of the Sacred Stone of Tucume, a site contemporaneous with Kuelap.

9   The literature on the brutal eradication of indigenous spirituality during the colonial period is quite vast. I would refer the reader to an excellent report on this from colonial time to the globalization current era: Baez, *El Saqueo Cultural de América Latina: De la Conquista a la Globalización.* See also Tzvetan Todorov's classic, *The Conquest of America.*

10   Personal communication in December of 2011.

11   Dr. Alfredo Narváez has not yet published his findings on ADE in the Chachapoyas archaeological area. This information is from a personal communication in Lamas, Peru, on August 11, 2012.

12   Gillespie, "City to Soil," 465–472.

13   Gillespie, "City to Soil," 465.

14   The phases of the moon affect the rising and falling of all liquids, from the sea with its tides to the sap in plants. A professor of agronomy at the national university of the state of San Martin, Dr. Jaime Alvarado Bremer, has made a scientific study of the effect of the phases of the moon on agriculture, published in a PowerPoint presentation; "Las Fases de la Luna y su Influencia en los Cultivos Agrícola." However, Prof. Alvarado does not include in this work Kichwa-Lamas practice and knowledge but successfully shows scientifically the effect of the phases of the moon on the growth of plants.

15   See for example the work of the French anthropologist/philosopher Bruno Latour, who titled one of his books *We Have Never Been Modern*.

16   On this topic see inter alia: Balée, *Cultural Forests of the Amazon*; Hecht, Morrison, and Padoch, *The Social Lives of Forests*; Posey, *Cultural and Spiritual Values of Biodiversity*.

17   Mauss, *The Gift: Forms and Functions of Exchange in Archaic Societies*.

18   This situation has recently begun to change under the influence of the work of quantum physicist Karen Barad that so inspired my 2011 book and is referred to as "the ontological turn."

19   For an argument on the entanglement of the material and the discursive, using Niels Bohr's understanding of quantum mechanics, see Chapter 4 in my 2011 book very much based on Karen Barad's work.

20   This contrasts sharply with the modernist view which thinks of them as not real but rather projections of the human mind. On this point see especially Chapters 5 and 6 of my 2011 book *Subversive Spiritualities*.

21   As Leora Batnitzky shows in her book *How Judaism Became a Religion*, the category of 'religion' is a protestant one since for Judaism, as for Hinduism and probably many other spiritual traditions, one's spirituality is not a private affair of 'beliefs' held in the privacy of one's mind and heart but a whole way of life. But she also shows how this new category became inescapable for everyone through the establishment by the Nation State of a separation between a properly political public sphere and a private sphere where 'religion' belonged. The secularization of anthropology—and for that matter of the modern education system as a whole—is part of this phenomenon. For anthropology, this development is both ironic and problematic since typically the people it studies do not recognize something like a totally secular sphere.

22   Mann, *1491: New Revelations of the Americas Before Columbus*.

23   Panduro and Rengifo, *Montes y Montaraces*, 12.

24   Coca is a traditional plant originating from the High Amazon region and used in the highland region for both medicinal and ritual purposes since time immemorial. The increase in coca production during the 1980s and 90s was due to the enormous increase in demand from the US for cocaine. The traditional uses require the unprocessed dried coca leaf with an alkaloid content of no more than 2% whereas the production of cocaine chemically treats the plant and transforms it into a drug with an alkaloid content of some 80% and requires a much-increased quantity of the leaf. Since the government of Fujimori imprisoned the leader of the Shining Path guerrilla movement (in 1994) and arrested the leadership of the other guerrilla movement, the MRTA, the growing of coca in the region has dramatically decreased.

25   Lecture in my study abroad program given by Agronomist Ing. Cesar Enrique Chappa S.M., of the Faculty of Agronomy at the University of San Martin in Tarapoto, January 2007.

26   Personal communication, Oro Verde Fair Trade Coffee co-op, Lamas.

27   I taped this speech, and this excerpt is verbatim. It was this request of Misael Salas Amasifuen that decided me to focus my center's work on the regeneration of Yana Allpa, a work that continues.

28   Cronon, "The Trouble with Wilderness or Getting Back to the Wrong Nature," 72.

29   Cronon, "The Trouble with Wilderness or Getting Back to the Wrong Nature," 79.

30   As Luis Vivanco points out in *Green Encounters*, biodiversity forest preserves "reflect and confirm authoritative concepts of museumized and unpeopled wilderness." For other similarly constructed and artificial so-called wilderness areas, see Haraway, "Teddy Bear Patriarchy," 26–58.

31   On this point, see Apffel-Marglin and Parajuli "Sacred Grove" and Ecology: Ritual and Science," 291–316.

32   We at Sachamama Center fully support the Kichwa-Lamas' efforts to have control over the Cordillera Escalera biological reserve.

33   Although the scholarly evidence does mention that this happens. See especially Eliade, *Shamanism* and Vitebsky, *The Shaman: Voyages of the Soul: Trance, Ecstasy and Healing from Siberia to the Amazon*, or Halifax, *Shaman: The Wounded Healer*.

Chapter 5. Implications for Society and the Non-Human World

1   I am grateful to my literature friend Robert Tindall for this reference.

2   Following Rupert Sheldrake, I will from now on use this term, which is more accurate and less misleading than the term 'scientific revolution.'

3   Scott, *Seeing Like a State: How Certain Schemes to Improve the Human Condition have Failed*.

4   As is by now welknown, Newton was secretly an occult philosopher.

However, he was an exceedingly ambitious man and knew to keep this interest of his successfully secret so as not to interfere in his achieving great state-recognized fame. It was not until the 1930s that his secret occult papers were discovered.

5   In her book *The Cultural Meaning of the Scientific Revolution*, Margaret Jacobs traces the history of four generations of Watts brothers starting at the end of the 17th century and shows that they pursued economic advantage from their discoveries based on the new science giving rise to the Industrial Revolution and eventually to the steam engine.

6   On this point see especially Michael Adas's book *Machines as the Measure of Men: Science, Technology, and Ideology of Western Dominance*.

7   See Taylor, *Sources of the Self*, 145.

8   Descartes VI:62, cited in Taylor, *Sources of the Self*, 149.

9   Hillman, *The Thought of the Heart and the Soul of the World*, 95.

10   Hillman, *The Thought of the Heart and the Soul of the World*, 93.

11   Hillman, *The Thought of the Heart and the Soul of the World*, 94. Emphasis added.

12   Cited in Maxwell, *From Knowledge to Wisdom*, 131.

13   Robert Proctor in *Value-Free Science? Purity and Power in Modern Knowledge* gives us a detailed history of the emergence of the separation between scientific pursuits and ethical concerns, as do Shapin and Schaffer's classic work on Robert Boyle's laboratory and his invention of the scientific experimental method Leviathan and the Air Pump, as well as Potter's book *Gender and Boyle's Law of Gases*.

14   Macaulay, "Minute on Education," 114–15.

15   Shiva, *Monocultures of the Mind: Perspectives on Biodiversity and Biotechnology*.

16   For a profoundly insightful critique of the notion that this is necessitated for technological reasons, see Stephen Margin's celebrated 1974 essay "What Do Bosses Do?" There he persuasively argues that it arose from the need on the part of the bosses to control the workers. See also his much later follow-up essay "Farmers, Seedsmen, and Scientists: Systems of Agriculture and Systems of Knowledge" (1996:185–248).

17   For two Andean examples see especially Chapters 5 and 6 in my book *Subversive Spiritualities*.

18   Barad, *Meeting the Universe Halfway: Quantum Physics and the Entanglement of Matter and Meaning*.

19   Particles are localized objects that occupy a given location at each moment in time, whereas waves are not properly entities but rather disturbances in some background medium or field. Waves have extension in space, occupy more than one position at any moment in time, and they can

overlap with one another to form interference or diffraction patterns.

20   Bohr, Essays, 59–60, quoted in Barad "Reconceiving Scientific Literacy as Agential Literacy, or Learning How to Intra-Act Responsibly Within the World," 232.

21   Foucault, *Discipline and Punish: The Birth of the Prison*, 1979.

Chapter 6. Spirits and Other Discarnate Beings

1   Beauregard, *Brain Wars*, 161.

2   Beauregard, *Brain Wars*, 168–169.

3   Beauregard, *Brain Wars*, 171–172.

4   One of the most dramatic NDE experiences is by a neuroscientist and neurosurgeon, Eben Alexander, during a week-long coma due to severe damage to his brain by an overwhelming bacterial meningoencephalitis. I recommend his latest book written with Karen Newell *Living in a Mindful Universe*. For these authors, consciousness/mind is the whole universe, and we are in it and part of it.

5   Which took place virtually on Tuesday September 15, 2020.

6   I have used here the Reader's Edition of the original without the paintings, translated by Mark Kyburz, John Peck, and Sonu Shamdasani, a 2009 publication of the heirs of C.G. Jung (page 127). But I also have had the opportunity to leaf through the original Red Book with the paintings and I own an edited and much smaller version of Jung's paintings that was published later.

7   Jung, *The Red Book*, 398–401.

8   Baring, *The Dream of the Cosmos and the Quest for the Soul*, 246.

9   Baring, *The Dream of the Cosmos and the Quest for the Soul*, 246.

10   Baring, *The Dream of the Cosmos and the Quest for the Soul*, 247; emphasis in the original.

11   Baring, *The Dream of the Cosmos and the Quest for the Soul*, 97. Those topics have been the purview of the discipline of anthropology which overall has interpreted such phenomena found in cultures where modernity has not thoroughly penetrated, in terms of expressing other aspects of the culture in which they are found, meaning that they are all about aspects of human society. Typically, they are not considered to have an intrinsic ontological reality but rather are seen by anthropology as originating from something like a collective cultural imaginary. With the more recent "ontological turn" this view has begun to change.

12   On this issue see Peat, *Synchronicity: The Bridge Between Matter and Mind*, 14; also Baring, *The Dream of the Cosmos and the Quest for the Soul*, 251 and passim.

13   Baring, *The Dream of the Cosmos and the Quest for the Soul*, 249.

14   David Peat, *Synchronicity*, 6–7.

15   Peat, *Synchronicity*, 4.

16   Peat, *Synchronicity*, 24.

17   Baring, *The Dream of the Cosmos*, 260.

18   Here I must note that Jacques Mabit has argued that Jung's archetypes are in fact desacralized spirits; see Mabit, "The Sorcerer, the Madman, and Grace: Are Archetypes Desacralized Spirits? Thoughts on Shamanism in the Amazon," 113–154.

19   Alexander and Newell, *Living in a Mindful Universe*, 238–39. The book is written in Alexander's first-person voice, but he writes extensively about Newell's fundamental contribution to his understanding of the implications of his NDE, crediting her for a major part of his current understanding.

20   Plumwood, *Feminism and the Mastery of Nature*.

21   See inter alia his book on Persian mysticism *Spiritual Body and Celestial Earth: From Mazdean Iran to Shi'ite Iran* and also his book on Ibn Arabi, *Alone with the Alone: Creative Imagination in the Sufism of Ibn 'Arabi*.

Chapter 7. Collective Memory in the Cosmos

1   Sheldrake, *The Science Delusion: Freeing the Spirit of Enquiry*. Rupert Sheldrake is a British biologist.

2   Morphic resonance depends on similarity and is not attenuated by distance in time and space, in this behaving in the same manner as particles in the nonlocality experiments of quantum physics. In those non-locality experiments, particles having been previously associated are then separated and sent in different directions, even at infinitely large distances, immediately react in the same way, with no intervening time having elapsed. This effect is what Einstein famously called "spooky action at a distance." Thus, morphic resonance works non-locally, while morphic fields are local, within and around the systems they organize.

3   Sheldrake, *The Science Delusion*, 99.

4   Bohm argued that the manifest world is the explicate order emanating from the implicate order, the latter containing a kind of memory. See David Bohm and David Peat's book *Science, Order, and Creativity: A Dramatic New Look at the Creative Roots of Science and Life*.

5   Sheldrake, *The Science Delusion*, 207–208.

6   Sheldrake, *The Science Delusion*, 335.

7   To make this clear, let me contrast Randy's case with that of Jacques Mabit, who apprenticed for several years with several local Amerindian shamans in the same area as Randy's. Although I have characterized Jacques' transformation as a conversion, I need to nuance this. Jacques Mabit came to the nearby city of Tarapoto with the desire to apprentice from local Amerindian Shamans since he had previously recognized the efficacy of

indigenous healers while posted by Doctors Without Borders to a remote community clinic in the Peruvian Altiplano. I have known Jacques Mabit since 2004 and became both a regular participant in ayahuasca sessions he and his wife direct at his nearby center, as well as a friend. When Jacques Mabit first approached an indigenous shaman to ask whether he could apprentice with him, he told him that he was from a totally different culture than his and asked whether this would disqualify him from learning. The shaman looked deeply into his eyes, took his pulse, and declared that he would make a better shaman than most people from his own ethnic group.

Jacques Mabit was and continues to be both a medical doctor in the sense that his MD degree has never been revoked, albeit a non-practicing one, hence a healer, and additionally a very devout Catholic. Given the history of the Catholic church in Latin America and with shamanism in general, one could not say that his faith inclined him to "believe" in sprits. I call what happened to him a conversion in the sense that through his own experience of the spirits of the forest who asked him to reciprocate for all the knowledge he had acquired from them by healing drug addicts, he converted to a form of Catholicism that included Amerindian spirituality, although not other forms of spirituality.

A crucial difference between Jacques and Randy's experience is that Jacques chose to become a shaman and actively sought out shaman teachers. Before acceding to the request of the spirits of the forest, he had been studying for some six years with several local shamans and he has never completely ceased learning from elder shamans. He and his wife opened Takiwasi center in 1992. Another fundamental difference between Jacques and Randy is that the former was deeply acquainted with the supernatural and the sacred whereas Randy was innocent of those two dimensions. Randy had, several years before his initiation, gone once or twice to a local mestizo shaman in Lamas mostly out of curiosity and strongly encouraged by a close mestizo friend of his who was supposedly apprenticing with that curandero. After only two sessions Randy gave up having realized that this local shaman was engaging in black magic mostly for financial reasons. He lost any interest he might have had in shamanism and that experience might explain his great reluctance to accompany me to the indigenous shaman I was taking a couple from the US to and insisted that he accompany me. I put great pressure on him to come and that is where and when he was initiated in this deeply painful and disorienting manner. So, if anything, Randy had a rather negative opinion of local shamanism and brought with him to that session with Don Aquilino a disposition opposite to that of Jacques Mabit.

Thus, the usual anthropological explanation cannot be used in his case, neither in the case of Jacques Mabit, the two cases being similar only in this one dimension of neither of them belonging to an Amerindian group. Jacques' and Randy's cases—both of whom became effective healers—suggest that explanations in terms of cultural dispositions, thoughts, or beliefs cannot be easily applied and are thus limited.

8   See Poole, *Our Lady of Guadalupe*, Introduction.

9   I must clarify that Randy kept his affairs private from me. However, when we first sat down so I could write down his initiation and visions, he first

started by telling me about many affairs he had had previously. I was initially baffled at his choice, but I later realized he wanted me to understand his previous life, where he was coming from, and how profoundly different it was from his current mindset.

10 Baring, *The Dream of the Cosmos*, 92.

11 Sheldrake, *Chaos, Creativity and Cosmic Consciousness*, 45.

12 Sheldrake, *Chaos, Creativity and Cosmic Consciousness*, 47, 49.

13 Sheldrake, *Chaos, Creativity and Cosmic Consciousness*, 101.

14 Sheldrake, *Chaos, Creativity and Cosmic Consciousness*, 101–2.

15 Sheldrake, *Chaos, Creativity and Cosmic Consciousness*, 106.

Chapter 8. Academia and its Discontents

1 And five more at Harvard, Wellesley, and later Wesleyan University.

2 Watanabe, "Unimagining the Maya: Anthropologists, Others, and the Inescapable Hubris of Authorship," 28.

3 Kuhn, *The Structure of Scientific Revolutions*.

4 This was especially so in the earlier years of the discipline. In late twentieth and twenty first centuries the study of complex and even modern societies has become widespread.

5 See Thompson, "Time, Work, Discipline, and Industrial Capitalism," 59–97.

6 See Marglin, "What do Bosses Do?" Also, by the same author "Losing Touch: The Cultural Conditions of Worker Accommodation and Resistance," 217–282.

7 Apffel-Marglin, "Rationality, the Body, and the World: From Production to Regeneration," 142–181.

8 John Connolly, lecture on the inauguration of Smith President Ruth Simmons, September 1995.

9 Kant 1798, cited by Connolly, "The Academy's Freedom—The Academy's Burden."

10 The one exception is the creation of National Parks after the end of the Indian wars in the US. The creation of National Nature Parks, first invented in the US, embodied an either/or logic where nature was either used only for human ends or it was left alone, never using any of it at all, so it could be "preserved" for human recreation, edification, or escape. Such a mutually exclusive relationship between utility and the complete lack of it is something seldom found in indigenous or peasant societies. In those places, the use of nature never precludes its inherent spirituality or sacrality nor does it entail its use for the sole purpose of increased productivity separated from its continued existence and thriving. In the Amazonian region and in other indigenous peasant societies the forest and the Earth are revered spirits or mothers whose continued life is carefully attended to through rituals and shamanic

ceremonies in full recognition of the inextricability of the life of humans from that of the non-humans. On the creation of National Parks in the US see William Cronon's classic essay "The Trouble with Wilderness or Getting Back to the Wrong Nature," 69–90. On the lack of a purely utilitarian approach to the earth or to forests or to nature in general see my introduction and essay in *Decolonizing Knowledge,* as well as Chapter 5 in my 2011 book.

11   More recently those concerns have again become relevant in some disciplines, especially those involved in the re-establishment of eco-systems that sustain the life of certain species, such as the salmon, for example, in the decision by some states to take down dams that have impeded the life cycle of that specie. The Harvard economist Stephen Marglin's book *The Dismal Science: How Thinking Like an Economist Undermines Community* is an eloquent argument showing how one discipline, economics, undermines human communities.

12   See *The New York Times,* December 7, 2020. I need to reiterate that sacrality or spirituality in such contexts do not mean lack of utility.

13   Espeland, *The Struggle for Water: Politics, Rationality, and Identity in the American Southwest,* 201.

14   For our contemporary ecological crises, the data is widely available not only in specialized publications but also in the media. For numerical data on the human epidemics of mental illness and addiction I can refer the reader to Michael Pollan's 2018 book How to Change Your Mind. I give some of those figures in the next and last chapter. In today's *The New York Times*—July 30, 2021—it is reported that from 2009 to 2019 the rate of suicide in the US has grown by 30%.

15   On this history see Proctor, *Value-Free Science.*

16   "University | Etymology, Origin and Meaning of University by Etymonline." Accessed September 18, 2022. https://www.etymonline.com/word/university.

17   Richards, *Sacred Knowledge: Psychedelics and Religious Experience,* 60–61. When Richards writes that "this threshold…is conceptualized by different people in different ways" he is referring to the conceptualization of the volunteers at John Hopkins or other northern universities or hospitals and not to people hailing from indigenous cultures.

18   Pollan, *How to Change Your Mind,* 263–4.

19   Pollan, *How to Change Your Mind,* 413.

20   Kopenawa and Albert, *The Falling Sky,* 418.

21   Kripal, *The Flip: Epiphanies of Mind and the Future of Knowledge,* 12.

22   Kripal, *The Flip: Epiphanies of Mind and the Future of Knowledge,* 68.

23   There is an ancient Hindu system of thought that is like the modern western one. It is known as the Charvaka school, also known as *Lokayata,* Sanskrit for "worldly ones," a school of thought which grounds its philosophy

in materialism and empiricism dating back to 600 BCE. It rejects notions of an afterworld, a soul, and any authority outside of the material world. It slowly but surely fizzled away and by the 12th century had disappeared and did not return until the 20th century, albeit as an import from the west rather than the reviving of an indigenous knowledge system. However, the charvaka school of thought did not create or invent a science along the European lines. This leads me to think that for that to occur the emergence of mercantilism was also crucial in the west.

24   One particularly vivid example is from anthropologist Richard Lee, *The Dobe !Kung.*

25   McGilchrist, *The Master and His Emissary,* 462.

26   Bauman, *Modernity and the Holocaust,* 13.

27   Weisskopf, *The Joy of Insight: Passions of a Physicist,* 147.

28   However, in editing my doctoral thesis for publication, I abandoned the third person and wrote in the first person, under the influence of feminist scholars.

29   Of course, I not only remunerated my collaborators, aka informants, for the time they gave me, but also after the publication of my first book gave the royalties to the women temple dancers/priestesses that were my principal "object of study." This however, seemed to me not at all adequate and commensurate to reciprocate for the incredible riches in understanding they had gifted me.

Chapter 9. Psychedelics and the Healing of Modernity's Ills

1   Pollan, *How to Change Your Mind.*

2   *The New York Times,* on April 14, 2021, reports the following statistic from the CDC: overdose deaths during the pandemic has surged by 29% over the previous 12 months.

3   I consider modernity to cover socialist, communist, as well as capitalist societies. Communist and to a sizable extent also socialist societies, follow Marx and Engels' ideology of dialectical materialism which has translated for example in the USSR and China into the persecution of religion and of shamanism. My colleague and friend Piers Vitebsky, who did fieldwork among Siberian shamans, told me that the Soviets punished Siberian shamans who had harpooned submarines in the North Sea, believing them to be some whale or other huge fish, by shooting them all.

4   As mentioned earlier, psylocibin has been voted to be legal for therapeutic reasons in Oregon in the November 2020 elections and I just received news that the Congress of the state of California has voted recently to make psychedelics legal in that state. Furthermore, peyote and ayahuasca are legal in the USA for the Native American Church and the Santo Daime and Uniao do Vegetal churches, respectively.

5   Pollan, *How To Change Your Mind,* 335–36.

6   Pollan, *How To Change Your Mind*, 377.

7   Swimme, *The Hidden Heart of the Cosmos*, 33.

8   See the volume edited by Takiwasi *Medicinas Tradicionales, Interculturalidad y Salud Mental: Memorias del Congreso Internacional*, Tarapoto 2009. This volume covers Latin America with many examples of shamanic or hybrid treatment for drug-addiction and other mental illness in major Latin American cities.

9   Pollan, *How To Change Your Mind*, 288. Emphasis in the original text. Pollan does not discuss his exclusion of the category of 'supernaturals' or even what he means by that term.

10   Pollan, *How To Change Your Mind*, 355. Emphasis in original.

11   Pollan, *How To Change Your Mind*, 413.

12   Richards, *Sacred Knowledge*, 145.

13   Yaden, "Of Roots and Fruits: A Comparison of Psychedelic and Nonpsychedelic Mystical Experiences." I am grateful to Jesús Gonzalez Mariscal for sending me this article.

14   Pollan, *How To Change Your Mind*, 336.

15   Pollan, *How To Change Your Mind*, 342–43. The three dots (...) are in the original and do not indicate that words have been omitted.

16   Pollan, *How To Change Your Mind*, 345.

17   Pollan, *How To Change Your Mind*, 334.

18   Looking at the extraordinary effect of these substances from another angle, it is not impossible to think that the spirits and sacred beings making their appearance through psychedelics are showing a vast compassion for our current predicament.

Of course, such a perspective is rejected immediately in the modernist dispensation or left to anthropologists to ponder their meaning but not their reality.

19   I came across an advertisement for investing opportunities dated Spring 2021 titled "Massive Market Trend is Forming in Psychoactive Drug Therapies" listing several companies that are already investing in that field to the tune of many billions of dollars. Of course, the commodification of such plants and fungi might prove to be quite problematic. However, their wide availability might transform modernity into something less lethal.

20   It is well to remember that LSD created by Hoffman in his laboratory is based on ergot, the fungi growing on barley and the one identified as used in the Eleusinian mysteries.

21   It may be necessary at this juncture to make clear once again that the ego is not deleterious or negative per se—it is in fact indispensable for most survival activities in daily life, as Iain McGilchrist and Jill Taylor have shown. But in non-modern cultures, this necessary boundedness of the ego is accompanied by, and subordinated to, cosmic reciprocity. In modernity we have developed the left-brain ego at the expense of the right brain, which is more feminine and

intuitive. As Jill Taylor argues, developing a whole-brain relationship to the world could change the thrust of modernity from destruction to peace.

22   I want to express my gratitude to both Funlayo Woods and Susan James for identifying this Orisha for me.

23   I am here echoing Swimme's 1996 book entitled *The Hidden Heart of the Cosmos*.

24   Pouillon, "Remarks on the Verb "To Believe,"" 8.

Conclusions

1   Bajaj, "Francis Bacon, the First Philosopher of Modern Science: A Non-Western View," 57–58.

2   China, as is well known, has completely abandoned this subsuming of rationality to the Tao in the 20th and 21st centuries. It is well to remind ourselves that communism arose from a western worldview in the 19th century, a materialist worldview which it has not discarded.

3   Shanon, *The Antipodes of the Mind*.

4   Armstrong, *The Battle for God*, 141.

5   As mentioned in an earlier footnote, even Hinduism with its built-in diversity is succumbing to the fundamentalist epidemic under the current BJP government. However, indigenous traditions seem to not have gone that way as the examples of the Dangaleat of Africa or the Sarayaku community illustrate, among many others.

6   See especially Panikkar, *The Cosmotheandric Experience: Emerging Religious Consciousness*. Panikkar has written some 60 books and it is difficult to choose among them. Toward the end of his life is when he embraced this multi-religious identity.

7   Armstrong, *The Battle for God*, 141.

8   I find the category of "recreational" very problematic in the legal terminology concerning psychedelics, since it leads one to consider the ingestion of shamanic plants and fungi as not requiring careful guidance as well as ritual, both being absolutely necessary.

ACKNOWLEDGMENTS

This book is the result of years of research, teaching, reading, practice, and conversations with a long list of friends, students, and colleagues. We would like to highlight Frédérique's friend Anne-Marie Codur, who read the first draft of this book. Her critical suggestions made for a fundamental rethinking of its organization.

Another dear friend and colleague of Frédérique's, Neela Bhattacharya Saxena, shared with her a long list of key references, along with her friendship. Other friends, colleagues and relatives gave us crucial information and feedback for part of this book. Several of them read the whole manuscript, giving us key suggestions.

We are deeply grateful to the following persons: Jennifer Browdy; Peter Cole; Thomas Cummins; Barbara Galindo M; Jesus Gonzalez M; John Grim; Susan James; Jacques Mabit; Elizabeth Marglin; Jessica Marglin; Alfredo Narvaez V; Pat O'Riley; Anel Pancorvo; Grimaldo Rengifo; Royner Sangama S; Robert Tindall; Mary Evelyn Tucker; Stefano Varese; Marc Weisskopf; Funlayo Woods.

Frédérique Apffel-Marglin, PhD. is Professor Emerita, Department of Anthropology at Smith College and has also taught at Harvard, Wellesley, and Wesleyan University. She founded the Sachamama Center for BioCultural Regeneration (SCBR) in the Peruvian High Amazon in 2009, which she directs. She has spent years in India doing fieldwork in Puri Jagganatha and in Peru working with indigenous peoples. She has authored or edited fifteen books and published some 70 articles and book chapters. In 1993 she decided for political and ethical reasons that she could no longer engage in classical anthropological fieldwork and ever since then has been invited to collaborate with activist/intellectual groups in Peru and Bolivia and with one of them, PRATEC, has published *The Spirit of Regeneration: Andean Culture Confronting Western Notions of Development*. Her 2011 book based on her work in Peru is entitled *Subversive Spiritualities: How Rituals Enact the World*. Other recent titles include *Contemporary Voices from Anima Mundi: A Reappraisal*, and *Sacred Soil: Biochar and the Regeneration of the Earth*, co-authored with Robert Tindall and David Shearer. Find out more at: http://asociacionsachamama.org

Randy Chung Gonzales has been working at Sachamama Center for Biocultural Regeneration in his native town of Lamas, Peru for some 10 years and has designed its buildings using indigenous styles of architecture and materials. He is a self-trained architect and visual artist. In June of 2016 he was asked by Frédérique to go with her and two visitors to an ayahuasca shamanic ceremony some two hours away quite against his will. At this ceremony Randy was initiated by disembodied spirits into shamanic knowledge and power very much to his own surprise. Such initiation by spirits are extremely rare, the most common method being initiation by an embodied, living shaman. Since then, he has been given powers by other indigenous spirits as well as the Virgin of Guadalupe and other sacred beings. He receives regular teachings from a disembodied Ashaninka shaman, offers healing to others, and directs an ecological center in the forest called in English "The Place of the Sacred Mountain," since it faces the mountain sacred to the local indigenous people, the Kichwa-Lamas. Find out more at: https://urkumamanwasi.com

www.ingramcontent.com/pod-product-compliance
Lightning Source LLC
Chambersburg PA
CBHW032050020426
42335CB00011B/265